FREEING THE WHALES

*How the Media Created
the World's Greatest Non-Event*

FREEING
THE WHALES

*How the Media Created
the World's Greatest Non-Event*

By Tom Rose

A Birch Lane Press Book
Published by Carol Publishing Group

Copyright © 1989 by Tom Rose

A Birch Lane Press Book
Published by Carol Publishing Group

Editorial Offices
600 Madison Avenue
New York, NY 10022

Sales & Distribution Offices
120 Enterprise Avenue
Secaucus, NJ 07094

In Canada: Musson Book Company
A division of General Publishing Co. Limited
Don Mills, Ontario

Manufactured in the United States of America

10 9 8 7 6 5 4 3 2 1

Library of Congress Cataloging-in-Publication Data

Rose, Tom, 1956-
    Freeing the whales : how the media created the world's greatest
non-event / Tom Rose.
        p.   cm.
    "A Birch Lane Press book."
    ISBN 1-55972-011-5
    1. Television broadcasting of news--Social aspects--United States.
2. Gray whale in press. 3. Wildlife rescue in the press.
4. Journalism--United States--Objectivity. I. Title.
PN4888.T4R67   1989
302.23'45'0973--dc20   89-22251
                                                            CIP

To IRWIN R. ROSE
A.K.A. Dad
Deserving his pride requires a lifetime of work, service
and commitment. Winning it just takes being there.

Contents

FREEING
THE WHALES

*How the Media Created
the World's Greatest Non-Event*

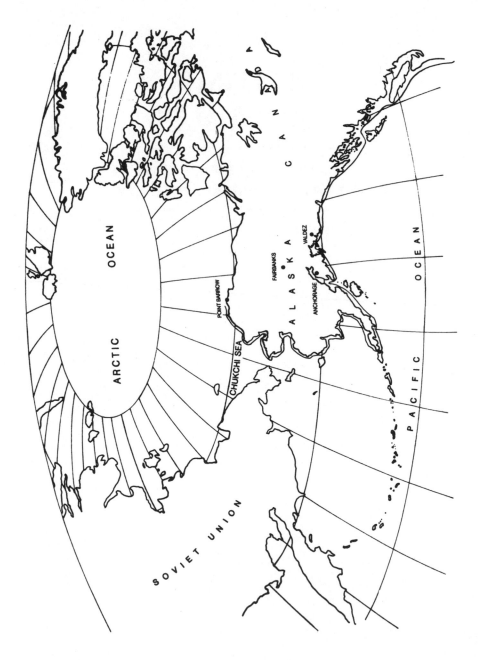

Chapter 1

The Hunt

The bitter weather came early along Alaska's North Slope in September 1988. The Siberian air that rolled in brought high winds and unseasonable cold. In one week the average temperature went from 10° above to 20° below zero. An unusually strong rim of ice formed along the shore sealing off America's northernmost coastline from the fierce Arctic Ocean.

Most of the thousands of whales that feed in these waters began to migrate south a few weeks early. Three young California gray whales did not. Two adolescents and one yearling were too inexperienced to sense the ice closing in overhead. Had they known what was in store, they would have joined the others. Instead, they continued to gorge themselves on crustaceans that lined the ocean bottom.

These whales were in no hurry to leave. This was their last chance to eat for five months. Once they began the trek to their winter home off Baja, California, they would fast until they returned to Alaska the following spring. By then they would have completed a 9,000 mile round trip, the longest migration of any mammal in the world.

During migration they would confront killer whales and great white sharks. As far as they knew, the Arctic presented no natural enemies. They were wrong.

The whales heedlessly rolled on their sides to suck the shrimp-like amphopods from the seabed just a few hundred feet off Point Barrow, a narrow sandspit five miles long. It was the very tip of North America. Four miles to the southwest stood Barrow, the largest, oldest and farthest northern Eskimo settlement on the globe. At any other time at any other spot on the Arctic coast of Alaska, the whales would have drowned unnoticed under the ice.

In a few weeks, these three creatures would become the luckiest animals in history, luckier than the whales who drown every year, luckier than the whales reduced to Japanese beauty products and Russian ice cream by armadas of high tech factory ships, luckier than the whales harvested by Eskimos.

After each spring thaw, carcasses of young whales were an almost common sight along Alaska's Arctic coast. The Eskimos who found them always assumed the ice trapped the whales who stayed too late in the fall. The dead whales were not wasted. Their remains were an important element in the Arctic food chain, feeding species as varied as polar bears and microscopic organisms.

The three whales occasionally stopped eating to scratch their ungainly snouts on the gravelly bottom for relief from the whale lice and barnacles infesting their skin. Ironically, it was these maddening parasites that would save them from the first of many obstacles they would face over the next several months.

For thousands of years, Eskimos have depended on the whale hunt for their survival. Over the centuries, they acquired a taste for the bowhead whale. Its clean skin makes for much better eating than its cousin the California gray.

While the barnacles annoyed the three grays, the tiny pests were nothing compared to one local Eskimo hunter. Despite a five-foot, three-inch frame, his prowess as a whaling captain earned him the nickname Malik which, in his native language of Inupiat, means "Little Big Man." He spent most of his 60-odd years roaming the ice off Barrow in search of the Bowhead whale. Most older Eskimos don't know exactly how old they are.

Until recently, hunting whales was the ony way to feed all the people who lived in this forlorn, frozen part of the world. The bounty from one 60-foot Bowhead whale could feed a village for an entire year. That's why the white man called what Malik does for a living "Subsistence Whaling."

By the beginning of September 1988, Barrow's whaling captains were starting to worry about what was becoming a dismal fall hunt. No one from Barrow had caught a whale since spring. Winter was nearly upon them.

Winter descends quickly in the Arctic. With it comes nine months of sub-zero temperatures and 67 days of total darkness. The Barrow sun set every November 17 and didn't rise again until the 21st of January, almost two and a half months later. In winter, temperatures regularly drop to 50, 60, even 70 degrees below zero. Factor in the howling winds that whip down from the North Pole or across from Siberia at speeds of up to 100 miles an hour, and the wind-chill reading can drop to 175 degrees below zero. Alaskans joked that they had two seasons: winter and damned late in the fall. The humor was incrementally lost the farther north you travel in America's biggest state. Barrow, Alaska, is as far north as you can get.

Barrowans proudly called their town "The Top of the World." For all intents and purposes it was. Located 320 miles north of the Arctic Circle, it could be reached only by air except for two or three weeks in the summer when the ice receded far enough for a thick-hulled supply ship to get through.

Malik and his people have called Barrow home since their ancestors paddled across the Bering Sea from Siberia as long as 25,000 years ago. These intrepid seafarers came in nimble open boats called umiaks made of dried walrus or sealskin. They were the first Americans. By 1988, there were 3,000 people living in Barrow, around 2,700 of whom were descended from those first explorers. They were Eskimos.

Malik assembled his six-man whaling crew on the night of September 16th. They gathered at Sam and Lee's on Nachick Street, the most northern Chinese restaurant in the world. They sorted their gear in the parking lot. When their preparations were complete, they would be ready to head out to the open waters of the Arctic Ocean in search of the migrating Bowhead whales.

In one of nature's most daring matches, these seven men sought to battle an agile 40-ton whale not from a umiak, but from an equally fragile aluminum dinghy. Even the slightest kick of a whale's gigantic tail or a slap from its powerful fins would dash the boat to pieces. Together, the whale's tail and fins, called flukes, propel and guide it with the precision and stealth of an advanced fighter plane, devastating nearly anything foolish enough to challenge it.

If struck by the whale, the jettisoned men would die almost the instant they landed in the eight degree Arctic ocean water. But the prospect of a winter without whale blubber, the important food source they called Muktuk, left these whalers little choice. Before Alaska's new-found oil money started pouring into Barrow in the 1970s, the Eskimos hunted whales only in the spring. Tradition taught that it was fruitless to try and seek out whales during the winter. Instead, the ancient whalers pitched camp on the ice and waited for the Bowhead to come to them. But tradition was beginning to give way to some of technology's crudest implements.

Now that they had outboard motors, Malik and his men didn't have to wait for whales. They could go out and look for themselves. Once they found and attacked one, they could pick up their portable radios and call for help to tow it in. While subsistence whaling was much easier for him than for his forebears, Malik was not about to call it a pleasure sport.

Malik's father and grandfather earned the title of Great Whaler. Even though the title usually followed in a family line, Malik had to prove to his people that he too was worthy of the same respect. He listened carefully to his elders. He learned their lessons well. With over 70 harvested whales to his credit, Malik was known in every whaling village in Alaska. His whaling adventures were a popular subject for elaborate epic poems celebrating the hunt. They were taught in schools, preached in churches, and retold on local radio and television.

On the morning of September 12, 1988, the wind died down considerably. But even with clouds insulating against colder air, the temperature remained at zero. To keep them warm in the unseasonably cold air, Malik and his six-man crew wore two layers of long underwear beneath their sealskin pants and parkas. As they launched their tiny boat from the beach in back of the Top of the World Hotel, the whalers wondered whether their shore access would be sealed off by ice formed in their absence.

After about an hour at sea, another whaling crew from Barrow reported over the radio that they had spotted a bowhead about two miles off the tip of Point Barrow. Malik squatted in the bow. He told the helmsman to travel the eight miles north at full throttle. At a top speed 20 miles an hour, it would take them around a half an hour to reach the site where the whale was reported. The wind chill brought the temperature to minus 50°. Malik rolled down the fur seal linings of his hood to protect his face from frostbite during the ride across the sea's writhing waters.

From more than a mile away, Malik could make out the mist on the horizon. The fine spray lingered 30 feet above the surface of the water before vanishing into the atmosphere. Two other whaling crews could be seen hovering around the area where the whale was last spotted. From his rivals' poor positioning, Malik knew that the whale had already eluded them on its way south for the winter. The whale was his for the taking. Malik signaled to slow the boat. He pulled off his hood and exchanged his fur mitts for the baggy blood-stained cotton work gloves he wore to kill many whales. The crew sorted the weapons they would use to strike their prey.

Before commercial whalers introduced the Eskimos to gunpowder, the only way to kill a whale was to keep stabbing it with ivory harpoons until it died. Malik now clutched a four pound graphite harpoon armed with a small bomb. Another member of the crew loaded explosive cartridges into a shoulder gun, a stubby brass rifle custom made for killing whales.

Malik prepared to strike with stealth. He and his men tried to remain invisible to the whale, or at the very least, distant and non-threatening. Even though not much can threaten a 40-ton whale, Malik didn't want to give the whale any more advantages than it already had. Malik looked at his watch: 10:30 AM. They had seven hours of daylight. If they killed a whale, everyone in Barrow with a boat would have to move fast to get there in time to help tow the whale back to town before nightfall. Darkness made worse the list of hazards all creatures must endure to survive in the Arctic: exposure, the cold, and the fearsome Nanook, the Polar Bear, a threat to every living creature from the tiny Arctic fox to the huge whale itself.

For the moment, the six men and their boat lay between the beach and the site of the whale. Malik ordered his rudderman, Roy Ahmaogak, to try and position the boat north and east of the whale so that they could run with the harpooned mammal toward the shore. They didn't want to tow a huge and unstable carcass any farther than they had to. But Roy knew that his main objective was to keep the boat close enough to attack the whale. If it meant a longer haul home, so be it.

Malik waved his paddle in an age-old sign to other whalers in pursuit of the same beast that his crew was readying a strike to try to kill it. Ever since Malik first spotted it, the 55-foot whale continued to surface and breathe regularly. Its hot breath formed a spout as if to beckon its pursuers and direct them toward the spot where they would receive the biggest gift of the season.

After watching the whale dive deep beneath the surface, Malik directed his crew to the site where he thought it would appear next. Trailing the Bowhead by little more than a hundred feet, Roy deftly piloted the boat directly into the whale's path. Malik held his breath, hoping it would surface close by. But despite all the modern technology at his disposal, he still needed to come within 10 feet of the moving whale just to have a better than even chance of harpooning it.

Malik's father taught him to aim the harpoon for a spot right behind the two perpendicular breathing holes in back of the skull. It is the most vulnerable part of the whale, a narrow cavity leading straight to the heart. If perfectly executed, the harpoon would pierce through the blubber, striking the unprotected heart. A lacerated whale heart pounded with such tremendous force that those few whalers lucky enough to land the perfect strike would hold onto the wildly pulsating shafts of their harpoons for as long as they could before being knocked off their feet.

Had the whale sensed the shadowy forms on the surface above, Malik asked himself. He expected the worst. He reached for his harpoon. The only sound to disturb his concentration was the idling of the Johnson outboard. The whole boat seemed to tremor with the anticipation of its crew.

Without warning the whale submerged deeper and longer than at any time since they first spotted it. Malik saw the bowhead's last intake of air and noticed that the blowholes did not open significantly wider than other shorter breaths. The whale would have to surface soon, and when it did, Malik would strike.

Malik grasped the harpoon firmly in his left hand, swaying from side to side. He fixed his attention on the point in the water where he expected the whale to emerge. Roy, the rudderman, expertly shuttled the boat into perfect position. Five seconds later, the shimmering black skin broke the surface of the Chukchi Sea precisely where Malik eyes were focused. He blinked and cocked his arms behind his round, thinly thatched head.

Malik's triceps tightened as he raised the hollow graphite harpoon. He knew the whale was most vulnerable the instant it started to exhale. A strong impulse ran through his wiry frame compelling him to lunge forward, launching the harpoon. The force of his throw nearly tossed him into the swirling black waters below.

The razor sharp tip pierced the gleaming skin of the magnificent creature. A primer charge at the end of the harpoon exploded with a bang as it lodged deep in the whale. Recoiling from the horror of bombs exploding inside it, the Bowhead bellowed in agony as it dove in a hopeless attempt to escape its fate. The next blast came seconds later. This bomb, on a five second fuse, ripped apart the whale's insides.

Roy, the rudderman, waited anxiously for the sound of that second blast. As soon as he heard it, he lifted the 40-pound brass shoulder gun. The whale surfaced, exhaling a fountain of blood. Roy stood ready to land still more exploding rounds somewhere near the whale's head. His target was so huge he could hardly miss. He aimed the lumbering weapon and jerked the rusty trigger towards him. The bomb, which should have gone off only after it was deep inside the whale, exploded on contact. Shards of blubber flew in all directions, falling back into the sea like a storm of crimson hail.

Roy fired again and again. The whale violently writhed in a frantic attempt to shake off the inflated sealskin floats tied to the harpoon. The turbulent water surged scarlet with bloody foam. A third shot entered the whale's arched back.

Malik ordered the helmsman to move the boat closer to the wounded whale. He was afraid that it might escape beneath the ice. If he could hit it with a second harpoon, the additional floats might slow it down long enough to kill it. As soon as the harpoon was loaded, he thrust it into the whale. The shiny black skin bloated again with the force of the bomb's explosion. The whale's huge tail caught one side of the boat. Malik pitched violently forward. His shoulder slammed against one of the seats. Drenched in the whale's blood, the men grabbed the gunwales to steady the wildly rocking dinghy. When Malik regained enough balance to look up, he saw a suddenly sluggish whale, its injuries too grave to overcome.

Afraid that the Bowhead might make one last attempt to dive beneath a patch of ice before it died, Malik reached for a third harpoon. He knew that while the crippled beast was mortally wounded, it was not yet subdued. The whale's size and its will to live could propel it onward for many miles, prolonging the ancient endurance test between whale and Eskimo.

But before Malik could ready the next shot, the limping whale succumbed. The men now had to work fast to keep their prize from sinking. Three other whaling crews out that morning had watched the strike through binoculars from key vantage points on the Chukchi horizon, cheering at each sight of blood. Now, taking up an ancient chant celebrating the kill, they hurried to help Malik and his crew make sure the dead whale did not sink to the bottom of the ocean.

Competition among Eskimo whalers has always been tempered by mutual respect and the need to join forces after the kill. When one crew got lucky, others dropped their own hunt to help their more fortunate comrades. All who contributed in any way got part of the slaughtered whale. Malik would repay those crews who rushed to his aid by letting their captains partake in the bounty, giving them choice sections of the butchered whale.

People have always been the most important resource in a subsistence whaling village. Everybody was expected to help the many different stages of a traditional whale hunt. Dragging the whale onto the beach for butchering is a monumental task. As word spread that Malik had a whale in tow, Barrow readied itself to help him.

Ten minutes after the call came in on the CB radio, news of the strike was broadcast on KBRW AM, the only radio station for 100,000 square miles. Regular programming was interrupted to broadcast the news of the whale kill. Volunteers with boats were urged to meet Malik at sea and help his crew ballast the whale and bring it safely to shore. Within an hour of the special broadcast, 80 people in 22 boats arrived on the scene. It took them four hours to haul the mammoth carcass the six miles back to the beach.

By the time Malik and his six-man crew arrived, it was too dark for them to see that practically the whole town was waiting. Three hundred. people ran out to greet Malik's crew as they sloshed their way to shore. This was the moment that the whaler dreams of as a child and cherishes as he grows old.

Over the centuries, Eskimos not only revered the whale, they worshipped it. In an unchanged ritual stretching back thousands of years, Malik gathered everyone on the beach around him. He said a prayer of thanks to the whale and its spirit which he believed would come to live within all who were sustained by it. Before the butchering could begin, Malik's wife performed another ancient ceremony. With a maternal touch, she gently poured water from a bucket, first into the dead whale's open mouth and then into its blowhole, letting the whale taste fresh water for the first time. Only then would the whale's spirit become part of the village.

Malik assigned several men to begin carving up the whale. If left unbutchered for even a short time, its massive unused energy would quickly turn to heat, causing the carcass to reach temperatures in excess of 300° Fahrenheit. The Eskimos had precious little time to butcher the whale before it cooked itself.

A half-dozen Eskimos climbed ladders mounted against the side of the dead whale, carrying Ulus, sharp fan-shaped knives mounted on traditional long wooden handles. They stood on top of the two-story-high carcass cutting the blubber in a checkerboard pattern. Hot putrid air hit them in the face as they ripped two-foot-thick squares of blubber from the whale's back with large iron hooks.

Plumes of steam belching out of the whale were visible for miles. Next, the Eskimos stripped long slabs of blubber from the carcass.

Within an hour, the 55-foot covering of Muktuk, the staple of the local diet, was removed from the decomposing whale. The slabs of Muktuk were quickly spirited into 22 neat piles reserved for each crew involved in the hunt. These piles were their reward and became the property of the crew's chief, to be dispensed at his discretion.

The butchers spent another few hours removing the whale's meat by repeating the same process they used to collect the Muktuk. By dawn the next morning, the entire operation, employing over a thousand people, was virtually completed. With a few more tasks here and there, the 40-ton whale, swimming carelessly just a few hours before, had been killed, towed to the beach, and thoroughly butchered.

In 1988, Barrowans no longer needed whale meat to survive. They could get through the winter even if they didn't kill a single whale. A dwindling remnant of traditional Eskimos remained uncomfortable with Barrow's increasing reliance on the outside world. Malik's catch insured them of at least one more year of independence.

Until the white man shattered their impenetrable isolation, subsistence whaling villages like Barrow killed only as many whales as they needed to survive. As World War II came to a close, nations with commercial whaling industries realized that the whales they slaughtered en masse teetered on the verge of extinction. In 1946, the International Whaling Commission (IWC) was formed.

Ostensibly, the IWC was created to protect and replenish whales. But in fact all it did was regulate their continued killing, albeit in reduced numbers. Exemptions became the rule. Nations like Japan and the Soviet Union successfully argued that their whaling industries were necessary to help their economies recover from the ravages of war. So did Norway and Iceland, although the former incurred almost no physical damage during the war and the latter suffered none at all.

Nations like the United States and Canada, with Eskimo populations that historically depended on whales for survival, petitioned the IWC to permit Eskimo whaling for subsistence purposes. Subsistence quotas were based on the size of each village and the projected number of whales in its area. As the number of whales increased, so too did the quotas.

The IWC created an odd and undeniable reality in subsistence Arctic villages. Instead of just hunting for enough whales needed to survive as they had for thousands of years, Eskimo settlements could treat their unfilled quotas like tradeable commodities, something of value to be bought and sold.

In 1988, the International Whaling Commission gave the tiny village of Barrow, Alaska, a quota of eight whales it could hunt and kill, far in excess of the number really needed for subsistence. With Malik's strike, Barrow took its fifth whale of the year. While all of them were Bowhead whales, there was no rule that said they had to be. In another of the IWC's many strange quirks, it was perfectly acceptable for Barrow whalers to fill their quotas with any whales on which they could get their hands.

Suddenly, the three California gray whales frolicking aimlessly off the coast of Barrow were fair game. Until the IWC imposed quotas, no one in Barrow would have given gray whales a second thought. But the byzantine provisions of the IWC created an artificial demand for any kind of whale meat. The organization established to save whales created new reasons to kill them. Once discovered, the three California gray whales could be killed just like the Bowhead. Even though their barnacled skin was virtually inedible and their meat was tough and acrid, Barrowans still had three more whales they could legally slaughter before the end of the year.

The IWC regulations didn't stop there. They went even further. Not only were subsistence whaling towns allowed to kill any kind of whales they could catch, the IWC also permitted them to trade their quotas with other subsistence villages. These towns could even hunt whales in excess of their own quotas if they did it to help fill that of another, less fortunate settlement.

With just under 3,000 Inupiat Eskimos, Barrow was the largest and most important Eskimo village in the world. It was also the oldest. It was the home of the greatest legends, and the greatest whalers, like Malik. It was also the home of a new and unintended creation of the International Whaling Commission: professional subsistence whaling.

On October 6, 1988, Roy Ahmaogak, a member of Malik's elite crew, got a phone call from the inland village of Nuiqsut, a tiny Eskimo settlement 80 miles south of Barrow. The Eskimos of Nuiqsut survived for centuries by roaming the frozen tundra in search of land animals. Before the IWC, whaling was as alien to Nuiqsut natives as tarpon fishing was to Barrowans. The Nuiqsut caller asked Ahmaogak if he wanted to hunt for more whales to help fill Nuiqsut's three whale quota. If Ahmaogak got lucky, he and his crew could make a tidy profit selling the whales back to Nuiqsut. On the quota market, one whale could fetch in excess of $50,000. More than enough incentive for Ahmaogak to give the offer some serious thought.

Within the next few days, the weather took a nasty turn toward winter. Temperatures plummeted to 20° below zero. Strong winds pushed the massive polar ice pack south on its annual foray toward the Barrow coast. With each passing day, the new ice forming around the shore was expanding farther out to sea. In the next few weeks, the new ice would blanket miles of the Chukchi Sea and stretch all the way out to the polar ice pack. When they met, the new ice would be consumed and incorporated into the floating pack, perhaps never to melt again.

Large as Australia, the polar ice pack is the biggest piece of ice in the world. For millions of years, the polar ice pack has floated frozen across the top of the world with some sections thousands of feet thick. For nine months of the year, it stretches from the northern coast of Alaska all the way to Norway, 3,000 miles away. In the summer, the outer edges of the polar pack melt away. Huge icebergs, some the size of small states, break off and float freely in the icy Arctic Ocean until consumed again by the encroaching pack during the next change of season. During July and early August, the last of the snow and ice melt away from Barrow's beaches. But by the beginning of October, those days are a distant memory.

Winter was back.

Ahmaogak told the caller from Nuiqsut he would take a look, but he thought that by this late in the year, all the whales would have left. Most of them were well on their way south to warmer waters for winter breeding and birthing. Ahmaogak spent Friday, October 7, 1988, fruitlessly searching for whales, riding his ski machine up and down the coast around Point Barrow. The temperature was dropping almost as fast as the light was fading. By the time he ended his futile search, the temperature had dropped to 25° below zero. Ahmaogak turned his ski machine around and headed back to Barrow across the 18 miles of glassy smooth Arctic Ocean ice, convinced there were no whales to be found.

But as he sped around the long sandbar north of Point Barrow, he spotted whales spouting off in the distance. Ahmaogak excitedly raced his ski machine to the site, hoping to find bowheads. Instead, he found the three California gray whales who were no longer frolicking. Now they were panicking, apparently trapped under a quickly growing patch of ice. The thin ice around the whales was too weak to support his weight, so all Ahmaogak could do was look at them from 150 feet away. It appeared that the whales were clinging to a hole barely big enough for them to stick their huge heads through to swallow a breath of air.

When the hole froze over, the whales would drown. As much as he wanted to help the stranded whales, Ahmaogak believed there was nothing anybody could do. The helpless giants were doomed. This kind of thing happens every year, he consoled himself. Countless numbers of whales die while making their annual migration from the icy Arctic waters. Their decayed carcasses washed up on shore every spring to prove it.

When he got back to Barrow, he unloaded his bear rifle and gear from the ski machine, and went inside to escape the sub-zero temperatures. After he had a warm bite to eat, Ahmaogak called his friends Craig George and Geoff Caroll, the biologists at the local wildlife management office, to tell them what he saw on the ice a few hours earlier. He could never have predicted that his routine report of a routine occurrence would lead to the most massive animal rescue effort ever staged by man.

Within three weeks, at least 26 television networks from four continents would come to Barrow to broadcast live, up-to-the-minute reports about the 'stranded California gray whales.' "Operation Breakout" became perhaps the most widely covered non-event in the history of electronic news gathering.

Of course, for Eskimos it wasn't news at all. Noah Webster defined news as "any information about anything previously unknown." Everyone in Barrow knew that gray whales died under Arctic ice. But the rescue of the three whales would still cost at least $5,800,000, personally involve both the President of the United States and the General Secretary of the Soviet Union, lead a fragile democratic government to the verge of collapse, and capture the imagination of hundreds of millions of people around the world before two of the whales were eventually freed. Journalists from competing networks would trample each other in pursuit of new angles while they missed the real story about Barrow and its Eskimos.

The whales would unite environmentalists and oil men, Eskimos and whites, Alaska with the Lower 48 states, the United States and the Soviet Union, and two people 7,000 miles apart who would meet and marry, all because of an absurd animal rescue.

Lucky whales.

Chapter 2

From the Edge of the Universe to the Center of the World

On Saturday morning, October 8, the day after he found the three whales, Roy Ahmaogak and Malik drove their ski machines along the Point Barrow sandbar to the spot where Roy found them. As they got closer, Malik's windswept face grew luminous with his child-like love for whales. He felt a strong kinship with the creatures he hunted. They were part of him. Two miles from the site, Malik could see three whale spouts hanging unusually close to each other in the bitter Arctic air.

Malik's excitement grew at just the sight of them. Roy was relieved to see the whales were still there. The two Eskimos parked their 500-pound ski machines on the snow-covered sand at the edge of the spit. The ocean ice was too weak to hold the machines. In fact, the area around the whales wasn't really ice at all. It was still only thick slush, but it was hardening by the minute.

The closer Malik got to the whales, the more he wondered why they didn't just swim away. The animals seemed paralyzed by fear.

Maybe they were afraid to leave the breathing hole to explore the unfamiliar water farther out toward the open channel. The Arctic autumn weather was the most unstable of the year. It was impossible to predict ice conditions beyond just a few hours. With the weather so uncertain, Malik knew that if the whales did not make a move within the next few hours, the ice could harden to the point where they might become genuinely stranded.

Malik sympathized with the whales' fear of the unknown. If they left this hole, they might not find another. What would happen if they ran out of air before they got back? What if they became disoriented under the ice? The whales instinctively knew that if they lost their way, they would drown.

No one knew more than Malik about the gray whales' cousins, the Bowhead whales. He knew they would not hesitate to break their snouts through the thick slush to breathe. Countless times they dove under large ice patches to dodge his well-aimed harpoons. He was surprised to see how different gray whales were from the species he knew so well.

Malik and Roy stood on the beach waiting for the whales to surface. They came up by turn every few minutes to breathe. It was their surfacing in the same place over and over again that kept the 10- by 20-foot hole from freezing over. In all the years he spent with whales, Malik never saw them act with such rational cooperation.

Malik instinctively wanted to touch the whales, but there was no way to reach them. The slush was too soft to support a man's weight and too thick for a boat. Unable to help, the two Eskimos climbed on their ski machines and headed back to Barrow.

Eskimo whalers from the tiny inland village of Nuiqsut, 80 miles southwest of Barrow, learned of the three whales from local radio reports. Several of them gathered at the hamlet's single telephone to call their colleagues in Barrow. Malik was dismayed to learn of Nuiqsut's eagerness to harvest the three helpless whales. He was from the old school which taught that whales are killed not for glory or profit but only for survival. And these three gray whales were not needed for survival.

The 20th century came to Barrow about 70 years late. But when it finally did appear, it thrust tumultous change upon everyone in the Arctic, and it did so with wrenching force. The sum of all the change meant that Barrow would never be the same. Whales would never again be the sole source of life. They would never again mean the difference between life and death. Instead, they would take on a whole new meaning: commerce, a concept as alien to the Eskimo as palm trees. The whales so sacred for so long suddenly became a commodity. Malik was ashamed of many things brought on by the modern era, but this view of life mortified him. The three helpless gray whales could be slaughtered not for food, but for the sake of the few hundred people they would employ for a day, something inconceivable just a few decades before.

As they thought about the whales desperately gasping for each breath, Malik and Roy realized they didn't find them by chance trapped in a tiny hole surrounded by thousands of square miles of ice. The very geography that threatened to entomb the whales allowed for their discovery and, in the end, their rescue. The whales were caught among the sand shoals at the very tip of a narrow sandbar stretching northward until it vanished into the sea. At its widest point, the five-mile Point Barrow sandspit was 100 feet across. The far end lay nine miles north of Barrow itself. It was a fragile earth barrier between two seas. It separated the Chukchi Sea and its fury from the Beaufort and its calm waters.

The whales probably gravitated to the sandspit because it served as a natural wind break. They could feed more comfortably in its shelter. But when the calm water started to freeze, the whales apparently thought they were stuck. If it had happened any farther from shore, no one would have found them, and they certainly would have died.

That night, over a few too many bootleg beers, some of Malik's whaling friends asked him what he thought about harvesting the three gray whales. Malik told his friends that as long as they had a chance to swim free, he couldn't see the point of killing them. He could only support killing the whales for humanitarian reasons. If they were going to suffer needlessly with no way to help them, then it would be the right thing to do. Malik deeply respected all the sea's great creatures. He insisted that others do the same.

Malik believed that if the whales could overcome their fear of ice they would have no trouble swimming free. Having never seen slush before, they probably thought it was just like ice. While the whales acted like they were trapped, as of Saturday afternoon, October 8, they were not. Later that night, reports of the stranded whales started to spread through town. Almost immediately, the newer whaling crews clamored for permission to harvest the whales.

But they weren't allowed to do anything until two white men named Craig George and Geoff Carroll had the chance to study them. They were out on the tundra hunting caribou and wouldn't be back until Monday. Craig and Geoff were professionals. Their job was to manage wildlife for their Eskimo employers. They helped start the local government's Department of Wildlife Management in the early 1970s. It offered these two adventurers a chance to study whales in a way other biologists could only dream about. But these two biologists had a bizarre price to pay for their chance to work in the Arctic. They were hired to help the Eskimos hunt and kill bowhead whales.

They conducted an annual census of the bowhead whale population for the local government called the North Slope Borough, a borough being Alaska's equivalent of a county. Their findings were the basis for negotiating the next year's quota with the International Whaling Commission. They came to Barrow to manage wildlife, but their most important task helped the Eskimos to continue hunting whales. Geoff and Craig exemplified a remarkable fact of modern Eskimo life. The Inupiat Eskimo lived primitive lives by conventional American standards, but they were sophisticated enough to hire the best modern expertise all their money could buy. The Eskimos recruited a cadre of professionals to manage their stormy relationship with the modern world.

The greedy talk of slaughtering the gray whales appalled Malik. He knew such brutal behavior would reflect badly on his people. The young whalers sounded like the white prospectors who were forever looking to stake another claim. It pained him to imagine all the careless whaling crews in a mad dash to senselessly kill three useless whales. At best, they would be used for dog food.

Before leaving on their weekend hunting trip, Geoff and Craig reported Roy's discovery to their boss, Dr. Tom Albert, 1,200 miles away in Anchorage. Albert wanted his two biologists to check on the whales before they left, and whether the animals would survive the weekend. Geoff assured him they would be fine. By Monday morning, the whales would safely be on their way south.

Geoff and Craig routinely investigated every reported stranding of any animal that appeared on the government's endangered species list. Protected from the rusty harpoons of commercial whaling fleets since 1947, the gray whales flourished. By 1988, biologists estimated there were 22,000 gray whales, the highest number in the history of the species. Yet they still figured prominently on the endangered species list.

Whale strandings were common. But if these three gray whales were as close to shore as Roy Ahmaogak claimed, their stranding would prove unique. Geoff and Craig would be the first biologists to actually observe gray whales trapped in ice. Although gray whales are familiar to nature lovers and whale watchers along the Pacific Coast of the Lower 48, biologists still knew very little about them. Depending on how close they could get, Geoff and Craig would have an opportunity to learn more about them, especially their behavior under extraordinary stress. Eskimos long believed the whales were killed by the ice, but until now, biologists could only theorize. On Tuesday morning, October 11, four days after the whales were found, Geoff and Craig would get to see firsthand.

The two bearded biologists loaded sleeping bags, flares, and emergency rations onto wooden dogsleds hitched to the backs of their ski machines. They needed a guide to direct them. Since Roy could not go, they asked Billy Adams, a skillful Eskimo hunter who knew the way. He had seen the whales on Sunday. Billy would be good company. He had a great sense of humor and his own ski machine. The three men were tightly bundled in a combination of modern and traditional cold-weather gear for the numbing minus 75° temperatures they could expect on their ride out.

As the sun rose just above the southern horizon, the trio sped alongside Barrow's only road until it abruptly ended seven miles north of town. From there, it was still another five miles to the whales. When they got as far as they could on the ski machines, Billy led them by foot the rest of the way. Craig stopped to marvel at the surroundings. He squinted past the ice's blinding glare to the sandbar. The tiny sliver of sand beneath him was all that remained of the North American continent.

As it tapered off into the sea, so too did the world of man. The utter solitude overwhelmed him. Not a trace of life. No vegetation, no variation in scene, no visible image of anything. Unending. Stark. White. Yet his Arctic was a bountiful natural habitat teeming with an immense variety of life. Walrus, seals, polar bears and, of course, whales. They thrived in a world so little explored and so little understood.

The three men stood on the frozen beach and watched for spouts. If the whales were alive and still clinging to the hole, sooner or later they would have to come up for air. If the men saw nothing in the next five or six minutes, there were only two possible explanations. The whales either swam free or they drowned. As much as they hoped the whales were free, Geoff and Craig longed to see them. They had already begun to map out in their minds the treatise they would write if only they could compile enough data.

As two minutes became three, Geoff and Craig knew they should have gotten there sooner. Just as they were about to give up, a low rumble came from a few hundred feet off shore. A whale's mammoth head poked through the ice. They were still here. Craig, George and Billy whooped with joy. They punched their fists through the minus 15° air and gave each other heavily mittened Arctic high-fives.

The whale exhaled. Unlike a locomotive letting off steam, this was the sound of something distinctly alive. Only a warm blooded mammal could make that deep gargle. "FFWWWSSSSHHH," the whale belched. As soon as it filled its giant lungs, the whale slipped its head again beneath the dark sea. The displaced water rippled through the weak ice surrounding the hole, freezing as it moved. A second rumbling began. Another huge head completely filled the hole's brief void. Looking through binoculars, Geoff could distinguish one whale from another by the pattern of barnacles on its snout. The beast swallowed its portion of air and vanished as quickly as the first.

From what Geoff and Craig could observe, the whales stayed under as long as they could. Protecting and guiding each other, they developed an efficient system for breathing. They pulled their heads back under and away from the hole to give their oxygen-starved comrades a turn to experience the hole's promised salvation. This behavior was new to Geoff and Craig. Neither of them could remember learning anything about whales reacting rationally to a life-threatening predicament.

After the second whale surfaced there was a long pause. Roy Ahmaogak reported seeing three whales. What had happened to the third whale? they wondered. A few seconds later, they got their answer. The third whale timidly emerged. It was smaller, almost fragile. It looked battered and tired. Its snout had almost no skin. It had rubbed off in its battle with the small hole. It swam with much less authority than the other two whales.

The larger and older whales stayed down longer to give the smaller one more time to breathe. When the baby had its fill, the cycle started all over again. Geoff and Craig noticed a pattern. When the two big whales surfaced, they rammed the edges of the hole. This self-destructive behavior puzzled them until they realized the whales were trying to expand the hole. Their ramming kept slush from turning to ice. Here was more astounding evidence that these whales possessed a keen intelligence.

Billy knew a bowhead would break breathing holes in ice up to half a foot thick. These grays had trouble even with soft ice. No wonder it was grays and not their Bowhead cousins that drowned under the ice.

Each whale took several turns breathing and then dove for about five minutes. Craig dug into his knapsack and probed for his 35-millimeter camera. He borrowed it from the borough to document the whales. Whatever photos he took would belong to the government. But this was a fantasy performance; he wanted copies of every shot for his photo album.

For almost an hour, the three men were transfixed. They stood as helpless as the struggling creatures they were desperate to aid. None of their training and experience prepared them for this. They knew how to study whales, not how to save them.

The whales were tantalizingly close. Billy, Craig, and Geoff stepped cautiously out to test the ice. Giddy at their unexpected good fortune, the three men carefully walked until the ice grew too weak to support them. They were just 50 feet from the whales. From what little they could see, the hole appeared about the same size as a whale's head.

Billy went to his sled to fetch the hollow aluminum pole he used to probe ice. He scampered nimbly back to where Geoff and Craig knelt at safety's edge. Billy carefully measured a few paces beyond his companions and pushed the end of his pole deep into the hardened surface. He had to lean hard to break the ice. Once through, the pole easily probed the slush. Billy knew it would not be long before it froze.

Craig held the camera under his parka to shelter it from the cold. His brittle film nearly snapped in the sub-zero weather. Learning from experience, he knew to wind it with tender care. The sun vanished behind a low lying bank of thick fog as he waited for the whales to begin their next breathing cycle. Hastily, he popped open the back of his camera to put in the proper film for the changing light conditions.

The forecast high for Tuesday October 11—four days after the whales were first discovered—was four degrees above. That was 12° warmer than the average for that time of the year. Since it was seldom that warm without insulating cloud cover, the men knew they might confront whiteout, one of the Arctic's most deadly conditions. The slightest wind can trigger it by whipping the dry, almost weightless snow into the air, blending it uniformly with the white sky. Whiteout blinds everything but the Arctic's most deadly predator: the polar bear. He actually uses the condition to attack his helpless prey. While well aware of the constant danger, the three men were experienced enough to be cautious and not to panic.

Right on schedule, the whales began surfacing after a four-minute dive, first the two large whales, followed by the smaller one. Craig excitedly shot a whole roll of film in one respiration cycle. He hurriedly reloaded his camera to shoot more before the whales dove again. He was flustered, but regained his composure when he remembered he was an expert, not a tourist.

The whales weren't going anywhere. He could hang around the edge of the spit for as long as he could stand the cold, taking his time, picking the best shots. When they came back, he could take even better ones.

For nearly an hour the men were speechless. When they tried to discuss the significance of their findings, all three spoke at once. Their exhilaration was tempered by their inability to help creatures of such intelligent majesty. The whales were sinking in what looked like a hopeless quagmire. Yet they were rational and deliberate. They avoided the panic they realized would doom them. Their fate was intertwined and they knew it. They had to work together to survive. It required leadership to devise and implement such an ingenious plan, but Craig and Geoff couldn't figure out which whale was in charge.

It was a mystery their science would not solve until just hours

before the whales were freed. Was it instinct that made them react to
the encroaching ice or was it rational thought? Was it genetic code or
sheer intelligence underlying this ingenious system? These were
some of the questions that would dog biologists, rescuers, reporters,
and millions of people around the world for weeks.

The whales' unusual surfacing was the most obvious unanswered
question Geoff and Craig asked about this strange and fascinating
phenomenon. The gray whales is noted for not only its migration but
also its habitat. As if not yet comfortable in its relatively new home
at sea, the gray whales rarely wanders more than a mile from shore.
Shallow water deters its two greatest enemies, the killer whale and
the great white shark.

Like all whales, the gray normally swims parallel to the surface.
To breathe, all the whale has to do is arch its back just enough to
expose its blowholes above the waterline. But the only way these
three whales could survive was to shoot out of the small hole like an
MX missile from a floating silo.

"We have to get this on videotape," Craig shouted. He wanted to
get back to town to borrow some equipment from the North Slope
Borough's TV studio. They tightened their hoods and pulled down
facemasks and goggles. Craig looked at his watch. He couldn't
believe four hours had passed since they first saw the whales. They
would have to hurry to return to town, fetch the equipment and get
back out on the ice before dark.

Back in his office, Craig picked up the seven-page Barrow phone
book to find the television studio's number. He called Oran Caudle,
the director of the Borough's state-of-the-art television studio and
asked him if they could take a video camera to photograph some
whales stranded at the end of Point Barrow. Oran was from
Texarkana, Texas, and didn't know much about whales. But he knew
what the Arctic could do to his expensive equipment and wasn't
about to let anyone borrow it.

The 31 year-old divorcé always wanted his Eskimo boss to make
better use of the lavish TV studio. His most exciting current project
was a training film explaining the North Slope's employee benefits
package. Oran was so desperate for hands-on television experience
he was willing to move to the end of the world to get it. Craig's story
piqued his interest. Then again, after four years in Barrow, just
about anything would have. He was always looking for local

programming to put on Channel 20, the North Slope's under-used television channel. Here was a chance to get some gripping pictures.

The more Oran learned, the more he wanted to help, but his hands were tied. He told Craig he could not lend out any equipment. He could assign a camera crew, but not until the next day. Hanging up the phone, Oran determined to go himself. Not only did the project sound interesting, but it would also be a welcome chance to get out of his office.

Oran was a big bear of a man. His ready smile radiated warmth. He endeared himself to almost everyone in Barrow, even Eskimos, many of whom resented a white man's success. Like almost 75 percent of all Barrow marriages, Oran Caudle's recently ended in divorce. He way trying to rebuild his life, but Barrow was about the worst place on earth to do it.

Every Barrow resident was a victim in one form or another. In addition to the highest latitude on the continent, the tiny town at the top of the world was afflicted with some of America's most notorious statistics: the highest rates of murder, rape, suicide, alcoholism and physical abuse of spouses and children.

If you somehow managed to withstand the isolation and cold, there were still the three insufferable months of darkness. Like everyone else in Barrow, Oran needed a strong support system to survive. But unlike most people whose only escape was drunkenness, Caudle turned to the Calvary Baptist Church. After service on Sunday, October 9, he talked with some of his fellow parishioners about the whales Roy Ahmaogak found two days earlier.

Caudle knew about gray whales not from books or PBS nature specials, but from seeing them frolic near the shore. Even when he didn't see them, proof of their presence washed up on the rocky beach in the form of slimy barnacles. If the footage was interesting enough, Oran would edit it into a 20-minute segment for Channel 20. Whales were more important to Barrow's economic life than cars were to Detroit. Barrow was a single industry town.

Wednesday morning, October 12, came too early for Oran. The division between day and night, taken for granted in the Lower 48, was a concept alien to the Arctic, something hard to adjust too, especially for a tunik (white) like Oran Caudle. Where midnight was broad daylight and noon was pitch dark, time was meaningless. Humans react like every other animal in the Arctic during the long season. They sleep. Psychologists call it "Seasonal Affected Disorder." Caudle called it "the winter blues."

It was all Oran Caudle could do just to sit up in bed to grab the remote control. In a daze he clicked on CNN, the Cable News Network. It was his link to the outside world. He showered, shaved and downed his daily breakfast: a granola bar and a can of apple juice. "Sonia Live" was his signal to be out the door. It was 8:00 AM, Alaska time. It was just as well. Caudle couldn't stand the host of CNN's mid-day talk show anyway. He wore the new felt-lined boots his mother sent him. Everyone in Barrow wore them. They were big enough for a family of four, but they were guaranteed to protect his feet down to 80° below zero. Caudle wasn't sure how long he would be on the ice, but at least his feet wouldn't get frostbite.

Craig told Oran that unless the ice grew stronger overnight, 50 feet was as close as they could get to the whales. Maybe now Oran could use the expensive zoom lens he cajoled the borough into buying. This was the first time he took it out of the box since it arrived air freight from Seattle three months before.

He packed a sensitive directional microphone which he stored along with the batteries, assorted cables, and plenty of blank videotape in special cold-weather bags. He loaded it all into the back of the TV studio's white Chevy Suburban.

Oran picked up Billy Adams and drove him to Craig and Geoff's office in the Naval Arctic Research Laboratory, known to everyone in Barrow by its initials. NARL was a sprawling complex of decaying World War II quonset huts and modern prefabricated buildings standing on wooden stilts at the northern edge of town. NARL used to be the center of town. Before its technology fell into obsolescence with the advent of satellite technology, NARL was the site of a massive radar station designed to warn against a transpolar nuclear attack. It looked like a space colony on a frozen planet at the edge of a strange and hostile universe. NARL was the last man-made structure this side of the North Pole.

When Oran and his crew arrived at 8:30 AM, the biologists looked worried. They thought time was running out for the whales. The National Weather Service said temperatures could fall to 40° below zero out on the ice. With such cold, the whales' only hope was wind, but the forecast predicted no wind. Without it, the holes would freeze and the whales would drown before the day was out.

The ride out to the whales lasted 50 grueling minutes. When the six of them brought their ski machines to a halt 10 yards from the snow-covered beach, Geoff and Craig were amazed at how much new ice had formed overnight. The whales continued their grim dance precisely where Geoff and Craig left them the day before. The baby seemed steadier, taking more regular breaths.

Billy Adams crept out to see how much farther he could walk. He went almost 50 feet beyond his earlier footprints. Remarkably, his tracks were still intact, proof of the stilled winds. At this rate, the whales had only a day or so left.

In his excitement, Oran almost dropped his camera. He was tripping all over himself. Craig told him to calm down. "The whales aren't going anywhere," he assured Caudle. "Take your time and do what you have to do to get ready. The whales don't have much choice, they have to wait for you."

Here were three animals in their natural habitat and Oran could treat them as if they were back in his television studio. Every other time he photographed animals, he was lucky to get any pictures at all. Oran painstakingly set up the camera. Equipment failure proved his main worry. At 40° below zero, any conceivable type of failure was not only possible, it was probable. Even if his gear worked, Oran wasn't sure how long he could last. It was more than cold, it was dangerous. When he breathed the bitter air too deeply, it singed his lungs. In weather this cold, bones become brittle and easily break.

When Oran looked into the viewfinder, he saw only fog. He knew from experience not to rip the camera apart to get at the droplets of water. He put the camera on the tripod and waited. In a few minutes, the inside would turn as cold as the outside and the condensation would vanish. Geoff and Craig noticed the whales fearfully reacting to the commotion on the ice. The animals most likely mistook the humans' reverberating footsteps for those of a polar bear. Breathing holes are favorite stalking grounds for the mighty bear in search of easy prey.

The trapped whales were extremely vulnerable. They had to know it. Every time they rose to the surface, they were dangerously exposed. A polar bear could kill a giant whale with one devastating swipe of its paw. The whales naturally tried to stay underwater as long as they could. But sooner or later they had to face whatever was stomping around on the frozen ceiling of ice above them. They had to breathe.

While Oran fiddled with the borough's expensive equipment, Geoff and Craig tallied the effects of the whales' predicament. They tried to think of ways to nudge the whales toward open water. The ultimate question was whether they could influence gray whales even if they wanted to.

Oran asked Craig to sit down so he could take his first pictures of the whales surfacing in the background. He lifted the 20-pound camera onto his shoulder, focused the zoom lens and squeezed his thumb against the soft rubber button that turned it on. Caudle lumbered about trying to record every aspect of the whales. He put the camera on the tripod and filmed Billy Adams testing the ice in the foreground with the whales bobbing their gigantic heads against the stark white background.

Since the water was freezing so quickly, it would be safe to walk right out to the edge of the breathing holes by the next morning, or so thought Billy Adams. In a guttural Eskimo accent, he said, "If the holes aren't froze over, we can probably pet 'em."

Oran had a sudden inspiration. "Let's do some interviews," he suggested. "We can edit them to go with the pictures of the whales for local TV. Which one of you wants to be interviewed?" Caudle inquired of his captive audience. Since the film would be shown on the local channel, Oran had to get some Eskimo flavor. That meant Billy or Marie.

Of the five people on the ice, Marie was the best one to conduct the interviews. She was Director of Public Information for the North Slope Borough. She was also Geoff Carroll's wife. In spite of her title, she didn't readily agree. Oran had to coax her. Geoff and Craig pretended to be completely absorbed in their various tasks. They did have lots of data to compile, but they were also both instinctively camera shy.

Oran assured Marie she looked great. Besides, if she made a fool of herself, only a few people in Barrow and some of the surrounding villages would ever see it. After more prodding and appeals to her vanity, she agreed to question her husband and then Craig. Before she knew what he was doing, Oran thrust the microphone into her hand and pushed the record button. "Go ahead," he said with one eye squinted shut and the other buried in the viewfinder. "Ask him what he is doing out here and what he thinks of the whales."

Marie regained her composure in time to pose some coherent questions. She asked Billy how the whales were discovered and what the chances were that they would be harvested. Billy said he didn't know if any decision would be made about harvesting them. All he knew was how they were discovered and what condition they were in.

When it was Craig's turn, he sounded professional, factual and concise, if a little nervous. His rugged face matched the terrain. With the whales active in the background, Oran reveled in the chance to finally shoot some compelling footage. Craig told Marie that the Wildlife Management office had a rare chance to study a phenomenon never seen before.

"Unfortunately, there just isn't enough data yet to comment with any authority as to how these whales got stuck or what their chances might be," said Craig, like a press secretary spitting out a 10-second sound bite.

Oran wanted Billy, an Eskimo, in front of the camera. It would make the setting much more authentic. As advance men for presidential campaigns were proving in the Lower 48, settings were critical to good television.

As Billy and Marie began speaking into the microphone, the whales rose to breathe and burst brilliantly into frame. Oran stumbled in the slush as he backed up for a wider shot. He couldn't imagine a more powerful image. These creatures had such a strong hold over the human imagination. Here they were fighting for each breath in front of people who risked their lives just to see them. Caudle's reaction was emotional, not journalistic. Could anyone maintain a hard-nosed sense of news under such extraordinary circumstances?

As Billy spoke, he motioned behind him to note the stressed condition of the baby whale. At that moment, the baby rose timidly through the ice and stole the show. Bloodied and tired, the desperate animal lay motionless. The pathetic creature seemed to appeal to the camera for help, as if it somehow knew its message would soon be transmitted to creatures of an alien but caring species.

The audio came across the bleak landscape perfectly, but Oran didn't hear a word. He was spellbound by the immense power of the pictures he was shooting. Billy and Marie called and shouted his name several times before they got a response. They were trying to tell him they were finished.

"What do you mean you're done?" he bristled. "Just keep talking, I don't care what y'all say. Just keep talking. Whatever y'all do, don't stop. This is just too incredible." Everyone was astonished. They never saw Oran so insistent. How could he possibly be so interested in hearing what they already said three times? Oran beseeched them to keep up the charade. Marie asked Billy the same questions over and over.

It was like an addictive drug. As much video as Oran got, he had to have more. He had long since forgotten about the cold. When he finally ran out of tape, the others convinced him it was a good time to head back to town.

If they needed any reminder about how cold it was this Wednesday, all they had to do was look down. In the four hours they spent on the ice, it had grown another 25 feet out toward the whale hole. If the cold kept up, they could walk all the way out to the whales in less than a day. The question was how soon the breathing holes would freeze. In any case, these shivering humans could brave it no longer.

The return trip on the back of the snowmobiles was even colder than the ride out. But after all the excitement, enough adrenaline pumped through their chilled veins to keep them from freezing on the way back to town.

After a chance to warm up and grab a bite to eat, Craig used Geoff's office to notify the Coast Guard about the trapped whales and to request their help in freeing them. Unfortunately, the closest permanently manned office was 1,200 miles to the south in Anchorage. He and Geoff thought the whales could easily be freed if there were a ship in the area to break a path through the soft ice. Maybe the Coast Guard could authorize one of its North Slope vessels to cut a channel to the open water which was only a mile away. On second thought, they wouldn't even need an icebreaker. The ice was so thin any medium-sized ship could do the job.

Craig mentioned the idea to Geoff the day before. It seemed like a small enough request. They left a message with the Coast Guard duty officer who promised to pass it on to the proper authority. Later that night, Susan Gallagher called the Coast Guard to see if anything newsworthy was going on. Gallagher was an Alaska night-beat reporter for the Associated Press. She phoned every night to find out if there were any late-breaking stories. The Coast Guard constantly mounted search and rescue efforts to find lost or stranded hunters. In Alaska, these life-threatening strandings were regular headliners. Within hours, this one would become the biggest in state history, and not a human life was at stake.

When he saw it on the wire, the night editor of the *Anchorage Daily News* thought enough of Gallagher's story to run it on page one of Thursday morning's edition. Six days after they were first discovered, the three whales were front page news. Gallagher wrote:

> A trio of whales trapped by ice in the Arctic Ocean used two openings for life saving air Wednesday as biologists sought help to free the animals. The three California gray whales apparently were swimming from the Beaufort Sea to their winter grounds off Mexico when they got caught in the ice east of Point Barrow a week ago, said Geoff Carroll, a biologist from the North Slope Borough. He said the whales' movement kept open two holes in the ice, but those openings shrank as temperatures plunged and new ice formed. By Wednesday, when Barrow's minus 13° set a record low for the date, the holes were 450 feet offshore.

The chain reaction had begun. Todd Pottinger was the next link. A television reporter at KTUU-TV, the NBC affiliate in Anchorage, Pottinger spotted the story on his way to the morning assignment meeting. The assignment meeting determined which stories were worth covering. At 26, Pottinger had already been in the television news business long enough to know that whales always mean news. The minute he saw the story, he was sold. People were fascinated by them. Whether they were beached, mating, or just swimming by, whales were always worth a segment on the Anchorage evening news, sometimes more. The news director needed no convincing. Whales were sure, safe. It was Pottinger's story. He could run with it.

He flipped through his Rolodex for Oran Caudle's phone number. Alaska was much too big for one local news agency to cover by itself. Newspapers, wire services and television stations relied on freelance stringers across the state to report on the areas they couldn't cover themselves. Oran Caudle was the one man Alaska TV stations could turn to for footage from the North Slope. He operated that region's only television facility.

When Oran reached his office that morning, he found a message from Todd Pottinger on his desk. Caudle beamed with excitement. Whenever anyone from Anchorage called, Oran could not help but feel important. Someone needed him after all. He watched Todd on the news every night and was proud to know him. That he would call did wonders for Oran's self-esteem. Part of Oran's job was to assist outside television stations covering Barrow. He was supposed to help make sure the coverage was favorable to the borough, but it was rare that anyone interested in the people of the North Slope had anything good to say. He couldn't imagine what Todd wanted. Since Barrow was so remote, the Anchorage paper arrived a day late. He didn't know the whales were headline news.

One of Oran's biggest frustrations running Barrow's TV studio was that whenever he thought he had a big story, he had to beg Anchorage to take it. Downstate channels covered only the bad news from the North Slope, and there was plenty of that: corruption, crime, alcoholism, polar bear attacks, or the weather. But Oran couldn't push that kind of news since his job was to help, not hurt the borough.

Oran could hardly contain himself when Todd asked him if he had heard anything about the three stranded whales. There was no way whales could be bad news. Pottinger wanted to find out more. He hoped Oran could help him. Not only did he know all about the whales, he spent several hours filming them. "You mean you've got video of them?" Todd Pottinger asked in amazement.

"Uh-huh," Oran answered proudly.

"Can you wait just one second?" Pottinger asked, unable to contain his excitement. He did not wait for an answer before putting Caudle on hold.

Todd's hunch had paid off. Before Oran could collect his thoughts, Pottinger returned asking how soon Oran could provide a satellite transmission to Anchorage. He knew Barrow was home to one of Alaska's biggest white elephants, a highly sophisticated sattelite transmission facility that stood just south of the runway. It was the main link in an ambitious, billion dollar, state project built in the oil-rich 1970s to connect Alaska's rural villages and settlements with the outside world. But like so many other ill-conceived projects of that free spending era, the transmission facility had almost never been used. Although the dishes constantly received, there was nothing ever worth transmitting.

Oran told Todd he wasn't sure if the system even worked. It stood idle for a decade, a misplaced fixture in the frozen tundra. Todd told him to find out quickly. Todd insisted that Oran call the instant he knew anything. In the meantime, Pottinger adjusted KTUU's satellite dish in Anchorage so it could receive the transmission from Barrow. Todd didn't have time to wait for Oran to call back. He needed to book 30 minutes on the satellite immediately. Otherwise, there wouldn't be time to re-edit the footage for the six o'clock news. He called Alascom, the huge telecommunications company that owned Aurora I, the $100 million satellite launched into orbit by the space shuttle Challenger in October 1982. Aurora I orbited 22,500 miles above the Earth connecting the once isolated 49th state with the rest of the world by telephone, radio and television.

Pottinger scheduled the feed for 1:30 PM, Alaska Standard Time. KTUU was committed to pay the $500 whether or not Oran could make his transmitter work. Oran checked the microwave relay connecting his studio to the transmitting complex. The lone borough technician tuned in the test pattern Oran sent him. The system worked. Oran called Todd to tell him the good news.

"Oh, by the way," Todd said before hanging up, "KING-TV in Seattle is going to downlink the fed for their news."

Aurora I was parked in geosynchronous Earth orbit high above the north Pacific. Seattle is the only city in the contiguous United States where a satellite dish can "see" Aurora I. Whenever someone in Alaska wanted to transmit or recieve from beyond the Pacific Northwest "gateway," the signal was transferred in Seattle to a different satellite. This process was called "looping." Even though looping added 45,000 miles to a picture's journey, at 186,000 miles per second, the slight detour took less than half a second.

By the time all the arrangements were made, it was 11:00 AM. Oran had only two hours to view all the footage he shot the day before and edit it onto a single 20-minute tape. For a network news producer, that would be the equivalent of a day off. But to Oran, it was an impossibly short deadline.

Terror quickly replaced his naïve enthusiasm. The footage he shot for local Barrow television was going not only to Anchorage, but also to Seattle. He always dreamed of working with real news professionals. This was his chance and the pressure was on. Oran locked himself in the edit suite where he frantically fast-forwarded through two and a half hours of tape, screening it for the best shots.

Todd called Oran back to reassure him. When they last spoke, Todd sensed Oran was on the verge of panic. Todd told him not to worry about making every edit perfect. KTUU's editors could clean up his mistakes. "Just relax and get it done," he said unconvincingly.

Oran finished at 12:15 PM. He called Todd for step-by-step instructions. Ten minutes later, he was told to put the edited cassette in the tape machine. He waited for a pattern of color bars to appear on his screen accompanied by the familiar sound of the test tone. When he saw it, he was looking at the picture coming back to him from Aurora I. Everything was working. Todd saw it at the same time on his monitor in Anchorage. Patiently, he talked Oran through his first live television transmission. "When you're ready, Oran," Todd said, "just hit the 'play' button and we're in business."

The transmission went off without a hitch. Todd couldn't believe how good the video was. The instant he saw the first show, Todd knew he was about to break a major television story.

Minutes later, KING-TV in Seattle called to tell Oran that NBC News was rushing to arrange an immediate transmission of Oran's footage to New York. Tom Brokaw wanted to run it on the "NBC Nightly News." At their boss' suggestion, Brokaw's producers were always looking for a unique, visually appealing story to end the show. When the three trapped whales came up during Thursday morning's conference call, NBC News bureau chiefs around the world readily agreed with the Los Angeles bureau that if the video was any good, the whales might make a good "kicker," TV slang for the story that ends each program.

Oran could hardly believe what he was hearing: His video on national television? He was glad Todd didn't tell him before they finished the transmission. He was already a nervous wreck. Now he was speechless. He had come a long way from the days not so long ago when he used to cover local beauty pageants back in Commerce, Texas. At 12:30 PM Alaska Standard Time, the three frightened whales concerned only a handful of people in a tiny Eskimo village straddling the top of the world. Just a few hours later, 15 million Americans watched them desperately gasping for air. It was a sudden diversion from the day's big news: the ongoing U.S. presidential campaign.

The moment the first image of a stranded whale appeared on a television screen at KING-TV in Seattle, no one was prepared to speculate that just days later, America would turn its attention away from its great quadrennial event and direct it instead toward the non-event of three California gray whales trapped in frozen waters off the continent's northernmost point.

But for those assigned to cover the story, it was even harder to prepare for the world they would soon enter, the world of Barrow, Alaska; a world like no other.

Chapter 3

The Eskimos: 25,000 Years Below 0°

In 1826, an Arctic explorer named Thomas Elson took one of history's great adventures. One day, while exploring Alaska's northern coast, Elson stepped 25,000 years back in time. He stumbled upon a string of prehistoric Eskimo hunting settlements along the edge of the world's northernmost periphery. What Elson did not know at the time was that he had discovered one of the most remarkable people who ever lived, a people whose very existence defied human logic. The Eskimos not only managed to survive longer than any civilization known to man, but they did so in an environment so brutal it all but seemed to rule out life itself.

Although the natives called their home Utqiagviq, Elson named it Barrow, after a British patron of Arctic expeditions. For 25,000 years, these nomadic tribes evolved in complete isolation. Their language of Inupiat and their peculiar culture was based upon a single primary influence: the whale.

The whale provided not only food, but heat, shelter and spiritual inspiration. The whale was more than a product, it was life itself. The whale was more than a creature. It was a spirit, its capture a gift. What other single source, the Eskimo asked, could provide them with everything they might possibly need?

Whale meat was the perfect food source, so rich with vitamins and minerals that its eaters were immune to nutritional diseases that ravaged other races. It provided a high concentration of vitamin D, a nutrient most people got from the sun, a source rarely seen and never felt in Barrow. The whale meat the Eskimos ate had the highest fat concentration of any food known to man, yet heart disease was unknown. The Inupiat Eskimos ate no fruits, vegetables or grains, yet their diet was filled with fiber.

They lived in the world's most brutal climate where the elements continue to claim the lives of even the most prepared. Before the non-Eskimos tainted them, the Inupiat enjoyed one of the longest life spans of any people on earth. But as time would prove, the Eskimos were a most fragile race. So long removed from any human contact, the Eskimo was unable to defend against diseases the white man carried. Like other native peoples in North America, the Eskimos were decimated before the first shot was fired.

Thomas Elson's visit lasted only a few days. But it would change the Inupiat people forever. It would inaugurate a perpetual decline. That decline would accelerate with each new outside influence, leaving the world's oldest known civilization vulnerable to the future's mortal blows.

At first the decline was insidious. The visits were few and far between. But like everything else in the once isolated world of Utqiagviq, the change was unstoppable. Eskimo civilization didn't start visibly deteriorating until several decades after Thomas Elson's first visit. By the second half of the 19th century, commercial whaling had become a booming industry. From heating oil to cosmetic products, the whale was a veritable goldmine to any man intrepid enough to hunt and kill one. Giant fleets of whaling vessels plied the high seas in search of glorious fortunes for captain and crew.

It was a glorious end, glorious for everyone but the victims: the whales. Before long, the greedy whalers culled the world's most fertile whaling grounds to near extinction. Their industry was one of the most prosperous of the post-Civil War era. But the demand for whale products reached such extraordinary heights that the richest New England whaling companies plowed millions of dollars into new ships that could spend years at sea looking for whales in waters stretching to the farthest corners of the globe.

The whales' last great sanctuary was under attack almost as fast as the sleek new vessels could make it up Alaska's uncharted coast. Its waters were the richest yet. They proved so fertile, in fact, that some companies established whaling stations along isolated stretches of Alaska's northern coast to service their fleets with fresh food and fuel. These stations would serve as the white man's first permanent inroad into Eskimo life.

The isolated depots quickly grew in importance. For the first time, the Eskimos began to trade for goods. The whalers introduced the Eskimos to unheard of luxuries like wood and textiles. The white man quickly learned the Eskimos' strengths and weaknesses. Their strength was their uncanny ability to survive in the Arctic. Their weakness could be summed up in one word: alcohol. The damage was both instant and catastrophic. The white man was destroying not only the great whales, but the people who depended on them.

Almost immediately after the white man arrived, Eskimos started dying. Early on, it was not unusual for hundreds to die of disease every year. Scores of Eskimos were taken into bondage by whaling crews anxious to exploit their skills. Countless others were murdered by competing whalers. And still more died from a previously unheard of phenomenon: starvation. Eskimos died because there were fewer and fewer whales to hunt, and because most able-bodied hunters were too drunk to catch the few whales that remained.

To make matters even worse, the town's addicted elders initiated a new, destructive form of barter that the New England whalers were only too happy to oblige. Eskimo leaders offered to give American sailors the servitude of their best whalers if the Americans would agree to give the Eskimos the molasses they needed to make their own liquor. Their fate was sealed.

In less than a generation, the self-sustaining Eskimo community Thomas Elson discovered had been almost completely wiped out.

All that remained of Barrow was an alcohol-ravaged shadow of its former self. In less than two decades, both the Eskimos and the whales had nearly been slaughtered to extinction. One thing had not changed. The Eskimos' fate was as inextricably tied to the whale as ever. As the whale suffered, so did the Eskimo.

Affordable petroleum products, which put an end to large scale commercial whaling, came too late to help the Eskimos. Barrow plunged into abject poverty. To survive, the Eskimos tried to resume their subsistence hunting ways. But the whales and the skills to capture them were nearly depleted. The Eskimos listed toward extinction.

Barrow remained unknown to all but a handful of missionaries and white traders until shortly after the Second World War. The growing threat of nuclear escalation and the Cold War gave Barrow a sudden, if short lived, position of strategic importance. By the early 1950s, the continent's northern periphery was the perfect site for the U.S. Air Force to build a Distant Early Warning Radar (DEW Line) station to alert against Soviet manned bombers flying overhead on their way to drop nuclear payloads on the United States. At its peak in the mid to late 1950s, DEW Line employed hundreds of Eskimos before being rendered obsolete in the 1960s by the development of the age's newest terror, the intercontinental ballistic missile. The rest continued their age-old hunt for Bowhead whales whose population was slowly recovering from the days of unrestricted whaling.

On February 18, 1968 Barrow's fortunes changed again. This time for good. After $125 million of fruitless drilling on the tundra 270 miles east of Barrow at a place called Prudhoe Bay, the Atlantic Richfield Company struck the largest single oil and natural gas field ever found. Geologists estimated there were 15 billion barrels of oil and 26 trillion cubic feet of natural gas lying just two miles beneath the frozen surface.

The Eskimo always thought that the black liquid they called Uqsruq that oozed from the surface of their frozen land was a lethal poison of an angry spirit. They watched as Uqsruq killed people, strong birds and mighty animals. But the white man worshipped it. So dependent was he on this rapidly vanishing resource, he would commit more than $20 billion, the largest private capital investment up to its time, designing and building the massive infrastructure needed to get the oil out of the ground and into an 825 mile pipeline

that stretched across of some of the world's most treacherous terrain
and then onto supertankers waiting at Southeastern port city of
Valdez.

Containing 25 percent of America's reserves, the Prudhoe Bay oil
field would provide, at its peak in the mid-1980s, nearly 20 percent
of all the oil consumed in the United States. So much revenue was
generated from a three dollar tax on each barrel of oil leaving
Valdez, that the oil industry alone paid more than 90 percent of
Alaska's bills. Alaskans were delighted. The oil companies spared
them from sales, property or income taxes so loathed by other
Americans. By the late 1980s, Alaska was America's least taxed
state.

Most Americans in the Lower 48 knew almost nothing about their
fellow countrymen settling the last, harshest and richest frontier. If
anything, Alaska, America's 49th State, was a paradox. A land of
contrasts, contradictions and above all beauty. Like no other
Americans, Alaskans thought of themselves and their great land as a
separate, distinct nation, a country all its own. They called people
who lived elsewhere "Outsiders." Any place beyond Alaska's
expansive frontier was referred to as "The Outside." Separated from
the Lower 48 by thousands of miles, Alaskans were also separated
by an ethic long lost in the Lower 48: the ethic of nation building.

And what a place it was. At more than half a million square
miles, Alaska was one fifth the size of the continental United States.
So vast it spanned two continents and three climatic zones.
Reaching deep into Asia, Alaska was both America's eastern-and
western-most state. Alaska claimed 17 of North America's 20
highest mountains, more than 100,000 glaciers, and an island chain
longer than the continental United States was wide. It was America's
first settled land. Yet by 1988, less than 30 years after its admission
to the Union, Alaska remained America's most sparsely populated
state: less than one person per square mile, one of the world's lowest
man to land ratios. In Alaska, caribou outnumbered humans 10 to
one.

Alaskans made more money than any other Americans. But
measured against their own material comforts, Outsiders considered
life in Alaska brutal, backwards and harsh. Many wealthy Alaskans
didn't have cars. Still more lived quite happily without plumbing or

electricity. It was the rugged spirit of adventure that drew thousands
to the last frontier.

But if Alaska was anything, it was remote. The state had only one
major road, the two-lane Parks Highway connecting Anchorage and
Fairbanks, which was regularly closed in winter, a nine-month
season in Alaska. Half of the population lived outside Alaska's two
urban centers. The only way they could get around was by air, sea or
dogsled. In an age of space shuttles and instant satellite communications, Alaska still remained remarkably uncharted. In 1988, less
than one twentieth of one percent of Alaska's magnificent terrain
had ever been touched by human hands.

For the rest of the country, Alaska, more than anything else,
meant cold and ice. Outsiders knew Alaska was big, but few had any
idea of how big or how remote the Great Land really was. Outsiders
knew that Alaska was home to exotic creatures like polar bears and
moose, but few understood the fragility of its magnificent ecosystem until the disastrous Exxon oil spill that devastated Southeastern Alaska's Prince William Sound in March 1989.

If Outsiders knew anything about the Alaskan Arctic, most of it
had to do with its Eskimo inhabitants. For even the best educated,
the history of the Inupiat Eskimo was a blank page. Most of what
Outsiders thought they knew about the Eskimos' ancient way of life
was wrong. Alaska's Eskimos never lived in Igloos, and they kissed
like everybody else.

Almost no Americans were familiar with Eskimo culture or
history. Still fewer were aware of present day conditions. They didn't
know that on a cash basis, the Eskimos were the richest people in
America. Nor did they know why: oil. Before they realized its far
reaching potential to change their lives, the Eskimos were against
oil development. They thought it would sound the death knell for
their subsistence way of life and wondered what could possibly
replace it. They found out with the passage of the 1971 Alaska Land
Claims Settlement Act.

The Act was the first and final settlement between the United
States Government and the natives of Alaska for all the land and
rights usurped from them since the U.S. purchased Alaska from
Russia in 1867 for the grand sum of $7.2 million, less than three
cents an acre. The settlement awarded the Eskimos a billion dollars

and 45 million acres of Alaska's choicest land. The Act gave Alaska's North Slope Eskimos power to tax their land, land that just happened to sit on top of a trillion dollars worth of oil and gas. Suddenly, Barrow was awash in cash.

For a town that had been using whale meat as its primary means of exchange, Barrow's sudden wealth brought enormous change. Not only were Barrow's elders ignorant about managing money, most of them had never even seen it. Illiterate subsistence whalers who didn't speak a word of English were suddenly overseeing multi-billion dollar portfolios from the earthen floors of their sod huts. Inupiat culture faced a new threat, something the white man called progress.

Smelling the opportunity from thousands of miles away, the cadre of whites who descended on Barrow reconstructed it in their own image. They came to build, manage and profit from one of history's most remarkable societal transformations. When the snow settled, Barrow had a new lifeline, a 7,000 foot runway that connected the town with the Outside on which it was now so dependent. Understandably, modern Barrow sprang up around the runway's southern edge.

The Arctic had a new bird, the construction crane. Modern prefab houses flown in from the Outside were assembled next to tiny driftwood hovels. Pathways were widened, sprinkled with gravel, and called streets. Several of them were laid out on tundra near the airport. For 11 months of the year they were frozen, snow covered and navigable.

But in the short weeks of summer, when the top few inches of the 1,200 foot thick permafrost melted with nowhere for the standing waters to go, Barrow's five miles of roadway were long thought impassable rivers of mud. Then a clever Eskimo mounted an old abandoned set of DC-3 aircraft tires on his pickup truck. The vehicle created a terrible mess, but the Eskimo got where he was going.

Barrow grew more in the 20 years since the oil discovery than it ever had before. Its population increased threefold to around 3,000. Although it was always the Arctic's largest town, Barrow's sudden wealth put it on the fast track to cosmopolitanism. It wasn't just get-rich-quick whites who came to Barrow, but Eskimos from impoverished Arctic villages anxious to experience life in the big city.

Its two billion Arctic-inflated dollars worth of growth notwithstanding, Barrow was still not much more than a tiny outpost at the top of the world. On foot, depending on the weather, the village was around five minutes wide by nine minutes long. The colder the temperature, the more the town shrunk. But with all their new found wealth, Barrowans grew lazy. As a result, new seemingly unnecessary industries arose. In a town as small as Barrow, taxis did a booming business. There were at least three companies that all charged $25 for the 500-yard ride between the Airport and the Top of the World Hotel.

Eighty hotel rooms sprang up to accommodate an increasing number of business travelers looking to hawk their wares to nouveau riche Eskimos. Barrowans didn't blanch at spending $200 million to build an all glass three story office building. Reputedly the most expensive per square foot building in the world. Nor did they balk at buying their children the world's most expensive school. But the $80 million price tag attached to Barrow High included a modern basketball arena and the Arctic's only swimming pool, indoor, of course.

Not only was Barrow on the fast track, it could eat fast food on the way. Arctic Pizza delivered for just $50 a pie. A cheap breakfast at Pepe's Mexican could be had for as little as $20, and there was even Chinese food. Wednesday nights Sam and Lee had their egg roll special: two for just $11.

An extensive gas main network pumped the heat giving fuel into rickety shacks. Women no longer needed to risk their lives collecting drift wood from the frozen shore. Dwellings were equipped with telephones and electricity. Even indoor plumbing was available, albeit at a nominal charge of $400,000 per hookup. Nimble ski machines whined past unemployed sled dogs. Barrow's high-tech television studio and satellite transmission and reception facility piped the world into the most modest Eskimo abode. Sonny Crockett and his vice-fighting cops were as popular in snowbound Barrow as he was in his bullet-ridden Miami.

Now Caribou, which migrated through Barrow backyards by the thousands, could be rendered lifeless during commercial breaks just by sticking a rifle out the kitchen window. Their carcasses, which hung frozen outside in the snow, could be quickly defrosted in Barrow's most ubiquitous modern appliance: the microwave oven.

In a place where the summer's highest temperature rarely rose above freezing, instant defrosting became a sudden necessity.

In less than a decade, Barrow went from being one of the poorest towns in North America to its absolute richest. In fact, by 1988, Barrow had the highest per capita income of any city on earth. Royalty payments alone from the Prudhoe Bay oil field amounted to more than $90,000 per person per year. But so inimical was this region to even the most basic elements of modern human existence that it took the world's highest per capita income to support a lifestyle the U.S. government correctly classified as impoverished.

Barrow was not only the world's richest town, it was also its most expensive. The one grocery store was nearly as well stocked as any of its counterparts in the Lower 48. But every item on the shelves was flown in from Anchorage or Fairbanks, where prices were steep to begin with. By the time groceries reached Barrow, the prices were high enough for families with six-figure incomes to qualify for food stamps. Fresh milk was $6 a gallon, corn flakes $7 a box. As long as the price of hamburger hovered near $5 a pound, subsistence hunting for many remained a necessity. Besides, most Eskimos, at least the older ones, preferred muktuk and caribou steaks to "white man's food" which they considered bland and unwholesome.

Barrow's rapid fire modernization gave the Eskimos the one commodity they never before had: leisure. Since the beginning of time, whaling had been the backbone of Eskimo life. Whalers were society's most important members. Now the only skill most Eskimos had was no longer crucial for survival. Seventy percent of Barrow's native "workforce" were put on the government payroll even though the vast majority of them did nothing. The only difference between them and the Soviet laborers who joke, "They pretend to pay us, we pretend to work," was that the minimum wage was $18 an hour and the workers didn't even have to pretend.

Contact with western society remained limited until the discovery of oil in the Alaskan Arctic. Suddenly, in the late 1960s, the Eskimos confronted wrenching change as they were forced to become part of American society. Barrow's sudden material wealth resulted in a monumental cultural meltdown. The Eskimos were collapsing under the weight of their own riches. The elders, who embodied Eskimo culture, were shunted aside by Barrow's new white masters. Their talents no longer necessary for their people's survival, the Eskimo elite fell into despair.

Alcohol, already a severe problem, now afflicted everyone: the third of the town that were alcoholics themselves, and the two thirds who lived with them. Alcoholism became a cultural calamity. The only difference between the late 20th century and the period following the decline of commercial whaling was that now Barrow could disintegrate in comfort.

Barrow voters overwhelmingly adopted a 1986 referendum outlawing the sale, consumption or possession of alcoholic beverages. The irony was that with such broad public support, many of those who voted in favor of the ordinance were alcoholics themselves. It instantly became the most widely evaded law in town. Consumption actually went up, not down. Enforcement was impossible because everyone continued to drink. Bootleggers thrived. They were so confident they would not get caught, they had listed phone numbers and plastered advertisements across town. Before the media arrived to jack up the price, a case of beer or a fifth of cheap whiskey could be had for as little as $100.

The Eskimos of Barrow had few role models. Their town was so ravaged by the scourge of alcohol and drugs, that it tolerated the outrages of its own mayor, George Ahmaogak, who was known for his violent drunken rages. In January 1989, he was arrested on an Anchorage street for seriously beating his wife with a metal briefcase after she reportedly refused to accompany him to another bar. News of his arrest ran on the front page of the *Anchorage Daily News*.

But news was nothing new to Barrow. The problem was that the news was always bad. Barrow was no longer just an isolated Eskimo hamlet on Alaska's northern rim. Its sudden wealth made it a household name across the state, a name synonymous with greed, corruption and crime. But outside Alaska, Barrow remained a mystery.

This was the world the media was about to invade.

Chapter 4

Here Come the Media

Oran Caudle wasted no time spreading the news. Immediately after KING-TV told him they were editing footage for the Thursday, October 13 edition of the "NBC Nightly News," he phoned home. He was so excited he dialed the wrong number twice before finally getting through to his parents back in Texarkana. He could hardly contain himself. "Mama, we're going nationwide!" he exclaimed in his North Texas drawl.

Half an hour later, Todd Pottinger called to ask for another favor. "Can you meet our crew at the airport?" Todd asked. Oran was confused. He didn't understand what Todd meant. What airport?

Todd told Oran that in the last few minutes NBC News and KTUU decided they wanted their own news crew in Barrow. They booked three seats on the day's last flight to Barrow on MarkAir, the only airline that served the town. It was scheduled to leave Anchorage at 3:30 PM.

While Anchorage TV stations occasionally sent television crews to Barrow, plans were usually made well in advance. KTUU had 12 months to prepare for the year's biggest story, the first sunrise on

January 21, which ended Barrows' 67 days of darkness. Now, KTUU told Oran that they would be in town in less than three hours.

Oran did not understand why Anchorage wanted more footage of the three whales. Oran just sent them a half an hour of video on the satellite. As remarkable as the whales were, Oran couldn't imagine why KTUU had decided to send its own crew so quickly. What could they do that he couldn't? For NBC, the answer was easy. For Oran, it was an unpleasant reminder of just how unimportant he was. While his footage was good, it was not good enough. Part of the problem was not Oran's fault. The soft ice just would not let him get close enough to the whales. But the real problem was that they did not think Oran had what it took to get the job done. NBC was so desperate for someone they thought they could trust, they offered to pay all KTUU's expenses until the network could get its own crew to Barrow.

KTUU sent Russ Weston, an experienced cameraman who had worked in Barrow before. But as his MarkAir 737 lifted off the Fairbanks runway after a brief stopover, he felt an undiminished sense of wonder at the scenery passing beneath. Below him lay nothing but virgin magnificent wilderness. For as far as he could see, forests of spruce and pine sprawled in every direction. He gaped at the winding Yukon basin, lit by the dimming light of the northland's setting sun. The Yukon was America's longest and greatest river, half again the length of the Mississippi. All this greatness, he thought, untouched by the hand of man.

The farther Weston flew, the terrain below grew more hostile. The heavily wooded wilderness thinned. As if a line was actually drawn in the earth, the vegetation vanished after crossing the imaginary Arctic Circle at 67° north latitude. Such extreme latitudes were more than even the hardiest trees could bear.

Then, out of the white void rose the stark magnificence of the Brooks Mountain Range that formed the Arctic's impregnable southern boundary. Russ could see only a fraction of the 10,000 foot peaks that constituted the world's northernmost and least explored mountain range. Its tranquil countenance belied an almost maternal desire to keep its virgin peaks uncharted. Almost all those who dared explore and uncover her treasures perished.

As the plane began its descent, the wonder of where it would land outweighed Russ's own experience of descending onto a sea of

Arctic desolation. No matter how many times he had done so, Weston still thought they might be making an emergency landing on a frozen lake bed in the middle of the tundra. It was as though a 7,000 foot airstrip was built at the edge of the universe.

As he looked out the south side of the aircraft, Russ saw the same expanse of white he saw from the air. Only the bizarre Buck Rogers look of the North Slope Borough television transmission site interrupted the bleak vision. It was the presence of this site that brought him. Stepping off the plane, Weston could not believe he had just travelled 1,200 miles without seeing a trace of man. It was 60° colder in Barrow than in Anchorage. He awoke that morning prepared for just another day as an Anchorage television cameraman. The day ended as one of the most remarkable of his life.

Biologists Craig George and Geoff Carroll were driving back to the Wildlife Department after sliding down their quota of greasy $13 quarterpounders at the local Burger Barn when they saw Oran descending the wrought iron steps of Barrow's city center, the airport terminal. Geoff and Craig were struck by the two strangers who accompanied him. Their bright ski clothes stood out in marked contrast to the drab but warm look of the locals.

Oblivious to his location, Geoff stepped on the brakes, bringing his Chevy Caravan to a stop right in the middle of Ahkoavak Street, one of Barrow's busiest roadways. Ahkoavak Street was crowded not with cars, of which there were few in Barrow, but with ski machines, and even these were infrequent. A car in the Arctic proved more trouble than it was worth. It needed special heaters to keep the engine from freezing even while it ran. The brutal cold destroyed transmissions with alarming regularity. And if the owner ever wanted his car to start again from October through May, he had to keep the engine running.

The fact that Barrow sat next door to the world's largest oil field did nothing to reduce the high cost of fuel which had to go all the way to Southern California for refinement only to be flown back to Barrow aboard special aircraft. At $3.00 a gallon it cost $200 a week just to keep a car running. Stealing a car wasn't a problem, but with no roads out of town, getting away with it was. Auto theft was rare in a town with one road and nowhere to go.

Geoff was curious to find out who was carrying the television camera. Craig was more interested in the reporter. When they pulled up alongside them, Oran introduced Russ Weston and Julie Hasquet, the KTUU correspondent. After sizing up Russ, they focused on his attractive but obviously uncomfortable companion. She looked as though she had fallen off a spaceship and landed on the wrong planet.

As strange as Barrow looked to her, her designer jeans, bright red ski parka, and blow-dried hair looked even stranger to Barrowans. She begged Russ to let her get back on the plane before it left her stranded in Barrow. If she missed it, she would be stranded in Barrow for the night. Her 15 minutes in Barrow was more than she could stand. She ran frantically to the check-in counter to see if she could still board the plane. She hurriedly climbed the stairs to the plane, sobbing in relief that her short Barrow trauma had come to an end.

When Oran told Geoff and Craig that Russ had come to town because of the whales, Geoff looked at Craig. They both thought the same thing. If the whales were news in Anchorage, then the Coast Guard might be more receptive to their request for a ship to break them out.

Fifty feet from where they said goodbye, Geoff and Craig's truck vanished in the thick ice fog. The only proof it was still nearby was the clear sound of the tires crunching crisply against the snow-packed road. Oran realized he forgot to tell them that the whales were going nationwide. But Oran didn't want to reveal his excitement at his sudden prominence to Weston. Caudle tried to pretend that the arrival of an outside TV crew did little to faze him.

It was Oran's job to escort outside media. The reason Barrow built the multimillion dollar television studio was to try to alter the town's sordid image. Barrowans used their state of the art technology to paint a single portrait that relayed two messages: a model Arctic community working hard to develop a hostile region, yet a town with deep social wounds that continued to need massive infusions of state aid to keep that model alive.

Helping outside news agencies report on stories from Barrow was one of the NSB television studio's most important functions. Nowhere else in the world could a news crew fly in and find a state of the art studio and transmission facility ready for their use free of charge.

As Oran drove the half mile up Momegana Street past the frozen litter-ridden cemetery, Russ marveled at Barrow's very existence. He followed Oran into the building that housed the TV studio. A familiar but incongruous sight took him by surprise.

"Oh, this," Oran remarked. "Welcome aboard the Arctic's only elevator."

Before leaving to fetch a cup of coffee, Oran told Russ to feel free to walk around but not to touch any of the equipment. He probably knew the equipment much better than Oran, but made no comment. When Oran returned, Russ asked him where he should stay. Oran picket up the phone and called the Top of the World Hotel.

"No problem," said the Colombian woman at the switchboard in her thick accent. "A hundred dollars cash per night, including running water." When Russ asked if they would take his American Express card, she rebuked him. Barrow was a "cash only" town.

In a place where some things, like construction, can cost up to a hundred times more than in the Lower 48, Oran realized the Top of the World was a bargain with rates only three times more expensive than those charged for similar accomodations in Texas. In part, the motel kept costs down because it stood on stilts above the frozen ground. Instead of digging an entire foundation, the construction crew saved millions of dollars by drilling holes just large enough for the stilts. The newly refurbished 35-room Top of the World Hotel was by far the biggest of the three motels in town. It was North Slope lodging at its finest.

The Top of the World was one of the first businesses to hook up to the $300 million Utilidor municipal water system begun in the early 1980s. But because of the arduousness of the project, less than half of Barrow's homes were able to take part in the Arctic miracle of flushing toilets and running water. It was by far the most expensive and sophisticated water system ever built.

Never before had such an ambitious construction project been undertaken in the Arctic. Special graphite pipes carried waste and drinking water 30 feet below the ground in tunnels dynamited through the permafrost. The tunnels were designed to prevent the permafrost from thawing and the pipes from freezing. If the permafrost did melt, the buildings above it would collapse into the sinking earth.

Oran asked Russ if he wanted to join him after the news for some tacos next door at Pepe's North of the Border. Mexican food 320 miles north of the Arctic Circle? Preferring indigestion to whale meat, Russ agreed to go along.

After Caudle checked Russ in at the hotel, it was nearly time for "NBC Nightly News." He wasn't about to miss his debut on national television. There was a big television set in the small but clean lobby of the Top of the World. It was already a little past six. KTUU tape-delayed the newscast so that it aired at 6:30 PM, Alaska time. Aurora I beamed the Anchorage stations to all Alaskan villages as part of the statewide Radio and Television Satellite Project, better known as RATNET.

Oran went next door to Pepe's to excitedly announce that Barrow "was going nationwide." As the newscast progressed, more and more people gathered around the set. The program's first and second blocks reported exclusively on the presidential campaign. The third segment was devoted to the Middle East, and the arms negotiations in Geneva, but still nothing on the whales. Oran would be mighty embarrassed if, after all his boasting about "going nationwide," the whales didn't make the news.

With Tom Brokaw's words "... and finally tonight," Oran Caudle was redeemed. Brokaw introduced the video reading a sentence from the TelePrompTer. "In Northern Alaska, Winter comes early. And for three California gray whales it may have come too early this year." With the words "gray whales," the NBC technical director ordered the technician to "roll tape." Oran's first pictures came on the screen. The audio engineer in the control room of NBC's New York studio turned up the sound of the first whale struggling to breathe in the middle of the frozen Arctic Ocean.

In the few seconds it took for the zoomed-in lens to capture the whale's head coming out of the water and exhale a lungful of air and water, the three trapped whales were no longer alone in the remote frozen waters off Barrow. They were now national news.

Because of the four-hour time difference between the East Coast and Alaska, the stranding was already old news in the Lower 48. Stung by NBC's first blow, every other news agency in the country immediately put reporters on the story. The Top of the World Hotel was immediately deluged with calls from news agencies trying to book rooms for the following night.

Todd Pottinger called Russ to tell him that NBC News had assigned Don Oliver, a veteran correspondent, to come to Barrow to cover the whales. Oliver was one of the world's best reporters. He masterfully covered the 1975 fall of Saigon where his furious outbursts earned him the nickname "El Diablo." Oliver's temper was complemented by the mild-mannered, congenial approach to news gathering of his sidekick, producer Jerry Hansen. After flying all night, Oliver, Hansen and their technical staff of four arrived in Barrow on Friday, October 14.

A week to the day after the whales were discovered, an American television crew was walking down the flimsy aluminum steps that would plant them squarely in the Arctic. When the first blast of cold air hit them, they knew they were totally unprepared for it.

When their NBC producers in New York and Los Angeles sent them to Barrow, Hansen and Oliver had no idea how long they would be there or under what conditions they would be forced to operate. There was nothing unusual about that. Such was life for these globetrotting professionals. Their job forced them to be ready to go anywhere, anytime. More often than not, the "anywhere" was someplace strange and remote, and the "anytime" was now.

After more than 25 years in the business, Oliver kept learning that just when he thought he had done it all, another story would come his way to prove him wrong. As he gazed out at his surreal surroundings, Oliver instantly knew he was in for another unprecedented adventure.

Unlike Russ who had worked in Barrow before, the NBC crew assumed that there would be no broadcast facilities worth using. So they brought virtually an entire TV station of their own packed tightly into 12 metal cases. The cases were filled with cameras, waveform monitors, vectorscopes, batteries, cables, editing equipment and camera heating pads.

But buried in the safest catacomb was the Los Angeles bureau's newest piece of equipment. They had been waiting for it for years. Only when the Persian Gulf tanker war calmed in late 1988 did the NBC Bahrain bureau agree to transfer their portable $17,000 gyrostabilizer. Attached to the outside of a camera, it allowed steady pictures to be taken from a flying helicopter. When Oran Caudle casually pulled out his own gyrostabilizer the next day, Don Oliver nearly fell out of the open-doored chopper. Barrow's gyrostabilizer was even more sophisticated than the one Oliver liked to brag about.

Before leaving Los Angeles, Jerry Hansen, the producer, checked to see that someone at the assignment desk would take care of accommodations and ground support once they arrived in Barrow. Hansen had one request, his own room. He couldn't stand Oliver's snoring. Lucky they were the first to Barrow. Had they arrived any later, Hansen would have been forced to use the snore proof earplugs he packed just in case. The town's 80 hotel rooms were growing scarce. To allow for late arriving competitors, the hotels no longer rented single rooms.

This wasn't the first time NBC News reported from the Arctic. But they had never before done it with so little preparation. Just as he was walking out the door of his Burbank office, Jerry glanced up at the map on his wall. Barrow looked like it was at the end of the world. When he stepped off the plane, his worst fears were confirmed. Barrow was the end of the world.

Even though there were only four miles of road in the town, Jerry, Don and the rest of the crew still needed a way to get around Barrow with all their heavy gear. To Hansen, the answer was obvious enough, rent a car. He thumbed through the seven-page Barrow telephone directory several times before he finally realized that there were no rental cars. The hotel manager suggested Hansen call the North Slope Borough, the local government. The NSB owned most of the town's vehicles. If anybody had any extras, it would be the NSB.

When word spread through the new all glass NSB building that NBC News was in town, everyone assumed they were assigned to cover the North Slope Mayor's Conference which Barrow was hosting. Locals were dumbfounded when Hansen told them that, in fact, he was in town to cover the stranding of the three whales.

"The whales?" one irate Eskimo asked, "What is so newsworthy about those whales?"

"I don't know," Hansen answered. "People just love them."

The man at the NSB gave Hansen a list of names of people who might have cars to rent. The first Eskimo he talked to wanted $1,000 a day for a 1975 Chevy Suburban. Hansen burst out laughing. But the last laugh was on him. The best deal he could find was with a character at the NSB who rented him three old pickups for the bargain price of just $600 a day. The ruddy faced operator was one of dozens of caucasians drawn to Barrow by its unique commercial opportunities, like charging the desperate Jerry Hansens of the world $600 a day to rent three broken down heaps. No one in the Lower 48 would have paid $300 apiece to *buy* them. In between his grimy exhalations of cigarette smoke, the man gave Hansen the keys and told him never to drive on the ice and never to turn the car off.

"Never turn the car off?" asked Hansen. "When is this bad dream going to end," he inquired in a failed attempt at self-amusement. That's when the white-haired Hansen remembered the surreal sight of a line of empty parked pickup trucks all with their motors running as he walked out of the Airport terminal.

The NBC Burbank desk asked Russ Weston to stay an extra day to produce the Friday story for "NBC Nightly News." Weston jumped at the chance. Producing a story for the network news was an opportunity he wasn't about to pass up. But to get the story, Weston had to see the whales. He saw everyone in town transporting themselves on the back of whining ski machines. Surely this was the best way there.

But when he tried to rent one, he ran into the same problem Hansen confronted looking for a car. The first man Weston found willing to rent a ski machine asked the same $1,000 fee Hansen was quoted for a car, except it would only purchase him one roundtrip. He couldn't even keep it for the whole day.

Weston turned to Oran in desperation. Could Caudle find him a ride to the whales? Oran offered a possible solution. He told him that sometimes the North Slope Borough's Search and Rescue (SAR) department took him up in one of their helicopters to take aerial pictures.

Russ's face lit up. He begged Oran to help him get one of those helicopters. He didn't care what it cost. NBC told him to spare no expense. Oran was as anxious to see Russ succeed as Russ was himself. This was the most exciting thing ever to happen to Oran. Of course he would help, he assured Russ, as he dialed his friend Randy Crosby. Crosby was the director and chief pilot of the North Slope Search and Rescue Department. Caudle asked Randy if they could get a lift out to the whales. Crosby said that barring any rescue emergencies, he would meet Caudle and Weston at the SAR airport hangar the next morning and fly them out for free.

After waiting in the large hangar for first light, Geoff, Craig, Russ, Oran, and Randy took off in a Bell 214 helicopter around 9:00 AM, for a comfortable, heated 12-minute ride to the languishing whales. For the first time, biologists Geoff and Craig would be able to survey the whales' condition from above. Neither mentioned the possibility that the whales might have died since the last time anyone saw them. The dark orange light of this early Arctic morning revealed the magnificence of a rare cloudless day. From the climate-controlled cabin of the helicopter, the rising sun looked deceptively warm. But it was above the horizon for such a short time and, at such a low angle, its feeble rays were powerless to lessen the bitter cold.

The helicopter flew due west from its pad at the airport and headed straight out to the ice covered Chukchi Sea parallel to the long Point Barrow sandbar. The group followed the sandbar north until the two holes in the ice came faintly into view. Their aerial reconnaissance gave Geoff and Craig an idea of what a ship might encounter in the unlikely event the Coast Guard dispatched one to break the ice. They could see that more than a mile of solid new ice stood between the whales and open water. An icebreaker seemed the perfect solution to freeing the three whales.

But Geoff and Craig knew the present circumstances made the use of such a ship impossible. The state of America's icebreaking capacity was a hot issue in Alaska at that very moment. In fact, the Coast Guard's bitter complaints against the Reagan Administration's refusal to authorize the construction of more icebreakers was on the same *Anchorage Daily News* front page as the first story about the Barrow whales.

Randy lowered the helicopter onto what looked like the last firm patch of sand on the spit before it drifted below the frozen blanket of ocean. Once on the ground, he had to keep the helicopter at half power so it wouldn't sink into the shifting sand.

Russ, Geoff and Craig jumped out the flimsy door and ran across the sand onto the ice. The ice had grown strong enough to support the weight of three men and their gear. Billy Adams' prediction was on the money. The ice was firm enough for them to walk right up to the edge of the hole. When they got there, the whales were waiting for them at the surface. The change in their behavior was obvious to

Craig and Geoff. When they left them a day earlier, the whales were not yet reconciled to the visits of these strange new characters.

It was a week since Roy Ahmaogak first discovered the whales swimming in slush on his way back from scouting for the Nuiqsut whalers. Now, they were genuinely trapped. The slush had turned to solid ice half a foot thick. The ice was so deceptively firm, it lulled the men into believing they were walking on terra firma.

Russ set his camera on the ice at the edge of the hole. He opted to shoot parallel to the sea's roiling waters rather than mounting the camera on a tripod. Russ knew that would make for a more dramatic shot. By rising squarely into the middle of the picture, the whale's head would fill the center of the frame much faster. Russ focused on the churning water in the middle of the hole, turned on the camera and stepped back. All he could do was wait for the whales to surface. When the first whale came up for air, Russ realized his plan for the shot was right on the mark. The focus Russ set flawlessly captured the whale. The shot brilliantly conveyed how cold it really was on the ice in a remarkable image. When the whale exhaled, Russ watched through his viewfinder as the water vapor of the whale's breath froze in midair and landed as ice crystals on the lens of the camera. A video veteran of many Alaska whale strandings, Russ himself was awestruck.

Russ raced back to the helicopter as soon as the baby whale sank beneath the dark water, completing the sequence. He was scheduled to transmit his story to NBC via satellite in less than two hours. He needed to get back to the studio to start editing the footage. Snow whipped by the helicopter lashed Geoff and Craig who remained behind as Randy lifted off for the trip back to Barrow.

Randy piloted his $1,250,000 swirling aircraft to hover just 200 feet above the whale's lone hole. Since it was too loud inside the cabin to speak, Russ tapped Randy on the shoulder and motioned that he wanted to take some pictures with Oran's gyrozoom. The aerials would confirm once again NBC's dominance of the early stages of the stranded whale saga. They broke the story, got the first close-ups, and now the first pictures that showed how small the hole really was.

Until Jerry, Don, and Steve Shim, the video editor, set up, NBC had no choice but to use Russ's film. They weren't sure what to expect of the Anchorage photographer. But Jerry was ecstatic when

Russ showed him his footage. He called NBC with the good news. They responded with good news of their own. The footage would run again on "NBC Nightly News," only this time higher up in the broadcast. Clutching a scotch on the rocks, Hansen warmly joked he didn't need his own crew as long as Weston was in town.

Chapter 5

A Whale in Every Living Room

When Oran Caudle returned to his office following his sojourn with the whales, he found a shell-shocked look on his secretary's face. There were messages on his desk from CBS, ABC, CNN, all the other local stations in Anchorage, and at least a dozen television and radio stations across the country. The soft-spoken Texan laughed in disbelief. He did not know what to make of his instant celebrity. In less than 12 hours, the story which he hoped to run on Barrow's local channel really had gone "nationwide." The world"s most remote television studio and the man who ran it were suddenly sought after by America's leading broadcasters.

Oran was treated like a hero when he reached the assignment desk. They called him "Mr. Caudle" and even "Sir." "Sir?" Oran thought. Waiters never even called him "Sir." But he was their only link to a story they were desperate to cover. NBC ran it. Now they had to cover it as well. If that meant resorting to flattery, so be it.

NBC's exclusive footage of the trapped whales the night before was immediately recognized as an industry "mini-coup." Network news producers loved animal stories. They gave the network anchors a chance to display, in the spirit of the '88 campaign, that they too were "kinder and gentler." But for a reason as obvious as it was elusive, whale stories were the best of all. Without even knowing it, Tom Brokaw impacted the psyches of even his most cynical viewers with his rueful smile at the end of Thursday's broadcast. The struggling whales couldn't help but touch the human heart.

If the other networks wanted in the game, they couldn't waste any time. If they worried about money, they could never play. By whatever means they could muster, they had to find pictures of the whales for their Friday night broadcasts. They tracked down Oran through a graphic NBC News superimposed on the footage it used the night before. It read "Courtesy of the North Slope Borough."

At first, nobody at the networks had a clue what the "North Slope Borough" meant. That was the kind of thing reporters were trained to find out. They called Alaska directory assistance and got the number for the North Slope Borough. When they asked for the person responsible for the video that appeared on NBC News the night earlier, the switchboard operator transferred them to Oran. The first calls Oran returned were from the networks. After talking to CBS, ABC and CNN, he found his freelance camera services at the center of a two-way bidding war. CBS and ABC crews were on the way to Barrow. But until they got there, they needed Oran Caudle to help them get the footage they had to have for their Friday night broadcasts.

Until the other networks put their own footage on the air, it was NBC's story. People interested in finding out about the trapped whales would tune in Brokaw and tune out Jennings and Rather. NBC had the obvious advantage. Don, Jerry and Steve were already on the ground and transmitting.

CBS and ABC desperately wanted Oran to go back for "fresh" video of the whales. Each time they spoke to him they raised their cash offers by hundreds of dollars. In the end, CBS won by agreeing to pay Oran the staggering figure of $2,000 to make one trip out to the whales. There was only one condition, he had to agree not to give any of the footage he shot to ABC or CNN.

"Wowee, I can't believe it," Oran exulted in his Texas drawl. He would make in one morning more than he would in a week and a half with the borough.

Oran knew CNN could never compete with the offers the networks made. But it was his favorite network. He watched it all the time. At 6:00 every morning, it ran the Barrow temperature.

Oran felt that any network that acknowledged Barrow deserved to be acknowledged itself. He would give CNN free use of the footage he shot for himself the day before as long as it gave the borough credit on the air. The 24-hour news network was only too glad to accept.

Oran barreled into Russ Weston as he ran out the door in his hurry to get back to the whales before dark. In his naïve excitement, Oran told Russ that the other networks were sending up their own crews. "Isn't that great?" he asked. Needless to say, Russ did not quite share the transplanted Texan's boyish enthusiasm. Russ' exclusive was coming to an end. From now on, he would have to compete with newly arrived journalists for the story that up to that point was his alone. The transmission facility was destined to heat up. Since only one signal could be transmitted at a time, Oran knew the task of handing out the time slots would fall in his lap.

Had Oran been at the Anchorage International Airport that Friday afternoon, he might have gotten a glimpse of the deluge that would descend on his quiet studio over the next two weeks. The normally quiet MarkAir ticket counter hummed with unexpected activity for the afternoon flight to Barrow.

MarkAir was more than the only commercial and freight airlines serving Barrow. In a village with no land or sea routes, it was Barrow's lifeline, its only connection to the outside world. Without it, the town would die. Outside of government, it was Barrow's biggest business, the source of everything from food and gasoline to transportation to all away games for the Barrow High School basketball team. The three daily flights carried much more than people. They carried the town's future, supplying virtually everything modern Barrow needed to survive its brutal environment.

MarkAir's new fleet of Boeing 737 jets had movable bulkheads. Usnally, the front two thirds of the cabin on Barrow-bound flights held cargo. Even at $337 for the cheapest one-way seat, MarkAir couldn't afford to give up the cargo space unless the plane was full.

But after this afternoon, the agents faced a rare problem. There were more people trying to get to Barrow than there were seats on the plane, including over a dozen people from CBS and the other Anchorage television stations. Behind them calmly stood the local representatives of the national wire services. To them, Alaska was home. But even they could not fathom what Barrow would bring.

Crates of heavy television equipment began to pile up in front of the ticket counter. Lucky for MarkAir, Ed Rogers was in the Anchorage office and not out checking up on cargo operations at one of the airlines remote sites deep in the Alaska bush. Rogers served as the Director of Cargo Sales for MarkAir and instantly saw the revenue potential of the unexpected passengers and their baggage. He wouldn't think of turning away full-fare paying passengers along with the fees he would collect from their excess luggage. He ordered the pre-loaded cargo off-loaded to make room for seats in the front two-thirds of the Barrow-bound Boeing 737. The cargo taken off the passenger flight was flown up later in the day on a special plane. Rogers made everyone happy and MarkAir a handsome profit in the process.

Instead of waiting impatiently for the aircraft to be reconfigured, several of the reporters wandered to the airport's watering hole for an afternoon pick-me-up. They had no idea this would be their last chance to buy a drink legally. Under most circumstances, Barrow was dry and drinking illegal.

In the cabin, mock panic accompanied word that Barrow was dry. One of the stewardesses sought help from the cockpit. The captain's sardonic announcement confirming the rumors only fueled the uproar. Stewardesses quickly took their serving carts to quiet the boisterous but good natured reporters clamoring for last shots. Within minutes, every bottle of alcohol on the plane was gone. The more seasoned Alaska hands calmly sat through the hubbub, reassured by the bootleg caches of liquor stashed away in their luggage. Once the administered drugs took effect, the cabin calmed down.

The pilot wakened his slumbering passengers on descent to Barrow with news that he had permission from Randy Crosby's air traffic control station in Barrow to fly over the stranded whales. The trapped whales were not just a national news item anymore. Now they were a tourist attraction worthy of aerial fly-bys.

The influx continued unabated for the next 10 days. The Top of the World Hotel started auctioning off occupied rooms to the highest bidder. People in town for the long-planned mayor's conference and other business returned to the hotel after their day's work to find their rooms taken by rude, ill-tempered media types. Since the invading hordes were willing to pay $300 a day, the hotel was more than willing to take the heat from their displaced guests.

Barrow had never seen anything like it. The current attention dwarfed the coverage of the only other event in Barrow to interest anybody on the outside, and this one had hardly begun. On August 2, 1935, the first plane ever trying to fly to the North Pole crashed ten miles south of Barrow, killing both of its famous passengers, legendary humorist Will Rogers and aviator Wiley Post. The few daring journalists who actually reached the unreachable site to report on the tragic accident aptly named it Desolation Point.

1988 was a different world. There were satellites, regularly scheduled jet flights, and ski machines. Modern Barrow had running water and a choice among Eskimo, American, Mexican and Chinese cuisine. With all its imported social ills, Barrow had so far managed to avoid one of the most pervasive problems in the Lower 48: homelessness. When the affliction struck, its source was completely unexpected. Suddenly the town was overrun by an influx of reporters with nowhere to stay.

Barrowans started clearing floor space to house as many Outsiders in their driftwood shacks as they could. The shivering and exhausted members of the Fourth Estate gladly subjected themselves to extortion if it meant escape from the unspeakable elements. They paid upwards of $100 each for the privilege of sleeping on a cold floor. These budget rates often did not include mattresses, sheets, blankets or running water. Many of these entrepreneurial Eskimo hosts were most selective in the compensation they would accept. The reporters learned quickly that what cash couldn't buy, whiskey would. A bottle of J&B secured a vacant bed faster than the crispest hundred dollar bill.

The lone loophole in Barrow's prohibition was seized with alarming speed. It was the top priority for many reporters. An obscure provision allowed non-residents to apply for temporary liquor import licenses. The applications were available at the Barrow City Hall which became the site of an almost endless line of those seeking an exemption from the harsh sentence of temperance.

Eskimos roamed the line offering hundreds of dollars to those willing to use their permits to help them illegally resupply their own caches. Once the reporters got their permits, they then made arrangements with their bureaus for immediate shipments of Barrow's primary medium of exchange. Thousands of dollars worth of beer, wine and hard liquor were shipped overnight express by the caseload. Ed Rogers' joke was that the MarkAir cargo storage area looked like a wholesale liquor warehouse.

Newsmen phoned their complaints to assignment editors, decrying Barrow's appalling lack of amenities. Some begged to be relieved. Others thrived on the hardship. Each privation suffered was a badge they could later point to as proof of their ability to report under a new level of adversity.

For veteran CBS cameraman Bob Dunn, it was a chance to prove that not even his graying hair and spreading paunch could stand in the way of his legendary bravado. Age and experience did nothing to temper Dunn's need to impress his colleagues. For several days, he pretended he was an Eskimo by adamantly refusing to wear gloves. Even several severely frostbitten fingers did not put a stop to Dunn's crusade. To protect him from himself, a group of Eskimo hunters gave Dunn a pair of polar bear-skin mittens. They did not want Dunn to confuse Arctic fortitude with lunacy.

Those reporters who arrived in town after their colleagues had commandeered the few available vans, trucks and ski machines, had a tough time getting around. The need of so many people to get out to the whales combined with their inability to do so gave rise to another short-lived Arctic tradition, daily transport auctions. Ride seekers congregated early each morning outside the Top of the World Hotel and shouted their competing bids to Eskimos with ski machines and dogsleds for rides to the ice. The most enterprising Eskimos fetched up to $400 each way. When the market stabilized, the going rate settled at around $200 or $150 cash and a fifth of liquor.

But, as KTUU reporter Todd Pottinger could attest, the high price guaranteed almost nothing. He paid top dollar for his crew and equipment to be dumped unceremoniously in the middle of the street after the driver somehow managed to plow into one of the Arctic's few telephone poles. Pottinger's insistence a refund met with an incredulous laugh.

Anyone without $200 for the return trip was stranded until Randy Crosby's Search and Rescue helicopter could pick them up. Those who could shake off the night's excess and get out of bed early enough stood shivering outside the SAR hangar for helicopter rides out to the whales.

As the Eskimo sled ride market matured, different levels of service emerged. First Class transport included sleds outfitted with polar bear blankets and down sleeping bags. Economy passengers were lucky to wrap themselves in a blood-stained caribou hide. Sometimes revolted passengers had to share the sled with a dead walrus or seal on his way to be butchered. Fortunately, it was so cold the carcass froze before it had the chance to emit its stench.

Just four days after the first nationwide broadcast on NBC, almost every newspaper in the United States featured the stranded whales on their front pages. All three networks led off their newscasts with updates from Barrow. The whales were the biggest story in America. They even eclipsed the presidential election. Compounding the non-event's absurdity, reporters from all over the world were immediately assigned to cover the story. If it was news in America, then it must really be news. I was one of those reporters.

Just moments before I unexpectedly found myself on the way to cover the story, I was ridiculing my friend Carolyn Gusoff for her unrepentant emotional desire to see the whales freed at any cost. Of course, I wanted them freed as much as anyone, but was too embarrassed to admit it. At 6:30 PM on Wednesday, October 19, just as Carolyn hung up, disgusted with my taunts, the phone rang again. It was Takao Sumii, the President of NTV, one of the three major Japanese television networks.

I ran N.Y. News Corp., a small television news service which offered custom television coverage of news events primarily for foreign broadcasters. He asked me how soon I could get a crew to Barrow to prepare and transmit reports back to Japan. I did not know what to say. The last few weeks, I was at home in bed with mono. I was barely well enough to go to the office let alone the North Pole. I stammered and stuttered in my halting Japanese. Since I could not figure out how to tell one of my best customers that I just would not be able to make it, I didn't. I told him I'd be delighted and frantically prepared to embark on my own voyage to the Top of the World. I called back Carolyn to tell her. She had the last laugh. I was going to cover the whales.

I assured Sumii-san we would be ready to transmit within 24 hours. Just like every other reporter hastily assigned to cover this story, I instinctively picked up the phone before realizing I had no idea whom I was calling. I remembered hearing Don Oliver refer to the Top of the World Hotel in one of his reports. The laughter that greeted my inquiry about vacant rooms was my initiation to a town gone mad.

I plaintively asked for the names of other hotels. The Colombian woman referred me to the competition, the Airport Inn. By the time I reached the Inn, the hotel operator told me they too were full. I beseeched this second woman for help. Did she know any names? What about paying for sleeping in someone's home? I desperately needed accommodations for my crew. She told me to call Rod Benson, the owner's brother.

Benson told me we could stay with his family for $200 per night. Unaware that the price he offered me was a bargain, I was aghast, but, like everyone else, hostage to his price. I asked him what we should know and what we should bring. His answer was a memorable one.

"Everything is expensive and no one takes credit cards, that is what you should know," he said firmly. "As for what you should bring, long-johns and liquor, not necessarily in that order."

I arrived in Anchorage 12 hours after leaving New York to meet with Masu Kawamura, the NTV reporter just in from Tokyo. He was assigned to work with us in Barrow. We waited at the Captain Cook Hotel for N.Y. News Corp. cameraman Steve Mongeau, who was expected to arrive after an all-night flight from Toronto where he was called in from another assignment. We were more worried about bringing enough liquor than we were about carrying the proper clothing. We spent over $500 on liquor from an Anchorage discount wholesaler, and less than $150 on boots that Barrow's cold would render useless anyway.

The Friday morning flight to Barrow was filled with reporters and oil professionals whose huge companies now were financing what had by that time became a full-fledged multimillion dollar rescue mission. I sat next to a striking Eskimo woman with jet black hair and deepset dark brown eyes sitting atop prominent cheekbones. She was Brenda Itta, an Eskimo leader returning home after participating in an Alaska Federation of Natives (AFN) conference.

This articulate but soft-spoken woman couldn't understand why her tiny embattled community had suddenly become the subject of the world's attention. She wished the whales well, but why were they more important than the AFN meeting she just attended or the North Slope mayors' conference presently taking place in Barrow?

Brenda Itta's unknown world and its fascinating people were of no interest to any correspondent. None of us came to Barrow to report on the extraordinary plight of the embattled Eskimo or the Arctic's hostile beauty. We came to tell the world about a common occurrence, the routine stranding of three whales under a patch of ice. The only thing that made this stranding extraordinary was that it happened just 20 miles from a satellite uplink earth station. Had the facility been located far away, these whales, like dozens of others each year, would have died ordinary deaths.

This brutal lesson was driven home on Saturday night October 22, 1988. Right across the street from the Barrow fire department, a flimsy driftwood house erupted in flames, killing three small children in one of the worst house fires in Barrow's modern history. The Karluk Street fire station was virtually empty that night. The men had gone home early for some much needed sleep. All week long they had worked exhausting hours helping save the whales.

An electrical short in the bathroom started the fire which killed eight-year-old Della Itta, her sister Irene, 2, and their baby brother, Miles Steven, 10 months. No one in Barrow accused anyone of negligence. The house's walls burned like dry tinder. The house was so quickly engulfed that even if the firemen had been in the station, there was nothing anyone could have done. There were no smoke alarms or adults in the house to alert the children who died before any help could arrive.

That very night Barrow played host to the highest concentration of journalists and television cameras on earth. With few exceptions, none of us mentioned the tragic deaths in any of our stories. It took us almost two weeks to start reporting on the more relevant questions about whether the naturally stranded whales deserved all the effort and attention lavished on them. We barely mentioned anything about our remarkable experiences at the top of the world, and appallingly little about the whales' real rescuers, the Inupiat Eskimos.

On the plane, Brenda spoke with passion and conviction about her people's proud history and the agony of the present. Her people were afflicted with a destructive addiction to alcohol. She could only predict a gloomy future. In Fairbanks she heard rumors about reporters smuggling in huge amounts of liquor. She asked me if they were true. My verbal fumbling could not hide a reddening face. I melted in my seat, all too aware of the whiskey I had stashed in the overhead compartment above Brenda's head.

Only then did I realize why Rod told me it was better to bring alcohol than money. Barrow was hooked. This event was an unprecedented opportunity to stock up and make a killing in the process. Not only did I confirm the rumors, but I confessed that she was chatting with one of the guiltier parties. I promised not to further contribute to the delinquency of her alcohol-ravaged people.

We all brought booze. Others brought it for the same reason I did, to help them do their jobs in a strange town. It didn't take long to realize why the Eskimos had such a problem with alcohol. Two days after we arrived, we had the same problems, some would say even worse.

Life in Barrow has one single objective, staying warm. We spent six to eight hours each day on the ice gathered around small holes in the middle of the frozen Arctic Ocean that grew more crowded by the day. We drank in the morning before going out to the whales. When we weren't fighting on the ice, we drank bourbon from each other's flasks to stay warm. When we got back to town we drank until we went to bed or passed out. "It is too cold to be sober," we reassured ourselves. The warmest buildings were rarely heated above 55 degrees.

The novelty and excitement of our new universe was short-lived. The overwhelming oppressiveness of Barrow almost immediately displaced wonderment. We were transported to a dark, cold and drunken world that defied the very laws of human existence. It took the Eskimos 25,000 years to drop to the inebriated levels we managed to reach in 48 hours.

Sensing a frightening change in their attitudes and performance, the American networks started replacing crews after their first week in Barrow. Those of us without such a reprieve managed to endure. All that was asked of the network replacements was that they replenish our depleted liquor caches. Just like the Eskimos we arrogantly mocked, we drank to revive our sagging spirits. Soon, we guarded our booze as zealously as our camera positions. Our rush-ordered refills were no longer for barter. They were for ourselves.

The next phase of our decline was the complete abandonment of western vanities. It wasn't long before we gave up any regard for our appearances. The hassle and expense of hygiene was nothing but an annoyance for most of us, especially me.

My first morning in Barrow, I took a long shower. It was an ordeal to undress in such a cold bathroom. Contemplating the paper-thin towel that promised a futile effort to dry myself quickly, I almost decided not to take one at all. But once I got in the shower, I was intent on staying in the warm, humid Eden for as long as I could.

More than the warmth, it was the moisture I longed for. Barrow was one of the world's driest deserts. Its cold, dry air parched the throat and cracked even the toughest skin. My escape abruptly ended when the steaming water turned to ice. Rod shut off the hot water in a surefire effort to get me out of his shower. Water was rationed and cost 15 cents a gallon. Any more long showers and he would jack up the already outrageous rent.

One local entrepreneur turned a tidy profit selling five minute lukewarm showers for $50. Remarkably, people paid it. Those of us unwilling to acquiesce to such extortion learned to live with even the worst odors. These indignities seemed mild when set against the unspeakable discomfort of traditional Arctic bodily elimination. It wasn't just the 25° below zero temperatures. Nor was it the fear of being seen. It wasn't even the danger of freezing vital parts. It was those damned dogs.

The first night in Barrow saw those of us from N.Y. News Corp. and NTV gathered around Rod Benson's formica bar for a late night bull session. Rod reveled in the excitement and we marveled at a part of the world none of us knew even existed. The heavy smell of scotch and stale cigarette smoke permeated the cold, dry air. Rod excused himself and quietly slipped away. On the way out, he casually picked up a roll of toilet paper and, strangely, a thick wooden club which were sitting together on an old metal chair next to the door. As soon as it slammed behind him, the unmistakable sounds of violently barking Alaskan sled dogs shattered the silence of the Arctic night. Not 30 seconds later, Rod, his aplomb perfectly intact, was back in his seat. We didn't dare ask what all the noise was about. Soon enough, nature would answer.

Alaskan sled dogs bore more resemblance to wolves than to pets. They were a tough, semi-domesticated breed reared to pull heavy sleds in the Arctic. They lived outside year round. Knowing that the hungrier they were the better they performed, owners purposely underfed their dogs. Consequently, the dogs are constantly on the lookout for any source of alternative nourishment.

Human scent often meant a dog's next meal in one form or another. Their keen sense of smell could track even the most well-hidden person at his most vulnerable moment. Almost the instant a person reached for his trousers, packs of canines were barking madly as they frantically raced toward their indisposed victim.

Snapping their ravenous jaws with no regard for what they might bite, the dogs fought bitterly amongst themselves to snatch the hastily dropped nutrients just inches from a person's most vital parts. It was at this point that the victim confronted the most unpleasant task of finishing his business with one hand while flailing the heavy club at the biting dogs with the other.

Lofty salaries and flashy bylines meant precious little to reporters assigned to Barrow. Here, skills perfected on the Outside were of little use. Those that considered long jet journeys arduous before arriving in Barrow looked forward to going through it all over again when it was time to leave. This was not Johannesburg, Beijing or even Beirut. There were no taxis outside the airport to whisk you to the comfortable hotel you would call home for the duration of the story.

There was nothing in Barrow to remind an outsider of the world he knew. Nothing seemed real. No trees, no grass. None of the earth exposed itself above the flat blanket covering of white that concealed the landscape's every inch. It took time to comprehend that if it weren't for man, nothing would break the terrain's completely uniform plain.

Suddenly the world's fickle attention focused on one of its most isolated places. Even with the miracle of instant satellite communication, Barrow seemed at least as enslaved to its harsh setting as the three whales trapped under the ice. Three hundred and twenty miles above the Arctic Circle, each day survived was a miracle achieved. No one occupied a more hostile, primitive and alien world than did the hearty Inupiat Eskimos.

Until the media adopted them as their own, it would have been impossible to save the whales. Because it was nature at work, most Barrowans did not see the point of trying to rescue the whales. But once the story went nationwide, the decision seemed out of their hands.

Whales stranded themselves for tens of thousands of years before the invention of satellite news gathering. They will most likely continue to strand themselves for thousands more. Everyone assigned to the whales' story knew this was a non-story, yet it was one the world was desperate to follow. The media monitored the whales as intently as they would a superpower summit.

The power of television alone could not account for the spellbinding influence of this story. The herd instinct led the news media to overtake Barrow. When NBC found good grazing, everyone followed. The valiant struggle of the whales and those who worked hard to rescue them would lead news programs around the globe for almost two weeks. But no group of news directors could have created this huge amount of interest. That power belonged to the whales, their rescuers, and the hundreds of millions who wanted them freed.

Since the white man's first unwelcome intrusion, Barrow was divided over the best tactics for dealing with him. Isolationists argued the Outsiders wanted the Eskimo and his ancient way of life destroyed. Modernists believed that the white man would welcome the Eskimos' entry into his world. For the Eskimo, the only question was how best to combine his own needs with what the white man designed.

Chapter 6

The Tigress From Greenpeace

Autumn 1988 marked the final days of Ronald Reagan's presidency. His administration had only a few months to complete its unfinished business and prepare for the transfer of power. Since most people thought there was little more he could accomplish, the nation turned its attention away from the lame duck President toward the race to succeed him.

No one knew this better than Interior Secretary Donald Hodel. Hodel realized that the period right before the President left office was his own last and perhaps best chance to push some of Ronald Reagan's least popular policies through Congress. Exploratory offshore oil drilling in some of America's most environmentally sensitive waters stood at the top of Hodel's list.

The oil companies promised it was safe, but few people believed them. Environmentalists countered that a single "blowout" at an offshore oil rig could spill millions of gallons of crude oil into a fragile ecosystem, causing catastrophic damage. Despite the President's overwhelming personal popularity, public opinion consistently sided with the environmentalists, eliminating any chance of enacting the President's policy through conventional channels.

With time running out, Hodel made one last effort to open up the entire U.S. continental shelf for offshore drilling. The biggest prize was Alaska's Bristol Bay. Separating the Aleutian Islands from the Alaskan mainland, Bristol Bay served as the home for more than three-quarters of the world's salmon, half the tuna, herring, halibut and countless numbers of other commercial fish species. Supplying the world with more than a billion dollars worth of fish each year, Bristol Bay was the backbone of Alaska's commercial fishing industry.

The oil industry and its geologist allies believed that some of the world's largest remaining undeveloped oil deposits lay just beneath Bristol Bay's floor. The oil companies were bent on tapping them, dismissing concerns over possible damage to America's richest maritime region. From the oilman's point of view, the quantity of oil and gas involved more than justified the risk. But the Alaskan fishermen, whose livelihoods depended upon the Bay's renewable resources, resolved to fight Hodel's plans to the bitter end.

Cindy Lowry was the Alaska field coordinator for Greenpeace, the most prominent environmentalist organization. Although it was created in 1972 to stop atomic weapons testing, its young group of firebrands burst into the world's consciousness with their risky stunts to save the whales. Greenpeace etched its indelible image in inflatable rubber dinghies. By placing their tiny craft between the huge harpoon guns and the helpless whales they were targeted to kill, the daring two man crews did more than risk their lives to save whales. They compelled the world to act. By 1989, Greenpeace was a household name. Its two million members were active everywhere. From the North to the South Pole, Greenpeacers fought for causes as broad as the world was wide. Controversy was their constant companion.

To Cindy Lowry, Bristol Bay was much more than a commercial fishery. It was the critical pathway for Alaska's sea creatures. All the animals that migrated to and from Alaska depended on swimming through and living in a clean, viable Bristol Bay.

Cindy believed that if the oilmen were given rights to develop Bristol Bay, they would threaten everything that passed through it, including two-thirds of the world's gray whale population. If there was a "blowout" at the wrong time, entire species could be irreparably devastated. For Cindy, it was the most offensive insult to weigh the survival of animal species against commercial considerations. The slaughter of whales, by whatever means, could never be justified. Cindy Lowry knew it was her job to stop it.

She didn't trust many people. But the people she trusted least of all worked for the Reagan Administration. Bristol Bay first appeared as a target in the federal government's gunsights back in 1985. The Interior Department solicited bids to buy lease rights in the pristine Bay. The outcry against the plan to extract oil from the rich ecosystem was so great, Interior Secretary Hodel agreed to cancel the process with a caveat. Instead of destroying the bids, Interior would keep them sealed in the event the administration "changed its mind."

Three months before President Reagan was scheduled to leave office, almost everyone thought the issue of offshore oil drilling in wildlife areas was dead. Both Presidential candidates publicly opposed it in Bristol Bay. Even the oil companies had given up. But Donald Hodel never did. Suddenly the Interior Department "changed its mind." Hodel's office announced that the bids would be opened and read at a hearing in Anchorage on October 11, 1988.

Cindy Lowry's distrust had paid off. While no one else seemed prepared for the sudden sea change in administration policy, Cindy was. Three years earlier, she submitted Greenpeace's own bid for lease rights in Bristol Bay. As her price for rights to drill in the Bay, she offered the value of the marine life that would be destroyed as a result. Cindy knew that if drilling went ahead, it would be the creatures of Bristol Bay that would pay development's price, not the oil companies.

Cindy didn't consider herself a rabble-rouser. But the oil companies, Eskimo subsistence whalers, and others with whom she frequently clashed thought that a perfect term for her. Cindy Lowry could easily be mistaken for a tough young banker. Her youthful attractiveness belied her 38 years. It was a label she detested and emphatically denied, but Cindy Lowry was a YUPPIE. She wore subtle perfume with her finely pressed, conservative business suits, drank expensive coffees, drove a Volvo and had a great big dog named after the tallest mountain in North America, Denali. Outsiders knew it as Mount McKinley, named for an American President who never set foot in Alaska.

October 11, 1988, came quickly for Cindy Lowry. She had only a few weeks to prepare for the hearing that would determine the fate of Bristol Bay and its creatures. Cindy prepared for the worst. So did the Mineral Management Service of the U.S. Department of the Interior which sponored the hearing. They hired 15 extra security guards to protect the proceedings and its participants from people like Cindy Lowry.

Cindy dressed as she always did for professional functions. But hidden away in her black leather executive attaché case was a sleek megaphone from Sharper Image. Before the doors were opened the security guards were warned to look out for "Greenpeace types," not smartly dressed business women. Suppressing a smirk, Cindy walked right past them to a seat at the back of the auditorium. She couldn't believe it. As Alaska's most notorious environmentalist, she expected trouble, instead, they didn't even recognize her.

The hearing was a big event. Controversy was all but assured. All the Anchorage media, the newspapers and the television and radio stations, were on hand to cover it. Earlier in the week, the Interior Department in Washington sensed trouble. They instructed the moderator to find whatever excuse he could not to open the Greenpeace bids. The tension was palpable. The moderator knew he wouldn't get away with it, but orders were orders.

Again, Cindy was ahead of the game. She had locked horns with the oil companies for too long to think the hearing would go as promised. To avoid being thrown out on a trumped up trouble making charge, Cindy made sure she was flanked by friends who would protect her. Fellow activists and fishermen trying to defend their livelihoods sat next to Cindy on both sides. When the moderator made his surprise announcement, Cindy slipped the megaphone out of her briefcase and quickly put it to use.

"What about the bids, why aren't you going to read the bids?" she demanded. The megaphone was louder than the auditoriums public address system. "Why don't you open the bids like the law requires?" Hundreds of heads turned in her direction to witness the outburst. Applause and cheers drowned out the smattering of boos from Alaskans who favored development as strongly as Cindy opposed it.

The security guards sprang to life. From all corners of the hall, they ran in Cindy's direction to eject her from the hearing. They fought and struggled with the phalanx of burly fishermen who rose with broad chests to shield her. After a heated exchange, the guards overwhelmed their opposition and yanked Cindy out of her seat. The crowd jeered as the guards dragged her kicking and screaming from the hall. Camera crews captured it all for the evening news.

Outside, they lined up to interview the hearing's frazzled star. Her performance became that night's lead story on all three Anchorage newscasts. After answering all the media's questions, Cindy walked to her car where her boyfriend Kevin Bruce was waiting. Kevin always tried to be on hand whenever Cindy planned any of her stunts in case he was needed to post bail. Knowing she was too upset to drive, he gave her a warm hug, took her keys and drove home.

On the way, they stopped to pick up Chinese Take Out to eat at home while watching Todd Pottinger's 11:00 PM newscast. They expected Cindy's expulsion to be the top story. But the surprise came when they heard Pottinger report it as a major victory. The uproar forced the Mineral Management Service to cancel the hearing. The sealed bids went right back to the same vault where they had moldered for the last three years. Cindy and Greenpeace had won. For the moment, Bristol Bay was safe.

Kevin was ecstatic. While she was still shaken by her ejection from the hearing, Cindy's pretty face lit up. She basked in victory not for herself, but for the otters, seals, and whales of Bristol Bay.

Opponents often accused Cindy Lowry of many terrible things. But none of her critics ever suggested that she generated her ubiquitous statewide publicity for self-promotion. Cindy Lowry was heart and soul an activist. Environmentalism was her life's abiding passion, often to Kevin's chagrin. While her tactics were sometimes questioned, her motivations never were. Her sole desire was to protect the creatures of Alaska's vast but shrinking wilderness. It wasn't a passion she acquired. Cindy Lowry was born with it.

She was a precocious environmentalist. By the time she was five, little Cindy was already cutting loose the fish her family caught on pleasure trips. The adults soon learned that if they ever wanted to eat any of their catch, Cindy was better left at home. By her 10th birthday, she displayed a dangerous but effective willingness to use deadly force to protect the animals she so loved. Patrolling to protect her Kansas farm against coyote poachers, little Cindy marched with her grandfather's heavy shotgun slung over her tiny shoulder. Shoving her loaded gun's double barrels into their stunned faces, she forced the marauding hunters to think twice before trespassing. Word of "that crazy Lowry kid" spread fast. Her militancy worked. The poachers never returned.

But when it came to her own life, Cindy was no martyr. After working long weeks on the Bristol Bay lease sale, she intended to take the rest of the week off. Nothing could spoil the hard-earned and long-planned weekend with Kevin she had already postponed several times. Thursday morning, October 13, Cindy Lowry slept in. Figuring she wouldn't miss the paper she disparagingly nick-named "The Anchorage Daily Snooze," Kevin took that morning's edition with him to the office. While casually glancing the front page, one headline caught his eye. It read "Ice Traps Three Gray Whales." He decided against calling Cindy who he hoped was still sleeping after her exhausting week.

A local Anchorage reporter named Jeff Berliner wasn't so thoughtful. He woke Cindy up at home to ask what she knew about the three whales. To the Alaska press corps, Cindy's phone was referred to as "enviro quote." Whenever reporters needed a source to quote on an environmental issue, Cindy would always oblige them, whether or not she knew any more than they did.

Jeff's call was the first she heard about the stranded whales. If Cindy didn't know, Berliner told himself, maybe it wasn't a story. Cindy thanked Jeff for the call and promised to get back to him as soon as she found out anything. The instant she hung up, the phone rang again. This time it was Geoff Carroll calling from Barrow. The biologist figured that if anyone could help him help the whales, it was Alaska's most famous whale hunter. Cindy Lowry was his man.

All Geoff knew for sure about the whales was that they were California grays. He didn't know their sex or ages although one was a baby and the other two seemed to be adolescents. Geoff told Cindy that unless a path through the ice could be cut to the open water, the whales would die. Any ship with a strong bow could do the job, he told her. The night before, the two biologists spent hours on the phone asking Coast Guard personnel around the country for help.

The United States had only two icebreakers, a fact known only too well to Alaskans, who had long argued unsuccessfully for more. Neither could help the biologists. One, the *Polar Star*, was limping its way through the 17-foot-high ice floes and blinding snow of the Northwest Passage, while the other, the *Polar Sea*, sat helplessly in its Seattle drydock.

Whale strandings were common events all over Alaska. When whales were imperiled near Anchorage, Cindy always tried to help. In fact, the last time whales became stranded nearby, Cindy and her dog Denali were almost killed trying to save them.

In August, a group of Beluga whales beached themselves just south of Anchorage. They were exposed and helpless on the mud-flats of Turnagain Arm, the body of water to the south of Anchorage. The Arm was known for its immense tidal surges called bore tides.

Unlike regular tides that gradually ebb and flow, bore tides form high-crested walls of water moving at up to 30 miles an hour.

The group of whales Cindy was trying to help had become stranded by a bore tide, finding themselves trapped on the Arm's deadly mudflats. Cindy knew that if they were not helped immediately, the whales would die before the next tide could bring the sea back in to save them.

Before launching her own private rescue, Cindy reported the stranded whales to the Anchorage office of the National Maritime Fisheries Service. NMFS was the federal agency responsible for enforcing the 1972 Marine Mammal Protection Act, passed by the U.S. Congress primarily to help endangered whales like those stranded on the Turnagain mudflats, and, later, the three trapped whales in Barrow. Even though NMFS rarely helped her, Cindy obeyed the law requiring citizens to report stranded animals.

NMFS employees took emergencies reported by Cindy Lowry with a grain of Greenpeace salt. "It's her again," they lamented, that crazy environmentalist who constantly cried "stranding." If NMFS responded every time, they would exhaust their annual budget in the first quarter of the year. They almost always told her there was nothing they could do. The Beluga whales stranded on Turnagain Arm proved no different. If they were going to be saved, Cindy Lowry would have to do it herself.

Out on the flats, dry skin was the biggest danger the whales faced. To a person, dry skin meant minor irritation easily alleviated by applying moisturizing cream. To a whale, it meant death. Without water to cool their warm blooded bodies, the whales would overheat and die. Cindy called her surprised boyfriend at work and told him she needed him to help her scoop water from tidal pools over the stranded whales.

Kevin was speechless. Was he hearing this suicidal suggestion from the same woman he was in love with? A woman he knew was slightly crazed but thought possessed at least a modicum of sanity? Anyone foolish enough to ignore the huge red danger signs warning people to stay off the mudflats stood a good chance of miring themselves so deep they couldn't get out. The mudflats were more dangerous than quicksand. The more you resisted, the deeper and firmer the mud would clutch you. If the mud did not pull you all the way under, you could watch until the incoming tide consumed you in a wall of water.

With the elections coming up, Kevin was too busy with his political consulting work to become a posthumous laughingstock. But he wasn't anxious for Cindy to become Greenpeace's latest martyr either. After repeated but unsubstantiated assurances that she wouldn't take any unnecessary chances, Cindy still could not convince Kevin the whales were worth the risk. Only when she threatened to go alone did he relent.

Like ice strandings in the Arctic, tide strandings of the kind Cindy and Kevin were now witnessing were natural and common occurrences. But their routineness did nothing to quench Cindy's zeal. Before he could unfasten his seatbelt, Kevin was reduced to screaming at Cindy out his open window. Seconds earlier, Cindy and her dog bolted out the open door and onto the deceptively solid floor of the Arm. In his haste to urge them back to safety, Kevin banged his head on the window frame.

Just a few hundred feet out on the dry waterway, Cindy screamed for help. Like a stealthy predator, the oozing mud grabbed Cindy's left leg and pulled her deathward. Between her frantic cries for help, Cindy desperately tried to reassure her dog Denali who was fighting his own losing battle against the deadly flats.

Sinking helplessly against the thunderous roar of the fast approaching bore tide, Cindy and her dog prepared to die. Her final solace was knowing that the force which was certain to kill her would redeem the beached whales.

The last thing Kevin Bruce wanted was to be eulogized as the "horn-rimmed hero." Vaulting across the protective guard rail, he bounded onto the dangerous flats in a daring effort to save Cindy and her dog. Finally reaching them, Kevin ignored Cindy's appeals to help her dog first. In just three minutes, the mud had already pulled Cindy waist deep. Cindy and her dog watched the wall of water threaten to consume them.

But Kevin turned his back, concentrating instead on pulling Cindy to safety. When she was free, she grabbed Denali by the scruff of his neck and pulled him out of the thick mud with one hard yank. They sprinted back to the shore. When they reached it, the water turned from demon to savior. They cheered as it rushed over the whales.

When she heard about the whale stranding in Barrow, Cindy immediately thought they must be beached like the Belugas in Turnagain Arm. Until it was explained to her, she could not understand what Craig and Geoff meant when they talked about "shore ice," "open leads" and the need for icebreakers.

By the close of business Thursday, October 13, Cindy did not know nearly enough to mount an effective campaign to save the Barrow whales. But by the time he got home, something told Kevin that his long-awaited weekend would go the way of all the others. That something was the look on Cindy's face. The seeds for still another mission of mercy had been firmly planted in her. This was just the sort of crisis Cindy lived for. Cindy loved Kevin. But it seemed she loved whales even more. Every time he started to think otherwise, there was another stranding and Cindy was off to the rescue.

At 6:00 AM Friday morning, Cindy's phone rang. It was Geoff Carroll in Barrow. After apologizing for waking her up, he told Cindy that the local television cameraman's footage appeared just hours before on the NBC Nightly News. The three stranded whales were a national story. Cindy Lowry was in business.

She jumped out of bed and into the shower. Before she could finish rinsing the shampoo out of her long brown hair, the phone rang again. It was Campbell Plowden, from Greenpeace's Washington office. He coordinated all the organization's whale activities. While he did not see the NBC report himself, he heard about it and wanted to know if Cindy thought Greenpeace could play a role. Plowden would leave the decision in Cindy's hands. If she could justify a realistic effort to help rescue the stranded whales, Greenpeace would pay the bill.

Plowden knew the International Whaling Commission's rules on the subsistence hunt allowed the Eskimos to kill any whales they could catch even though they usually ate just bowhead. He was afraid the Eskimos might claim the whales before anyone tried to rescue them. He urgently wanted Cindy to find out if the Eskimos had any plans to kill the whales to fill their quota.

In his long fight against it, Plowden learned as much as any white man about Eskimo subsistence hunting and he didn't like what he knew. The ardent whale advocate did not think the Eskimos were subsistence hunters at all. Missile launchers, time-released bombs and outboard motors did not bear even a remote resemblance to traditional whaling.

While Plowden couldn't understand how Barrow with its $80 million high school and $300 million water system could call itself a subsistence village, Barrowans couldn't understand how a K Street liberal 7,000 miles away in Washington, D.C., could pass judgment on how they lived their lives.

Cindy called Geoff and Craig back and asked them if they knew of any local plans to harvest the three whales. The biologists confessed that even if there were plans, they would likely hear nothing of them. Barow's white minority often charged the Inuits with furtively keeping to themselves. Critics complained that Eskimos would never confide in a white man, particularly one with environmental leanings.

The International Whaling Commission empowered the Alaska Eskimo Whaling Commission to represent North Slope whalers and to regulate their local hunt. Craig called AEWC headquarters in Barrow to see if any of the captains wanted to harvest the three trapped whales. Craig learned to his great surprise, that yes, in fact, there were lots of people interested in killing the whales. Several local captains had asked the AEWC for permission to harvest them. Since the whales in question weren't Bowhead, a committee had to approve the captains' request. A meeting was scheduled for 7:30 PM Saturday October 15, in a classroom at Barrow High School.

Craig was shocked. After three days with the stranded whales, he couldn't help but feel attached to the helpless giants. These creatures had struggled against fantastic odds to survive as long as they had. His boss always reminded him never to get emotionally involved. Why did he feel so attached to three whales foolish enough to strand themselves under the growing Arctic ice? Craig knew that if presented with data on the stranding in the abstract, he would say the whales' death was a good thing, natural selection, survival of the fittest, a cleansing of the gene pool. But knowing the whales as well as he did, Craig suffered with them. He couldn't bear the thought of a few greedy Eskimos sharpening their harpoons to slaughter three whales for which he believed they had absolutely no use.

Craig called Cindy and told her that the whale's fate would be decided at a special meeting the next night. Cindy promised to get on it as fast as she could. The NBC News report could only improve the whales chances, she reasssured Craig. She told him to tell NBC's Don Oliver about the meeting. Maybe he would cover it. It was the same tactic human rights campaigners used to aid political prisoners in repressive lands, Cindy explained. The more people on the Outside who knew about the whales, the more pressure they could put on the Eskimos to spare them.

Craig and Geoff knew the mere fact that a meeting would be held meant chances were good the committee would grant the whalers permission to harvest the three young grays. Cindy and her allies had less than 24 precious hours to mount a campaign effective enough to block the Eskimos. If the vote was in favor of harvesting, the whales would be killed the next afternoon, right after the Eskimos changed out of their Sunday church clothes.

The defiant whalers weren't threatened by a few Outside television cameras. The Outsiders were always giving the Eskimo a hard time about his whaling. What business was it of his anyway? In fact, if the meeting went as planned, some whalers would probably offer to take Dan Oliver and Russ Weston on their ski machines to film the great Eskimo victory.

Since she thought she was taking the rest of the week off, Cindy felt it would be an opportune time for the contractors to remodel Greenpeace's Anchorage office. They were busy with buzz saws and power drills and she couldn't get any work done there even if she wanted to. Instead she holed herself up in Kevin's H Street condo and started working the phone. The simplest way to free the whales was to have a ship come in and break the ice. Campbell Plowden told her he would try to find an icebreaker from Washington while she should use her Alaska contacts.

Cindy started at the top. She called Alaska Governor Steve Cowper's Juneau office. Whenever Cindy was in situations where no one else would help, she called the Governor's executive assistant, David Ramser. Sometimes he helped, more often he didn't. Cindy voiced an impassioned tone of determination as she told Ramser the story of the trapped whales. Environmental activism was a lot like sales. Cindy had to convince the people in power that taking action was worth the investment in political capital.

She enticed Ramser with some tempting political bait. If the pro-development Cowper could use his influence to get the Coast Guard to divert an icebreaker to Barrow, Cindy promised that the first-term Democratic chief executive would win badly needed points with an environmental constituency in which she had tremendous influence.

Ramser remained unmoved after impatiently listening to Cindy's well articulated offer. "What do you want us to do about it?" he asked in a tone which made it clear he had more important things to do. "I'm not interested and the Governor's not interested."

From previous dealings with the Governor's top aide, Cindy knew Ramser had an impatient streak that didn't mix well with her hunger for action. Instead of trying to reason with him, Cindy upset him more by barking back. While her mind told her that aggravating him was counterproductive, she went on.

She relented only when she knew she was arguing in vain. Cindy promised Ramser she would find other means to save the three whales. At the last second, Ramser didn't want Cindy to hang up mad. Instead he offered to listen to whatever requests Cindy made, with the proviso that neither he nor Governor Cowper could be used to lure others into promising help.

She walked into the kitchen to refill her coffee mug when the phone rang again. It was the wife of an oil executive who made Cindy promise never to identify her. Cindy jokingly called her "Jane Whale." Ms. "Whale" asked if she knew anything about those whales that appeared on NBC News the night before. When Cindy said she knew quite a lot about the whales, "Jane Whale" was thrilled.

"You see," she said, "I know a way we can get them out." Cindy's back straightened as she pressed the phone closer to her ear. The woman on the other end of the line said she knew Pete Leathard, the president of VECO, Inc., Alaska's largest oil construction company which had a huge operation at Prudhoe Bay. "Jane" told Cindy that Leathard saw Brokaw's broadcast the night before and was so moved by the pictures of the whales that he wanted his company to help save them.

"How can he help us?" Cindy asked. She didn't understand why an oil man, the enemy, would be interested in helping three trapped whales. It must be a stunt, a hoax, or a P.R. ploy, she said.

"No, no," the woman insisted. "Leathard's dead serious."

Jane told Cindy that VECO owned a huge ice-breaking hover-barge designed to supply construction materials to build offshore oil rigs. In 1984, amid predictions of a great discovery, three oil companies joined forces to build the only platform stable enough to withstand the shifting ice and howling winds of frozen Arctic ocean. The hoverbarge supplied materials used to build Mukluk Island, a man-made gravel island in the middle of the raging Beaufort Sea. Mukluk Island was the biggest and most expensive oil rig ever built. But when the billion dollar investment struck seawater, it marked the end of North Slopes drilling activity. The $4 million hoverbarge commissioned to manage the ill-fated boom was consigned to early mothballs.

Leathard was sure the barge could cut through Barrow's new seasonal ice. Designed to float on a cushion of air, the heavy barge broke through the thick ice by displacing the water beneath it. Since it was of no use to anyone, Leathard thought VECO's chairman and founder Billy Bob Allen wouldn't object to deploying the hoverbarge for a day's work in Barrow.

Leathard thought if Allen had any doubts, he could assuage them by pointing out the fact that NBC News was covering the story, almost guaranteeing VECO national exposure. The "Industry," Leathard prepared himself to argue, couldn't put a price tag on the positive publicity. An oil company helping rescue three stranded whales was like money in the bank. Leathard was convinced the hoverbarge would work and was determined to prove it

"Jane Whale" told Cindy all Leathard needed was a helicopter powerful enough to pull the 200,000 pound barge out of the frozen berth it has been mired in for four years. The barge sank a few feet deeper into the thawed permafrost during the few short weeks of each Arctic summer. In the winter, the barge froze deeper into the ground.

Cindy's contact needed help locating a helicopter suitable for towing the barge 270 miles northwest to where the whales were stranded.

"The only type of Helicopter that can pull a load that big is the Sky Crane," she said. "A Sikorsky CH-54 Sky Crane."

"Well, where would I find one of those?" Cindy asked.

"The only people that have them in this state are the Air Force and the Alaska National Guard."

"How long will all this take?" Cindy wondered aloud.

"Once you get the helicopter, VECO can have the barge in Barrow and the whales freed in 40 hours," Jane promised.

For a reason Cindy would never understand but never violated, the woman asked Cindy not to reveal her name. "Just trust me," she pleaded. "VECO really wants to help." She instructed Cindy not to call her unless it was urgent. Otherwise, she might have to withdraw the offer.

Puzzled but excited, Cindy hung up and looked into space. Why would an oil company want to help three whales, she asked herself again and again. After fruitlessly trying to come up with reasons why the plan wouldn't work, Cindy realized she had no choice. She had to trust her source. She didn't know how, but by God, Cindy would get that helicopter.

She called back the Governor's office. She told Dave Ramser that an oil company was willing to donate the use of its icebreaking hoverbarge to cut a path for the trapped Barrow whales. All they needed was authority to borrow two Skycrane helicopters from the National Guard or the Air Force.

In no uncertain terms, Ramser told Cindy that the political situation in Juneau made it impossible for anyone in state government to help. As for every other oil dependent state, 1988 was a bad year for Alaska. Alaska's economy walked a financial tightrope. One false move could mean sending the state into an even deeper recession. Oil company tax revenues were way down at the moment they were most needed. After the Governor had asked Alaskans to bite the fiscal bullet, why would he risk his dwindling political clout on three non-voting whales?

Only a few weeks earlier, the Governor was roundly criticized for moving too slowly to rescue seven North Slope Eskimo walrus hunters trapped on a huge piece of ice that broke away from the shore and drifted out to sea. Ramser thought if the Governor suddenly led a rescue effort on behalf of three animals after doing so little to save the lives of seven native Alaskans from Kotzebue, it would smack of anti-Eskimo racism. It would be an act of political suicide.

Cindy became enraged when Ramser asked why she was so concerned about the fate of animals that weren't even endangered. Suffering is suffering, Cindy insisted. The suffering of a specific animal isn't mitigated by the state of its species, she argued. Cindy reminded Ramser that people were far from endangered and the whole country watched the extraordinary 1986 rescue of little Jessica McLune from a well in Midland, Texas. By the way, Ramser suddenly remembered, the Governor was out of town and couldn't be reached until Monday.

Ramser laughed out loud when Cindy asked him to request the assistance of Soviet icebreakers in accordance with an existing American Soviet maritime treaty. "The Coast Guard wouldn't even let us ask the Soviets for help when the Kotzebue hunters were trapped," Ramser responded. "You actually think they're going to allow it for three whales?"

Not wanting Ramser to hear that she was on the verge of tears, she angrily hung up the phone and called Geoff and Craig for consolation.

Ramser wasn't lying when he said the Governor was out of town. In actual fact he was in Barrow, right across the hall from Geoff and Craig's office in the Naval Arctic Research Lab's hearing room.

For Governor Steve Cowper, his initial refusal to help marked the last time he would be asked to take any part in the drama about to unfold. From that moment until the rescue was over, Governor Cowper was neither heard from nor consulted again.

But how could he or anybody else in their right mind know that this seemingly insignificant event would turn into the biggest news story in the history of the state of Alaska? That it would capture the imagination of hundreds of millions of people at all ends of the earth? That it would personally involve both the President of the United States and the General Secretary of the Communist Party of the Soviet Union?

Had it not been for the real news of the ill-fated voyage of the Exxon Valdez which spewed 11 million gallons of toxic North Slope crude oil into the pristine waters of Prince William Sound just five months later, it might well have been the kind of blunder from which many politicians can never recover. Cowper fumbled the media attention which came with the rescue, but he proved himself a take charge administrator during Alaska's next big news event.

Cindy Lowry was endowed with a fearless determination and an ability to get things done. Friends couldn't connect her with the despair that accompanied her slightest failures. Her best political contact in the state delivered a shocking blow. She could count on no help from the Governor or anyone in his office.

Cindy looked out her east window and gazed at the snow-covered magnificence of the Chugach Mountains. They seemed to stare right back at her with a wondrous attraction. But it was a facade. The sun's orange afterglow lent the rugged mountains the appearance of warmth and peace that she knew did not exist. Nothing in Alaska, Cindy mused, neither its nature nor its people, was as benign as it appeared. Cindy Lowry was alone.

She thought about the three whales as if she knew them. She already felt deeply for them. Never before had she seen these California grays, not even in pictures. Yet she started to cry, the first of many tears to come.

The moment Cindy started to believe there was little left to do, the phone rang. It was 7:00 PM, Friday, October 14, 1988, exactly one week after the whales were first found. A man named Kent Burton was on the line. If he was telling the truth, he had the most grandiose title of anyone in the United States government. He identified himself as the Under Secretary for Oceans and Atmospheres for the United States Department of Commerce. He was calling from his Washington, D.C., office where it was 11:00 PM.

"Hello, Cindy?" he asked tentatively. "Commerce Secretary William Verity suggested I call you and offer our help in your efforts to save those three whales."

A perfectly timed miracle. It was the critical call that would lead down an irrevocable path toward freeing the whales.

Kent Burton didn't get involved because he loved whales. He got involved because Alaska Senator Ted Stevens urged him to. Stevens was one of the longest serving and least recognized members of the United States Senate, just the way he liked it. Anonymity was the tool Stevens used for 20 years to build his unique position of quiet power. It was that power he would use behind the scenes to help save the three whales. Stevens answered almost every reporter the same way. In his native Hoosier twang, Stevens repeated his maxim time and time again. "If you're gonna get things done next time, you better keep your mouth shut this time."

Cindy, like most Alaskans, knew why the Commerce Department was the critical arm of government responsible for dealing with endangered species and animal protection. Unlike Outsiders, nearly every Alaskan has experience with wild animals. Even in the heart of Anchorage, the state's urban and cultural center, moose graze in public parks. Just outside town, grizzly bears stand comfortably in any hundreds of salmon rich streams, showing amazed human onlookers why bears are the world's best fishermen.

Although the most powerful, Senator Stevens wasn't the only one to lobby the Commerce Department that day. Earlier, Campbell Plowden had done the same. He told Burton that Cindy was trying to get an icebreaker to cut a path for the whales to swim through. It worked. Commerce was interested in helping Cindy Lowry help the whales.

Cindy didn't need that hapless Governor. Now, she had a major oil company and the United States Government on her side. The rescue of the three lucky whales was about to begin.

Chapter 7

Billy Bob's Last Frontier

Alaskans call their great land the Last Frontier. America's America. A place where even the darkest past need not stand in the way of a new and better future. The unique Alaskan ethic glorifies above all those who triumph over adversity. The more they overcome, the greater their claim to Alaska's romantic mystique.

In 1988, no one embodied the Alaskan ideal more than Billy Bob Allen. While Alaskans loved to boast of the obstacles they surmounted, few would dare impose tales of their own hardship on Bill Allen. When Bill Allen disembarked at the Port of Anchorage in 1968, he was little different from most migrants flocking to the Last Frontier in search of a new and better life. A troubled past and a burning desire to stake his own claim were his only companions. Alaska was the last place big and young enough to accommodate dreams his size. Alaska was Bill Allen's last best hope.

Never did his family's grinding poverty dim the young Allen's vision of a future he thought would be as wide as the open range of his native New Mexico. Like most young boys, Billy Bob Allen dreamed of quitting school. At 14, Billy Bob's idle daydream was turned to a nightmare when his daddy walked out. The unprepared teenager had no choice. He had his mama and seven brothers and sisters to feed. Billy Bob Allen quit school and went to work.

The desperate youngster found work helping a local welder lay oil and gas pipelines. After 15 years toiling under a broiling desert sun, Bill Allen saw his life cruising in the fast lane to nowhere. Allen's long dormant dreams sprang back to life with stories of an oil boom that loomed on the Alaskan horizon. It was 1968. Alaska was about to take off and Bill Allen wanted to get in on the ride. He and a partner founded a small oil supply business called VE Construction. His partner had the money, Allen the brains. Before long the 31-year-old New Mexican landed his first contract building a small offshore oil platform in waters near Anchorage. He was so good that, in less than a decade, Bill Allen had built Alaska's largest oil construction company.

No one could tell by looking at Allen that he was one of the richest men in Alaska. He prided himself on his ruggedness. Only after he achieved success in Alaska could Allen afford to spend time at his ranch near Grand Junction, Colorado.

On Saturday morning, October 15, 1988, two days after the whales first appeared on NBC News, Allen and a number of his ranch hands were checking and fixing the shoes of some of his 50 thoroughbreds. Through the backlegs of one of his horses, Allen could see his ranch manager's pickup approach the paddock. He brushed off his Wrangler Jeans and pulled out a faded red bandana to wipe the sweat from his dusty face.

"Mornin' boss," the ranch manager said. "Pete Leathard's on the phone from Anchorage. He said it's important."

Allen told his men they could go to lunch as soon as they finished shoeing the horses. He walked across the meadow toward the heavy black rotary phone that was probably older than the stable it was in. Allen knew Pete Leathard would not have bothered him unless it was important. In the "all bidness" (oil business), unexpected news is almost always bad news. Allen's mind raced to concoct the worst possible scenario. Perhaps there was a blowout at one of the offshore rigs VECO built. He wondered how many men had died. Allen thought he was hearing things when Pete asked him for permission to authorize the National Guard to tow the hoverbarge to Barrow on a whale rescue mission.

"You wanna do what?" he asked in a thick Texas drawl.

It was the ease of taking close-up pictures like this that transformed the whale stranding from a routine Arctic occurrence to an international media extravaganza. (Micheal Echola, Alaska National Guard)

Eskimo hunter Ralph Ahkivgak (second from right in baseball cap) was better known to his Inupiat comrades as Malik, the Little Big Man, one of the greatest whalers in the Eskimo world. For two weeks in October 1988, Malik worked not to kill whales but to save them. (Randy Brandon for SIPA)

The combined ease of great pictures and the immediacy of instant satellite transmission made Oran Caudle, the director of the North Slope Borough television studio, a critical link between the isolated Arctic village of Barrow and the rest of the world. (Randy Brandon for SIPA)

The Eskimo campaign to save the three whales was led by Arnold Brower, Jr. It was Brower's idea to use chain saws to cut a path to freedom. (Frank Baker for BP Exploration)

Local biologists Geoff Carroll and Craig George were the first scientists to study the whales. They were also the first people to try saving them. Their efforts to locate an icebreaker was the subject of the rescue's initial news story which appeared in the *Anchorage Daily News*. As the story grew, so did their celebrity. Reporters followed them everywhere. (Randy Brandon for SIPA)

The chain saws Arnold Brower used as an experiment quickly became the whales' lifeline. Here, an Eskimo pull-starts a saw in minus 25 degree weather. Masu Kawamura, a Japanese television correspondent, wonders when this will ever end. (Tom Rose, NY News Corp.)

Of the many who came to save the whales, Cindy Lowry was the most important. The Greenpeace environmentalist brought all sides together, creating the consensus needed to sponsor a wide-scale rescue operation. When the adolescent whales first stranded themselves, they may have been orphans. But when Cindy learned of their plight, they immediately had the mother of their dreams. (Jeff Shultz for SIPA)

The Alaska National Guard dispatched its top field commander to take charge of the military role in the rescue. Here Colonel Tom Carroll, with aluminum seal pole slung across his shoulder, confers with an amused Eskimo. (Micheal Echola, Alaska National Guard)

Like millions of his fellow countrymen, the President is enthralled with the plight of the whales. He orders Bonnie Mersinger, shown here, to coordinate contact between the White House and Alaska National Guard Colonel Tom Carroll. At first she thought the colonel was a jerk. Later she married him. (White House)

VECO Inc.'s donation of a 185-ton icebreaking hoverbarge to free the whales was all the cover the United States Government needed to authorize a full-blown rescue. For three fruitless days, Colonel Carroll and his National Guard unit tried to tow the barge across the frozen surface of the Arctic Ocean from Prudhoe Bay to Barrow with a cargo helicopter. After attempting everything else, Carroll ordered the first-ever double helicopter pull. It too failed. (Denise Quinn for ARCO)

On October 18, three days after first seeing the whales on the evening news, President Ronald Reagan phones Colonel Carroll in Prudhoe Bay to offer his support for the rescue. (AP Worldwide)

The two larger whales, Siku and Poutu, seen surfacing together, were healthier, stronger and more vital than the third, a baby named Bone. (Micheal Echola, Alaska National Guard)

Before they had perfected their new art, it took dozens of Eskimos to cut open new breathing holes for the whales. (Micheal Echola, Alaska National Guard)

The Top of the World Hotel and Pepe's North of the Border were the northernmost hotel and restaurant on Earth. For two weeks in October 1988, this complex housed and fed most of the Outsiders who made Operation Breakout one of the greatest non-events of all time. To make things even easier for them, Oran Caudle's state-of-the-art television facility was just across the street in the modern glass office building. (Randy Brandon for SIPA)

Two brothers-in-law from Minnesota paid their own way to Barrow so they could try their portable de-icing machines to keep the small holes from freezing over. Here Greg Ferrian (left) and Rick Skluzacek prepare to drop one of their six de-icers into an open hole. (Frank Baker for BP Exploration)

Not only had Bill Allen not heard a word about the whales, even if he had, he wouldn't have given a Texas damn. He loved horses, not whales. Those damned environmentalists always talked about whales whenever they tried to stop one of his new projects. He listened impatiently while Pete Leathard tried to convince his boss that VECO might get some unexpected mileage out of helping free the whales.

"Bill," Pete said. Allen had only recently begun to insist on a single, more dignified first name. "That barge can do the job. It can free those whales and win us some needed points with the environmentalists. I hate to do this to you Bill, but we need you back here to take charge. The media's gonna jump all over this one."

Allen didn't need to be reminded that the hoverbarge had turned into a financial disaster. It was his signature that validated the $4 million check used to pay for it. No one likes losing money, including Bill Allen. Better to use it than to let it sink further into the frozen tundra. Pete Leathard was right. Bill Allen signed on. The rescue was official.

The oilman reluctantly cancelled the rest of his stay at the ranch and booked a flight back home to Anchorage. He stored his ten gallon cream-colored Stetson in the overhead compartment, said "howdy" to his fellow first class passengers and stretched his long legs in his specially requested bulkhead seat of the 757 widebody jet. During the six hour flight from Denver to Anchorage, he started having second thoughts about the unusual project he just authorized. What in the "hail" was an oil construction company doing working with environmentalists to save three whales? Whenever someone from the Outside asked him how folks in his business got along with the state's environmentalists, Bill Allen used an industry metaphor. "Since 'all' don't mix with water," he would say, "we don't mix."

Just about the time Pete Leathard called Billy Bob Allen in Colorado, Kent Burton from the Department of Commerce again got in touch with Cindy Lowry in Anchorage. Burton was waiting for instructions on how to help save the whales. Cindy told him she still had to hear that VECO had officially donated the barge.

The moment she put down the phone it rang again. It was Pete Leathard from VECO. He told her his boss Billy Bob Allen just authorized the release of the barge and was on his way back to Anchorage.

Cindy Lowry didn't realize that her acceptance of VECO's offer to use the hoverbarge would create one of the oddest coalitions in the history of the environmentalist movement: VECO with its barge and Greenpeace's Cindy Lowry with her contacts to save three California gray whales. She was elated. Cindy called Kent Burton at the Commerce Department in Washington to tell him the good news. She asked him what she should do about the helicopter since the governor turned down her requests for assistance. Burton said that only an elected official requesting military assistance could set the cumbersome bureaucratic wheels in motion. Once that was done, Burton could take the next step.

Why bother with her senators? Cindy asked. She expected even less interest from them than from Governor Cowper. Surely, if any of Alaska's four statewide office holders would help, it would be Governor Cowper. After all, he was the only Democrat. Everyone knew that Republicans secretly conspired to further damage the environment. Within the environmentalist movement, it was all but an acknowledged fact. When was the last time, Cindy asked herself, either of Alaska's senators or its lone congressman, all of whom were Republicans, ever supported anything she worked for? Although unreliable, Democrats were Cindy's only potential political allies in her war to save the world. Or were they?

Not having much choice, Cindy took Kent Burton's advice and called Senator Ted Stevens' office. She began to realize she might have misjudged her erstwhile adversary when Senator Stevens' assistant, Earl Comstock, told Cindy that his boss would be delighted to do whatever he could to help. According to Comstock, Stevens had been following the story of the trapped whales on television.

On Saturday, Comstock called the senator at home to ask if he would be interested in relaying Cindy's request for National Guard helicopters to tow the frozen barge. The senator was more than interested. To his wife's chagrin, he cancelled plans to spend a quiet Saturday with his family and rushed to his office on Capitol Hill.

Cindy was too excited to wait for Senator Stevens to respond. She wanted to find out for herself who had the helicopters and how long it would take to make them operational once they were put on active duty. She called National Guard headquarters in Anchorage expecting to get another answering machine. Instead, she reached General John Schaeffer.

General Schaeffer was much more than the highest ranking military officer in the state. He was an Alaska legend. The full-blooded Eskimo from the small subsistence village of Kotzebue on Alaska's northwest coast was the unrivaled hero of his people. The 51-year-old general was the most accomplished Eskimo ever to enter the white man's world. His achievements were taught in all of Alaska's schools and Inuit communities throughout the Arctic fringe. Schaeffer was perhaps Alaska's most celebrated public figure. He turned a half million dollar grant to his local Native corporation by the 1971 Alaska Land Claims Settlement act into more than $50 million. He managed this astonishing feat in less than a decade, and he did it by employing 700 people in a village that had never before used money.

His military career was even more impressive. Two years before statehood, a 28-year-old Schaeffer enlisted in the famous Eskimo Scouts, officially known as the Alaska Army National Guard's First Battalion. By 1988, General John W. Schaeffer was Adjutant General for the Alaska National Guard and Commissioner of the State of Alaska Department of Military and Veteran Affairs.

Many Alaskans felt Schaeffer's next stop would be a term in Juneau as Alaska's first native governor. Opinion polls showed Schaeffer winning almost any political office he sought.

Cindy was startled to hear his unmistakable voice answering the phone that Saturday morning. Before she could respond, the general had to repeat his greeting a second time. Cindy didn't know at the time that General Schaeffer had gone to his office because of the plight of the whales. Senator Stevens had already asked him to put together the logistics needed to support a rescue operation.

"We're here trying to save those whales," the full-blooded Inuit general told Cindy. She was impressed. She didn't know how or why, but all of a sudden, the "bad guys" were marching to her tune.

In less than 24 hours, Cindy Lowry had achieved the impossible. She enlisted the support of a giant oil construction company, a United States Senator, the United States Department of Commerce, and Alaska's highest ranking military officer, all to help save three stranded whales gasping for air at the top of the world. But this was hardly the time to celebrate. The rescue hadn't even begun. The constantly ringing phone never let Cindy's exhaustion catch up with her. If it wasn't the National Guard, it was Senator Stevens. Kevin's bedroom had become the headquarters for the genesis of the most massive animal rescue in history.

She couldn't even grab a cup of coffee before the phone rang again. It was Ben Odom, one of Bill Allen's biggest clients. Odom was among the most powerful men in Alaska. As the senior vice president of the giant Atlantic Richfield Company, he ran ARCO's multibillion dollar North Slope oil installation. Though Ben Odom and Bill Allen had become close friends, the two men could not have been cut from more distinct cloths. Ben Odom was born into the bustling and elite world of the great Oklahoma oil boom of the 1930s. Refined and educated in the ways of etiquette and industry, Odom was destined to rise to the top. After 35 years at ARCO his style and charm were frequently compared to his oilman friend James A. Baker III, who in just a few weeks would be nominated as Secretary of State by yet another old Texas oilman friend, President-elect George "Poppy" Bush.

Early Saturday morning, the casually-dressed Odom had arrived in the executive suite on the top floor of the 23-story ARCO Alaska building in downtown Anchorage. The night before, Pete Leathard had asked permission to use some ARCO equipment to remove the hoverbarge which sat at ARCO's East Dock in Prudhoe Bay. Odom was intrigued not so much by the whales as by the technical challenge of a rescue. The Arctic was the world's most difficult work environment. Any chance to try something new could only help. He built his career by accomplishing things people said couldn't be done in such harsh conditions. Odom also knew it wouldn't hurt ARCO's image to finally be a good guy. Trying to save whales could only win points in a much larger industry battle.

For almost a decade, ARCO and all the major oil companies had lobbied hard for the right to drill for oil in the Alaska National Wildlife Refuge. At 20 million acres, ANWR was North America's last and largest virgin wildlife refuge. The oil companies wanted to drill on 1.5 million acres of Arctic coastal plain located right in the heart of 200,000 strong Porcupine Caribou Herd's central calving area. Proponents argued that ANWR's estimated 3.2 billion un-tapped barrels of oil due east of the existing Prudhoe Bay fields was the last best hope for a major domestic oil discovery.

Ben Odom and Bill Allen believed that refusal to exploit ANWR would increase America's growing dependence on foreign oil. They also believed development could make their companies fabulous sums of money. On both counts they were right. Both President Ronald Reagan and candidate George Bush felt refusal to tap the last remaining domestic sources of oil would weaken the United States, something they resolved never to allow.

Environmentalists like Cindy Lowry argued that the threat to the environment had become too great. Allowing oil drilling in a National Wildlife Refuge was an obscenity. Before the Exxon Valdez disaster of March 1989, the oil companies bragged about their distinguished environmental record in the Arctic. But even the pro-development Reagan administration disagreed. In 1988, the Environmental Protection Agency charged that the oil companies regularly violated many strict federal standards. The EPA claimed that oil and chemicals had spilled over and ruined 11,000 acres of tundra.

During the 1988 presidential campaign, George Bush argued for development by actually claiming that caribou "loved the pipeline." The U.S. Fish and Wildlife Service disagreed. The USFWS said the negative impact on the migrating caribou was much greater than originally thought.

At the time of the whale stranding, it looked like the oil industry had gained the critical upper hand in the decade-long battle to open the Arctic National Wildlife Refuge (ANWR). Ben Odom, Bill Allen and the United States government knew that positive coverage of oil companies working to rescue the whales might push them over the top. Good public relations could sway the few fence-sitting senators whose votes they needed to start drilling.

Knowing what might be at stake, the conservative Odom didn't want to take any chances. He offered more than the use of some facilities. He told Cindy that ARCO would be delighted to donate all the fuel the National Guard helicopter would need to tow the 400,000 pound hoverbarge.

Based on Pete Leathard's estimates, Odom figured it would cost ARCO $35,000 to provide the fuel needed to pull the barge out of the ice and tow it on the 40 hour trip to Barrow. For a company that did $25 million of business a day in Prudhoe Bay alone, it wasn't even a rounding figure.

Odom told Cindy that he would meet with Allen as soon as he got back to Anchorage. If all went well, the hoverbarge could be on its way to Barrow as early as Monday night, October 16. Two days later, the whales would be free.

Cindy anxiously wanted to talk to Geoff and Craig. In just a few hours, Barrow was scheduled to hold a special meeting to decide the whales' fate. The International Whaling Commission granted the local representative, the Alaska Eskimo Whaling Commission (AEWC) the right to control their own IWC quota. They could continue to hunt as long as they made sure Barrow whalers obeyed the law. If they didn't, the IWC had the power to impose tough sanctions on AEWC members, including probation, heavy fines, and, most severe of all, reduced quotas in upcoming seasons, a cultural death penalty for a village whose culture many believed was already long extinct.

To best police itself, the AEWC board included all of Barrow's top whaling captains. The consensus approach made sure that each captain shared an equal stake in the committee's decisions. Every so often, the captains met informally over Chinese food. Visits by IWC representatives to discuss the local whale hunt marked the only time anyone in Barrow was ever formal about anything. Whalers reluctantly stepped out of their heavy native garb to climb uncomfortably into ill-fitting western clothing that hadn't been worn since the last IWC meeting. Inuits weren't much for western-style meetings. Only the most unusual situation could get them to participate in one. The stranding of the three California gray whales had become such a situation.

Nuiqsut whalers wanted the three animals harvested and offered Barrow whalers the chance to make good money. The quota and IWC regulations allowed it. So did tradition. But the whales were quickly becoming a national media story. How would the whalers appear to Outsiders if they killed animals the world wanted saved, and all for a just few thousand dollars? The leaders of the whaling crews knew they possessed the power to decide whether they would harvest the trapped grays or let them die and become part of the normal food chain. But what they did not know was that they also had the power to create or abort one of greatest media non-events of all time.

To Alaska wildlife management professionals, harvesting the struggling creatures seemed the humane thing to do. Most Barrow lay people agreed. Conventional wisdom convinced them that an extensive rescue would doom the whales to prolonged suffering and the taxpayer to wasted expense. Geoff and Craig knew little chance existed that the whales would survive. Cindy also was not convinced that the whales could be rescued. But she had to try. She was afraid the whaling captains wouldn't give her the chance. She did not want them to change their lives or ways. All she sought was a little time to learn whether a successful rescue could be mounted.

Dr. Tom Albert, the North Slope Borough Wildlife Management Director, asked Cindy for a progress report. He wanted to know if the prospects for rescue were real. His job was to work with the Eskimos—if they wanted to harvest the whales. Albert didn't want his men, Geoff and Craig, to stand in the way if their rescue seemed unlikely. Provocation without cause could only hurt relations with his Eskimo employers.

When Cindy told Albert about the plan to break the ice with VECO's hoverbarge, she said enough to convince him to side with her attempt to save the whales. He knew that Geoff and Craig would have to take on a new, broader mission. Research was still important, but their task was no longer aloof observation. Now Geoff and Craig had to do whatever they could to keep the whales alive. For the first time since the animals were discovered 10 days before, man was about to take his first active step toward freeing them.

Although Cindy had drawn the outline of a rescue plan, it still had to be implemented. She had to follow up on the promises of support to ensure they were delivered. Even though the efforts of the rescuers could be rendered moot by an Eskimo decision to use their remaining quota of strikes to kill the whales, it was time for everyone on her side to get to work.

Like any new organization, the one born Saturday morning, October 15, 1988, needed a leader and a name. Kent Burton of the Commerce Department knew that power is exercised by those who assume it. The United States Government would lead the rescue and it would be called "Operation Breakout," a name that would be officially changed to "Operation Breakthrough" without explanation on the eve of the whales' eventual rescue.

As Undersecretary for Oceans and Atmospheres, Burton oversaw the National Oceanographic and Atmospheric Administration (NOAA). Under the 1972 Endangered Species Act, NOAA was the final legal authority on any matter concerning all marine mammals, including, of course, whales. Burton wanted a NOAA representative on the scene in Barrow to coordinate the new government policy, freeing the whales. He needed a figurehead, someone able to let the world know that NOAA was in charge of the big rescue. Anyone could do it, Burton convinced himself.

Tom Albert told Burton he had already spoken with someone from the NOAA Fisheries Anchorage office named Ron Morris. Albert wanted Morris to help him out at that night's Barrow whaling captains' meeting. Morris thought the overnight trip to Barrow a pleasant diversion. He packed a few things and drove down Minnesota Drive to Anchorage International in time for MarkAir's noon flight to Barrow. Kent Burton had his man. Ron Morris was on the way.

Bill Allen's plane landed in Anchorage two hours after Morris' took off. Pete Leathard met Allen at the gate. On their way into town, he briefed his boss. The National Guard was busy putting together a team, NOAA claimed a federal role and already had a man on the way to Barrow, and ARCO promised to supply the fuel for the whole operation.

On the way in from the airport, Allen nodded his head and pointed the rough edged tip of his Tony Lama cowboy boot resting on Pete Leathard's dashboard in the direction of Alaska's tallest building. The rancher's way of saying he wanted to see Ben Odom. Odom was in that Saturday afternoon busily working on the rescue. The three of them began mapping out the operation as it had shaped up so far. Odom asked how much labor would be needed to break the barge free of ice and how much it would cost. Leathard reminded them that at $50 an hour, labor alone could soon cost VECO tens of thousands of dollars. Earlier that day, Allen committed himself and his companies to freeing the whales and that is exactly what he intended to do.

The three men called General Schaeffer, who told them he was having trouble assembling a logistics command to run the operation from Prudhoe Bay. General Schaeffer wanted a sharp 40-year-old Colonel named Tom Caroll to head the operation. He was the finest field commander in the state. Carroll had taken the weekend off and wasn't scheduled to report to HQ until 0800 Monday morning. General Schaeffer wasn't going ahead with the operation until he reached his best man.

Chapter 8

A Great Eskimo Hunter Saves the Whales

There was nothing Tom Carroll loved more than the smell of fresh-cut wood. When he wasn't covered in military fatigues, he was usually covered in sawdust. At headquarters, they joked that the only way to keep Colonel Carroll clean was to keep him green. Saturday morning, October 15, was no exception.

The boyish-looking colonel's glasses were covered with a layer of dust so thick he had to use his hands to "see" along the edge of the cabinet door he had just put through the lathe in his garage. Carroll, his glasses opaque, knocked over nearly everything between him and the ringing phone.

It was General Schaeffer calling to tell him the National Guard had been asked to help save those stranded whales everybody was talking about. "They're calling it Operation Breakout," the General said. "Are you interested?"

Because he loved field operations, Colonel Carroll remained in the military after he returned from his decorated tour in Vietnam as an Infantry Commander. Therefore, he welcomed any opportunity to leave his cloistered desk in the Anchorage Frontier Building. The General told Carroll to report to headquarters. Carroll hung up the phone, showered, donned his standard issue Alaskan National Guard Colonel's camouflage fatigues, and headed out the door.

Colonel Tom Carroll possessed an unshakable sense of professionalism. His father was a military man, a legacy passed to Tom. The colonel evoked an almost mystical can-do spirit. Adventure, risk and daring were nothing new to the colonel. Neither was loss. He first learned what that meant when he was only 15.

On the morning of March 27, 1964, Prince William Sound erupted as the epicenter of the most powerful earthquake ever to strike North America. Its 9.2 reading was the highest ever recorded by the Richter scale. Eighty times more powerful than the 1906 San Francisco earthquake, it made history for moving more earth farther and faster than any other one on record. Its force was so devastating that it killed people up to 700 miles apart. The Black Friday quake was Alaska's greatest modern tragedy. From Port Ashton to Nellie and Anchorage to Seward, 131 people died that morning. One of them was Tom Carroll's father.

Tom Carroll was one of the few people in the Last Frontier of the late 1980s actually born and raised in Alaska. He was called a Sourdough. Alaska's earliest white pioneers used to cherish this versatile mixture and carry it with them to make bread and biscuits. Since it replenished itself after each use, the dough stayed fresh indefinitely, just like those early pioneers who settled and remained in Alaska. It became the state's namesake. Becoming a Sourdough required a right of passage no other state could match. Other than birth, Sourdough status could only be conferred to those who had survived at least 25 Alaskan winters.

Colonel Carroll drove down C Street through one of Anchorage's many strip malls built in the oil boom days of the early 1980s. He thought about the strong images of the whales he saw on Todd Pottinger's newscast the night before. Carroll was no environmentalist, but like almost everybody in Alaska, he wished the creatures well. But he wondered why the National Guard had joined the rescue.

Civilian passersby stared at Tom Carroll dashing through the lobby of one of Alaska's modern office buildings dressed in jungle combat fatigues. When the colonel walked into his office he was surprised to see General Schaeffer lounging in his chair, using his phone. The general was talking with Senator Stevens in Washington. Like an unexpected visitor, Carroll offered an apologetic salute to his superior officer and quietly backed out of his own office.

Eight days after the whales were first discovered trapped in the ice, General John Schaeffer joined Colonel Carroll, a contracting officer, two Arctic logistics specialists and a press aide in the conference room down the hall from his office. He explained to the hastily assembled group that the purpose of their mission was to tow a 185-ton hoverbarge from Prudhoe Bay to Barrow. Tom Carroll, whom Schaeffer had put in charge, had to decide what equipment was best suited for the massive tow. Carroll knew that pulling 185 tons over nearly 300 miles of jagged ice could prove to be quite a tricky operation. Privately, he wondered whether it was even possible. But Colonel Carroll was paid to do, not to doubt.

Pete Leathard assured General Schaeffer that the most difficult part of the task would be digging the barge out of the frozen tundra where it idly sat for the last four years. Once free, the barge could easily be towed across the ocean's solidly frozen surface. Or so everyone thought.

Carroll checked with all the armories across Alaska to determine what equipment was available and best suited for the job. In calligraphic script, Colonel Carroll listed the options on a yellow legal pad christened for his new assignment. The colonel weighed his options and, like all good commanders, sided with caution. He chose the Sikorsky CH-54 Sky Crane helicopter. The Sky Crane was capable of lifting more weight than any other helicopter. If it couldn't do the job, nothing could.

Carroll wanted to make sure that the necessary fuel, the Sky Cranes' biggest requirement, would be available. It guzzled a staggering 650 gallons an hour. That meant it would take at least 30,000 gallons to get the barge out of the frozen earth and across the ice to Barrow. Before he ordered the helicopter, Carroll checked with Schaeffer to see whether he was authorized to use that much fuel. The General told Colonel Carroll to guzzle away: ARCO was donating all the fuel he would need.

When Ben Odam learned his offer was being taken most seriously indeed, it was too late to turn back. By the time the rescue was over,

ARCO would become by far Operation Breakout's largest private cash contributor, donating more than $500,000 worth of fuel to help save the three trapped whales.

Next on Colonel Carroll's list was office support. Between the pilots, public affairs, and ground personnel, Carroll would need a command post and living quarters for nearly a dozen people. After checking with Ben Odom, Carroll learned that ARCO would also provide office space, telephones and rooms for the National Guard and VECO in the company's ultramodern Prudhoe Bay installation 1,700 miles from the North Pole.

ARCO spent hundreds of millions of dollars to build a sumptuous habitat for their workers on the North Slope. To keep up morale, they equipped it with every conceivable comfort—movie theaters, maid and room service, bowling alleys, and cafeterias serving the finest steaks and lobster flown in fresh from Anchorage. Until the Eskimos in Barrow spent $15 million to build one in 1986, Prudhoe Bay had the only swimming pool above the Arctic Circle.

It took several hours for Colonel Carroll and his men to arrange for the aircraft and personnel to support the Sky Cranes. When they finished, the Colonel told his men to go home. "Don't forget to get some sleep", he reminded them. "You're all due back here at 0500 hours." He wanted to get an early start. "Wheels up at 6:00 AM." Tom Carroll had asserted his command.

Colonel Carroll wanted to check the ice conditions around Barrow before making a final decision to go forward with the hoverbarge tow. For all the talk about how smooth and solid the Beaufort Sea ice was between Prudhoe and Barrow, no one had actually examined it.

Pete Leathard promised that the barge could break ice up to two feet thick. Any ice thicker than that would have to be cut by something else. Leathard didn't have to elaborate. There was nothing else available capable of cutting ice more than two feet thick. Tom Carroll was not about to risk his men, equipment and his own rank on an operation that didn't have an excellent chance of success. If he ever thought the deck was stacked against him, Operation Breakout would end.

General Schaeffer walked with the colonel to the Xerox machine across the hall. Carroll glanced at the document the general was about to copy. The yellow note paper contained Schaeffer's hand-written call sheet with the names and numbers of everyone involved in the rescue. The colonel was prepared to find the names of some of Alaska's most prominent citizens: Senator Stevens, Governor Cowper, Bill Allen and Ben Odom. But he was not prepared to read the name that topped the list—Cindy Lowry.

"Isn't she the Greenpeace gal with the bullhorn?" he asked the general.

"She sure is," Schaeffer responded. "And, like it or not, you'll have to work with her. She's the one that started this whole thing in the first place."

Colonel Carroll had nothing against Cindy. But he wondered how someone so well known for her vocal opposition to plans or positions of the United States Armed Forces in Alaska could be so suddenly interested in involving herself in such an unabashedly military operation.

Tom Carroll tried to reach Cindy Lowry during the next half hour. But he couldn't get through because she was on the phone to Geoff and Craig, who had just gotten back from a day on the ice with the whales. They were discussing strategy for that night's critical Barrow whaling captains meeting. They confirmed what she had been watching all morning on her television. The whales were fast becoming a local phenomenon, a tourist attraction and a national news event all in one.

By Saturday afternoon, October 15, eight days after they were first discovered, the once isolated whales now had almost constant company. Some Eskimo hunters and the few media crews already in town joined Geoff and Craig to spend the entire day with the animals. The whales would never again go unattended during daylight hours.

Geoff and Craig told Cindy that as they were about to leave, they discovered the youngest whale had trouble breathing. The baby whale wheezed, coughed up lots of water, and looked exhausted. Until that moment, Geoff and Craig were ordered to observe the whales, not to interfere. The whales needed more room to breathe. The hole they depended on for survival was once 60 feet by 30 feet. In the eight days since the whales were first discovered, it had shrunk by two thirds. The hole would soon completely freeze over.

The two biologists desperately wanted to help. If they could just slightly expand the hole, the whales could breathe easier and buy some precious time. They shouted their ideas for expanding the holes over the deafening whine of their ski machine as it raced across the bleak Arctic landscape on the long, cold ride back to Barrow.

Before ending the conversation to clear her line, Cindy asked Geoff and Craig if they had heard anything yet from Ron Morris.

"Who?" they asked.

"Ron Morris, from NOAA fisheries. He's the project coordinator," Cindy answered. Morris was due in on the 3:30 PM flight. She didn't know if living arrangements had been made for him once he got to Barrow. The few hotel rooms were going fast.

She would soon face the same predicament. Campbell Plowden called from Washington. He told her to pack an overnight bag and get up to Barrow on the next flight. By the time she had her cue, it was already too late. The last flight to Barrow left Anchorage at 3:40. The next flight would not leave until Sunday morning.

About the same time Cindy commenced her own scramble to get to the top of the world, Ron Morris' plane began its descent. He was about to enter a world that after many previous visits still remained on the periphery of perception. Just five years short of becoming a naturalized Sourdough, the 54-year-old Morris could never quite figure out how a town like Barrow ever got started. Morris couldn't imagine a more depressing place.

When the pilot turned on the no smoking sign signaling the final approach into Barrow's Wiley Post Memorial Airport, Morris nearly strained his neck to recover the last drop of his drained Bloody Mary. Satisfied he had polished it off, Morris popped a couple of Tic-Tacs in his mouth. He wanted to make a good first impression. He stroked his beard as the plane taxied to the terminal. He liked the rakish nautical air it gave him. With his thinning silver hair, Morris looked like one of those little wooden carvings of Maine lobstermen sold in souvenir shops down in the Lower 48. All he needed to complete the image was a bright yellow slicker.

If he wasn't convinced already, Morris needed no further reminders of where the 737 landed once he stepped off the plane. It was nearly 50° colder in Barrow than it was just a few hours before in Anchorage. Barrow and Anchorage seemed like two different worlds. In many ways they were. Anchorage was closer to Seattle than to Barrow. Separating them were more than a thousand miles of wilderness. Man and his ability to fly over it were all that connected the two vastly different realms.

No one waited for Ron Morris at the airport. He had no idea where to go or what to do. After grabbing his frozen nylon bag from the rickety ten foot stainless steel luggage chute, Morris looked out the smoke-stained terminal window into a Barrow street scene shrouded in the steam of man set against the Arctic dusk's heavy bluish gray backdrop. He made out an "Airport Inn" sign across the street. As he pushed open the light lacquer pine door, Morris noticed no trace of his breath condensing on the window just inches from his face.

"Must be Arctic plastic," he thought. Ordinary glass would have shattered in the bone-chilling temperatures. The first blast of Arctic air hit him, as it does every visitor, square in the face. Grimacing, he sarcastically mumbled, "Not a bad day." Remembering earlier visits when things were really bad, he regained his perspective. At least they haven't lost the light.

Ed Benson still had a couple of empty rooms at the Airport Inn. But by the time Morris showed up, Benson could ask and get $225 a night for a warm bed and a shower. Born and raised in New York City, Morris knew when he was being conned. But he also knew when he had no choice. He dropped his American Express card on the shelf atop the half-open dutch door to the service counter.

While Morris unpacked his overnight bag, Ed Benson shouted to him from the bottom of the stairs. Tom Albert from Wildlife Management was calling to tell him about the whaling captains' meeting that night at Barrow High School. Before hanging up, Ron asked Albert where he could get a bite to eat and a beer before the meeting.

Morris wanted to find out more about the issue of harvesting the whales. He saw reports of it on the news in Anchorage. If a competent Eskimo could convince him there was no hope of saving the whales, and Geoff and Craig would agree, then Morris wouldn't argue against them.

Tom Albert, the Director of Wildlife Management for the North Slope, arranged for the newly assembled rescue team to get together at Pepe's before going to the high school for the whaling captains' meeting at 7:30. Over dinner, Ron Morris could debrief Geoff and Craig. If the whalers voted to spare the three California grays, Ron wanted to make sure everyone knew that he would be in charge. NOAA appointed him coordinator of a rescue, should it be approved by the whalers.

Geoff and Craig looked exhausted as they pulled up their chairs in the crowded restaurant. Five days on the frozen surface of the Chukchi Sea at 35° below zero had started to take its toll. The human body needs at least 7,000 calories a day to stay warm in the Arctic. Morris watched in wonder as the two men devoured more of the world's most overpriced Mexican food in a single sitting than his salary could afford in a week. Between the two of them, their bill came to almost $100.

A few reporters spotted the biologists. Now that they were off duty, they couldn't refuse to answer one or two questions. At every opportunity, Geoff and Craig reminded the press that the fate of the whales lay in the hands of the whaling captains. No one could help the animals if the Barrow elders decided to kill them.

"But what if they decide not to kill them?" NBC's Don Oliver asked in gravely voice. "Could anything be done to save them?"

Before either Geoff and Craig had a chance to answer, Ron Morris faced directly into the blinding glare of the NBC crew's lights that reflected dazzlingly on the top his hairless head.

"My name's Ron Morris," said the man from NOAA. "I was appointed earlier today as the coordinator of Operation Breakout. As you know, the whaling captains meet in just about an hour to figure out what they are going to do. The meeting is open and you're invited to attend. Once it's over, I'll be available to answer any questions."

Geoff and Craig appeared relieved. Finally, someone had arrived on the scene who could handle Oliver and his constant questions. They were impressed with the way Morris invited him to the whaling captains' meeting.

No matter how badly some of the younger Eskimos wanted to harvest the three trapped whales, none could ignore the presence of media descending on Barrow. All three major networks were getting their acts together. By the next night, Sunday, October 16, they would all be in Barrow. Even cash-strapped CNN found a way to send its own crew to cover the stranding.

Malik wanted to arrive at the meeting early. He sought to talk some sense into the brash young Eskimos clamoring for a chance to strike the stranded whales. Malik knew that killing the animals could shake subsistence whaling to its very core.

To the newly arrived press corps, Malik might have been just another Inupiat Eskimo living at the Top of the World, but he was smarter than any Outsider would realize. Walking into the high school on Takpuk Street, Malik wore a warm outer garment called a parkee. it was made from the skins of light brown caribou fawns and the shimmering gray fur of male Arctic Squirrels. His traditional lightweight boots, called mukluks, were made of bearded seal skin, or Oogruk.

When Malik entered the school, several reporters were already there. Most of them had just gotten to town and stopped by the High School. Few thought the meeting worth more than superficial coverage. Almost none had ever seen anyone dressed like Malik.

As he walked out into the hall way to pour himself a cup of hot coffee, NBC cameraman Bruce Gray lifted his heavy equipment back onto his shoulders. The powerful lights affixed to his camera nearly blinded a stunned Malik when he came back into the room. Gray focused his lens on Malik's mukluks, then on his parkee, while at the same time preparing to take pictures of Malik's archetypal Inuit face.

Before Barrow's top 20 whaling crews could make their way into the classroom assigned to them, it was clear they would have to move to accomodate all the people interested in attending the public meeting. There were more than a dozen Outsiders and around 50 Barrowans anxious to see what would happen to the trapped whales. They moved across the hall to a state-of-the-art semicircular audio visual projection auditorium filled with around 100 padded theater chairs. That room was just big enough to seat everyone.

A short, powerfully built Eskimo man, wearing wide silver frame glasses over dark sunken eyes and a rounded but robust face, waited patiently to start the meeting. His name was Arnold Brower, Jr., and he was one of the most successful young whaling captains in Barrow. He was perhaps the top young subsistence whaler alive. His crew killed five Bowhead whales during the spring season alone; an almost unheard of accomplishment, even for his mentor Malik.

Arnold Brower, Jr., was part of one of the world's largest Inuit families. In fact, many of the hundred or so people in the auditorium were named Brower. It seemed that nearly every Eskimo in Barrow was either named Brower or had close relatives that were. The Browers could trace their Eskimo lineage back thousands of years, but their name came from modern times. Their patriarch was a brash young explorer from New York City who came to Barrow in the 1880s in search of adventure. Brower discovered much more than even his burgeoning dreams could fathom. He found an immense fortune and a stunning legacy. The former came from selling coal to new steam powered commercial whaling ships plying through cold Arctic waters in search of bounty. The latter, legend has it, came from Brower taking prodigious advantage of the Eskimo's most famous cultural trait: spouse sharing.

No one knew for sure how many Amero-Inupiats were actually sired by Charlie Brower, but within a generation, there were literally hundreds of them. They were everywhere. Brower had dozens of "family" trading posts stretching all along Alaska's North Slope. They were all run by people who claimed to be Browers. Soon there were so many Browers in and around Barrow, they built their own section of town and named it, aptly, Browerville.

What started as a haphazard collection of traditional sod and whalebone huts had become a veritable Barrow suburb by 1988. Browers of all shapes and sizes lived in heated homes with running water. There was even a shuttle bus to take them the 400 yards to "downtown" Barrow. When they expired, Browers were laid to rest in their own family burial ground.

Like many of Barrow's subsistence hunters, Arnold Brower, Jr., took pay from the North Slope Borough. But unlike most, Brower actually worked. He was one of Mayor George Ahmaogak's top aides. Since the mayor was out of town attending an Alaska Federation of Natives annual meeting, and the deputy mayor, Warren Matumeak, was unavailable that night, Arnold Jr. was left to run the whaling captains' meeting.

Emergency whaling meetings were rare. But if ever there was an occasion that could be called an emergency, this was it. No Barrowan was threatened with starvation. Nor were there massive fleets of commercial whaling vessels just off shore killing all the whales Barrow used to depend on for survival. This threat was uniquely modern.

To the reporters dazzled by his strange-looking boots and classic Inuit face, Malik appeared to be a primitive Eskimo whose countenance would make colorful national news footage. They would soon learn that Malik was much more than a great video sound bite.

Malik knew that, for whatever reason, tens of millions of people in the Lower 48 were glued to the saga of the three stranded whales gasping for breath at the top of the world. This was Barrow's first and probably last chance to make any kind of impression on so many Outsiders. Malik also realized that if the cameras captured the image of a cruel band of Inuit hunters, no matter how small, out to kill a few more beloved whales, it could mean the end of Eskimo whaling, and hence the end of traditional Inuit life. Once the gruesome pictures came down off Aurora I, the damage would be done. The only question left to answer would be the severity of the consequences. Malik had to do all he could to make sure it never happened.

Just before Arnold Jr. moved to open the meeting, Malik gently but forcefully pushed the startled Brower into a corner. Malik insisted on talking privately with a group of four stubborn young whalers still clamoring to slaughter the trapped animals. Speaking in his native Inupiat, Malik told the young men, his own disciples, that the stakes of their impetuous action were far too high. Shaking his head in stern, somber rebuke, Malik demanded they cancel their request to harvest the whales.

The young whalers huddled together and quickly reached a consensus. One of them approached Arnold Brower, Jr., and whispered something in his ear. Brower sat down in front of the three television microphones hastily taped down on the table. "Is everyone ready?" he asked.

"The whaling captains of Barrow have decided to use our best efforts to save the three Agvigluaqs," he said using the Inupiat word for gray whales. The room broke into a wild cheer.

Arnold Brower's short declaration removed Operation Breakout's last and biggest obstacle, the local Eskimo whalers. For all of Colonel Carroll's military expertise, Ron Morris's camera presence, and Cindy Lowry's fearless determination to mount a rescue, the critical move belonged to the Eskimos.

As an increasingly anxious world would soon see, the Inuits would do far more than approve the rescue. They would carry it out.

Chapter 9

Colonel Carroll's Impossible Task

The instant Arnold Brower, Jr., made his startling announcement, he completely transformed the local Eskimo debate about what to do with the three stranded whales. The media on hand would record the whalers' 180° turn. It was no longer a question of whether to kill the whales. Now the Inuits wanted to save them.

Roy Ahmaogak, the local hunter who discovered the whales eight days earlier, nervously leaned over to speak into the portable public address system. His words were the first spoken after the whalers decided to help free the three leviathans.

Speaking in the thick guttural accent characteristic of Inupiat Eskimos, he said, "It seems to me that before we can free the whales, we have to figure out a way to keep them alive until the barge gets here. Does anybody have any ideas?"

Geoff, Craig, and Ron Morris sat together facing the whalers. Unaccustomed to speaking in front of bright lights and rolling television cameras, Craig George looked around apprehensively before mustering the courage to offer his suggestion.

"Arnold, what about the saws you used today?" Gaining confidence with the nods of approval from people around him, Craig continued. "Arnold Jr. was out there today and his chainsaw opened up the hole real good. I can't see why they couldn't go right on doing it for the next couple of days until the barge gets here."

Chainsaws were among the first tools the Eskimos bought with their new oil money back in the early 1970s. They have been one of the most important weapons in the Inuit arsenal ever since. Unlike the lumberjack who viewed the chainsaw as a time saver, the Eskimo saw it as a lifesaver. Ice was more than an inconvenience. It was the constant barrier separating the hunter from the food and furs he needed to survive. The power saw not only saved the Eskimo from the arduous chore of manually chopping through thick ocean ice, it saved him much precious energy which allowed him to hunt for longer periods of time.

On Friday afternoon, Brower had an idea. If he could cut holes in the ice with his chainsaw to hunt seals, why not use it to enlarge the whales' hole? The lone hole was shrinking several feet each day. By Friday, it was only 10 feet wide by 12 feet long, barely larger than the head of a single whale. Unless the rescuers did something fast, the hole would completely freeze over.

Without bothering to tell anyone, Brower loaded one of his chainsaws and a rusty gas can onto a wooden dogsled and hitched it to the back of his ski machine. Impervious to blinding winds and bone-chilling temperatures, the hardy Eskimo drove out to the whales.

After fiddling with the carburetor, Brower brought his rusty chainsaw to life with a roar in the minus 25° cold. He carried the saw to the middle of the longer side of the rectangular hole and cut several blocks of ice from the edge. After Craig described Arnold's success earlier in the day, the whalers decided to use a couple of their own saws to further expand the hole.

Ever since they found themselves imprisoned in a small hole in the ice, the whales had to make a choice. They could learn to dramatically alter their standard breathing pattern, or they would die. They chose to live.

Because of its distinct habitat, the gray whale developed an equally distinct breathing pattern. Rarely, if ever, would the gray whale swim more than a mile from shore. Hugging close to the ocean's edge, it lived almost exclusively in shallow waters. Gray whales spent most of their lives in water not much deeper than the length of their bodies.

Other whales, like the magnificent humpback, lived farther out from shore. Their immensely powerful breaches could vault 80,000 pounds and 40 feet of whale clear out of the water. The force of the humpback crashing back into the water smashed off more barnacles in a second than a gray whale could shake off in a year of gravel rolling. This spectacle delighted increasingly numbers of tourists who came to Alaska. Their hosts became flourishing entrepreneurs in a growing industry Outsiders called whalewatching.

Biologists long thought gray whales didn't breach because they lived in shallower waters than other whales. They never deviated from their traditional pattern of arching their backs just enough to expose their blowholes above the waterline and breathing horizontal to the surface. The moment Roy Ahmaogak spotted three heads popping in and out the one small hole eight days before, he learned something new. A gray whale could lift its huge head clear out of the water if it meant survival.

On Sunday morning, Geoff revved up the power saw to cut the ice around the middle of the hole. Malik vigorously motioned for him to stop. Geoff knew more about whales than most whites, but Malik knew more than Geoff. Shoving a buzz saw into the middle of the water where the whales needed to surface would surely drive them away. With nowhere to go, the whales would swim to their deaths, unable to breathe. Malik wanted to proceed cautiously. He sensed the whales had to become accustomed to the roar of the tools man would use to free them.

Malik took two running saws and placed them on the ice at opposite ends of the hole. Then he motioned the few onlookers to wait quietly. If the whales saw that the water above them looked unchanged from the last time they surfaced, they might take a chance.

Malik was right. After an abnormally long dive, the whales approached the open hole with trepidation. They tentatively lingered just a few feet below the surface before cautiously breaking the water's roiling plain. This time, there was no lounging in the open water. Just as they had breathed in shifts when they were first discovered, the whales started to do so again, first the two larger whales, then the baby. Each whale breathed deeply and quickly dove back down under the ice.

Only when the whales started to grow accustomed to the saw's loud vibrations did Malik figure it was okay to start using them. He slowly pushed his saw's sharp point into the edge of the thick ice. Malik, perhaps the most seasoned Eskimo whaler alive, was unprepared for what he saw.

Moments after shying away from the sound, the whales seemed to relish it. Perhaps, Malik thought, they sensed that the loud and ungainly surface instruments were miraculously splitting the ice threatening to entomb them. Malik had a new worry: How to keep the three whales from accidentally rubbing up against the lethal blades of a chainsaw at full throttle.

Geoff, Craig and Ron were relieved when they saw how quickly the whales overcame their fear of the saws. But they were astonished at the way the whales seemed to embrace the tools as their salvation. Craig mentioned to Geoff how much Cindy Lowry would regret not having been there to see it. But by early that Sunday morning, Cindy was already en route to Barrow.

Her anxious wait the night before paid off. As soon as the whaling captains' meeting adjourned, Geoff and Craig excitedly rushed to call Cindy from one of the newly installed touch-tone pay phones in the bright lobby of Barrow High. It was the call she and Kevin had nervously awaited all night. She told the biologists to call the minute there was any word. She tried not to watch the phone as she breathlessly waited for it to ring. Kevin left to pickup take out food and a video cassette. He was glad to get out if only for a few minutes. Watching Cindy strut so anxiously about was more than he could bear.

Anticipating Cindy's restless mood, Kevin scanned the shelves of the local video shop looking for any movie capable of keeping her mind off the silent telephone. He heard Cindy mention she wanted to see "No Way Out," about a young naval officer's steamy relationship with a beautiful Washington politico. Only after the rescue was over would the irony of that selection reveal itself.

"They want to save them," Craig exultantly told Cindy. Already clutching Kevin's elbow, she almost punctured his skin with her fingernails. Not only was she denying him his long-promised weekend, now she was causing physical harm.

Cindy could hardly sleep. She was booked on the noon flight to Barrow and she hadn't even started to get ready for her journey. Although she lived in Alaska, Cindy didn't have the proper clothes for the Arctic. She didn't have any food either. From what little she knew about Barrow, if she failed to bring her own, her choices would be limited to whale, walrus or seal meat.

Cindy had not read a newspaper since she first devoted herself to saving the three whales. Her only source of news came through a cable hooked to the back of Kevin's television. None of what she saw or heard prepared her for the remarkable and unique stage upon which the drama was being played out. There was no mention of the ironies or the Eskimos, and there was certainly nothing about Pepe's Mexican Restaurant, Arctic Pizza, $200 dollar ski machine rides, or toilet paper with wooden clubs.

It was as though there was no human existence, just the forlorn images of an endless white ocean melting imperceptibly into an equally infinite white tundra. Although she was the one to propel the three naturally stranded whales into the national spotlight, Cindy Lowry had not learned a thing about the Arctic's largest and most important town where she would arrive nine days after the whales were first discovered.

As she climbed into bed, Cindy realized she did not have to reset her alarm clock. She got up at 6:30 every morning to train. Running marathons was one of her tamer hobbies. Sunday morning, however, Cindy would get plenty of exercise racing to complete last-minute chores in time to catch the noon MarkAir flight to Barrow.

Kevin had his own errands. He worried about what Cindy would eat in the remote whaling village, but for different reasons. He knew that if her culinary selection was limited to an assortment of marine mammals, Cindy would die before indulging. Cindy liked to tell people she ate only health foods. Kevin knew that wasn't exactly true. She secretly craved preservatives, cholesterol, and lots of sugar.

Kevin wanted to avoid the acrimony which attended most discussions of Cindy's diet, particularly on the morning of her big trip. Shortly after she left the house to buy a suitable hat, gloves and boots, he slipped out to quickly assemble some wholesome foods for her to eat. Fruits, vegetables and a high energy peanut and raisin trail mix would be Kevin's final present to Cindy as he kissed her goodbye at the gate.

Like most MarkAir flights to Barrow that weekend, reporters filled Cindy's plane. And, like all MarkAir flights to Barrow, this one made an intermediate stop in Fairbanks. An hour by jet north of Anchorage, Alaska's second largest city marked the northern end of the state's limited road system and the completion of slightly less than a third of the journey to Barrow.

Walking around the world's most northerly modern airport terminal, Cindy figured she'd parlay the 25-minute layover into her last meal before descending into the dreaded nertherland of Barrow. Seeing a Mexican food stand across the concourse, she briskly walked over, looked at the menu and ordered a taco salad. Surely, she thought, this would be her last chance to indulge in her favorite cuisine.

While Cindy waited in Fairbanks for her flight to continue to Barrow, Ben Odom and Pete Leathard were flying high above the Alaskan frontier aboard the ARCO executive jet. VECO's North Slope operation had been hard at work. En route to Prudhoe, Pete Leathard talked regularly by phone with Marvin King, VECO's ground operations manager. King and his men spent the whole night out in the minus 30° temperatures. First they had to determine whether the barge would even work. Then they tried to free the 185 tons of sunken barge from its frozen berth at ARCO's East Dock.

King told Leathard he could make the barge seaworthy, but he needed the one thing Leathard didn't have: time. He knew the boss was on his way and assured him he would keep the operation fully staffed until the job was done.

Using chainsaws, ice axes and picks, King and his dozens of men worked feverish shifts in the bitter cold, chopping, sawing and chipping away four years of impregnable Arctic ice that had built up around the barge's hull. These hardy men were specially trained to perform manual labor in the world's most hostile climate. At up to $100,000 a year, they were among the highest paid laborers in the world.

Each man knew it was foolish to measure the tasks he performed in the Arctic by what he could accomplish under normal conditions. Here the rules were different. Man and his vast powers were severely diminished. The Arctic was the last place on earth where nature defied his mastery. If a white man wanted to call the Arctic home, he either accepted the limits of his adopted habitat or he died. A man could endure such taxing elements only so long.

The two VECO crews working in shifts in the brutal cold arrived at the same predetermined fate: quick and inexorable exhaustion. After only a few minutes, even the ablest could work no longer. The battered men took sanctuary in a prefabricated shed that was supposed to provide the wearied laborers with warmth and nourishment. The donuts, coffee and cigarettes were about as nourishing as the 40° temperatures were warm. Not unlike the creatures they were spending themselves to free, the men entered the shed bewildered by their own numbness and pain. Their lungs were singed by the bitter cold. They doubled over coughing, gasping for breath.

The shed's only sounds came from the footsteps and wheezes of the exhausted men. They didn't say a word. Their jaws were frozen. Moving their frozen joints even slightly caused tremendous pain. By the time their jaws thawed enough to allow single word speech, it was time to get back to work.

On their way out, the mildly rejuvenated workers were met and replaced by the other beleaguered crew struggling to escape the cold. At great personal peril, VECO's Arctic construction workers toiled through the night to pry loose an ungainly device that would attempt to free three whales stranded 270 miles away.

All four American television networks were either in Barrow or had crews on the way. Tens of millions of Americans already following the story, were anxious for action. The fancy of a few Outside news executives had transformed a routine gray whale stranding into a serious rescue campaign. Now, for the first time since they were discovered eight days before, a tangible step was finally being taken to free the three whales. But ironically, none of the media that generated the interest to justify the rescue could find a way to get to Prudhoe Bay in time to cover the rescue's first real story. It would not be the last time the TV reporters missed the real story.

Don Oliver and his NBC crew were the first reporters on the scene. Frantic for a way to get there, producer Jerry Hansen rented the Arctic's only available helicopter at the going rate of $6,000 per day. But by the time they arrived, it was too late. Most of VECO's backbreaking work was already done. The first footage to appear on American television showed the hoverbarge seemingly free of ice. Since no one could compare that event against what the barge looked like frozen and buried, the American people would never know how much the VECO crews sacrificed and accomplished.

Billy Bob Allen appreciated his men's effort. "There is no

substitute for effort," he always preached. His men believed him because he never let them forget that he was one of them. At first, Allen told friends he wanted to help the whales because "it seemed like the right thing to do." For the next two weeks, Bill Allen and the giant company he led concentrated on virtually nothing else. Pending business was shelved while anxious executives throughout the industry wondered why Allen and his people were so passionately committed to something that had nothing to do with pumping oil and could only *lose* them money.

Allen worked well into Saturday evening in his Anchorage office familiarizing himself with the operation's evolving details. The first crisis occurred when Marvin King called from the workers shed out at the East Dock. He told Allen that the ice removal was going better than planned but his men were exhausted.

"Rest 'em up," Billy Bob answered. "We can't have none of them dropping dead on us."

King told Allen there were many things left to do before the barge would be ready, not the least of which included the removal of 600 tons of ice entombing the vessel. The ice could only be cleared by hand. King didn't know what to do first. Colonel Carroll and his special National Guard unit were due to arrive in Prudhoe late the next morning. Allen told King to combine whatever tasks he could. Any tests that didn't require the barge to be ice free should be performed as soon as possible. It didn't take long for King to figure out his boss was right.

King had just started to put the engines through their paces, before he discovered his first problem. One of the turbochargers which gave the barge enough power to hover above the surface of the ice was dead. Allen thought finding a replacement would be damned near impossible. His hoverbarge was the only one like it in the world. Allen called the barge's Japanese manufacturer to see whether they might find a replacement. When he told them he needed it immediately to help save three stranded whales, they thought their cowboy client had lost his mind.

Two hours later, Allen had received no response. He lost his patience. It was early Sunday morning Tokyo time when he called the president of Mitsui Shipbuilding. Fifteen minutes later, Mitsui's equipment network located a machine in Long Beach, California, that could be airlifted to Anchorage.

The amorphous effort to save the whales was still a marginal operation. Any minor obstacle could have provided a perfect excuse for any party to back out, leaving the whales to their fate. Since the hoverbarge was the rescue's only option, the inability to find a turbocharger would have been sufficient grounds for VECO to abort the rescue.

Learning he would need to charter a special cargo aircraft to fly the turbocharger to Prudhoe, Allen pressed both his thumbs firmly against the side of his balding head in a fruitless attempt to ward off the headache he invariably got whenever he ran into major unexpected expenses. The smallest plane that could fit the huge engine was the C-130 transport, a military mainstay. If the Hercules, as the C-130 was known, could transport troops and tanks in and out of trouble spots around the world, Allen knew it could get his turbocharger safely to Prudhoe.

Five minutes had passed since the turbocharger crisis was resolved when King called Allen again with still another disaster. No one in Prudhoe knew how to operate the hoverbarge. Only one man at VECO had operated the ice crusher and now Allen had to find him. No one at VECO had heard a word from barge captain Brad Stocking since the billion dollar exploratory well at Mukluk Island turned up dry in 1984.

Using electronic databases listing the whereabouts of oil construction sites and their employees, Pete Leathard initiated a worldwide manhunt to locate the elusive captain. After three days of intensive search, VECO gave up. Brad Stocking was never found.

Bill Allen called around the state to find out what could pull a 185-ton craft from Prudhoe to Barrow. The answer he got most frequently was uniquely Alaskan: the "Cat train."

Cat trains resupplied remote inland villages during the nine months of winter, by using the surface of Alaska's hundred thousand miles of frozen rivers as its roadway. In a state with no roads, the rivers were the resupply life line for settlements and homesteaders that otherwise could not be reached. Long snow sleds crammed with supplies and provisions were attached to heavy Caterpillar earth movers fitted with extra wide tank treads to grip the ice and pull their cargo across the surface of frozen rivers.

But the size, weight and destination of Bill Allen's icebreaking hoverbarge ruled out the Cat train almost as soon as it was mentioned. Even if there was a wide enough river close by to pull it along, the barge was much too big and heavy to be towed by a Caterpillar. The nearest river leading toward Barrow was 65 miles west of Prudhoe and its mouth had not completely frozen. In the event Colonel Carroll and his CH-54 Skycrane helicopter could not do the job, Cindy Lowry would have to find some other way to save her whales.

Colonel Carroll had made plans for that Saturday night and he was not going to cancel them just because he had to lead a mission to the Arctic early the next morning. The 40-year-old colonel was filled with boundless energy. He capered about Anchorage reveling in temperate R&R until well after 0300 hours. He waited to get home before indulging in his one noticeable vice: coffee. He drank the day's final cup, reached into his fastidiously kept closet and pulled out a couple pairs of Army-issued longjohns and other cold weather gear he figured he would need for the two day trip "up to the Slope." He neatly packed it all into a large green canvas duffel bag. Carroll quickly fell asleep.

When his alarm rang 45 minutes later, the colonel woke up rejuvenated. He leapt out of bed and poured himself the day's "first cup" from the still fresh pot of coffee he made less than an hour earlier. He showered, shaved and quickly cleaned up what little mess he made and left the house.

He met up with his crew of six and boarded the Alaska National Guard's C-12 King Air executive turboprop for the five hour flight to Barrow. Before pulling the hatch closed behind him, Carroll ordered the two Sky Cranes moved out of their Elmendorf Air Force base hangar to be readied for a quick sendoff.

After awaking from a short nap, Carroll contorted his athletic frame around in his front row seat to pass back sweet rolls and coffee while briefing his men about Operation Breakout. Knowing he was about to enter the fray of a developing national news event, Carroll brought along Mike Haller, the National Guard's Public Affairs Officer to "handle" the media.

Colonel Carroll told Haller his mission had one purpose. Keep a competitive press from interfering with the rescue. The best way to do that, Carroll said, was to befriend the media. Haller planned to hold regularly scheduled press conferences so the media could feel like they were getting all their questions answered. Carroll warned Haller to avoid giving the press the idea they were being manipulated. The minute that happened, the coverage of the National Guard could turn nasty.

They knew that everyone would immediately seek to get on the barge. They discussed setting up and coordinating press pools so only one television crew, still photographer and print reporter would be allowed access at a time. Any footage, pictures and quotes taken by the pool reporters would be made available to every news agency.

Carroll's pilot checked with Barrow air traffic control to see if they could get clearance to fly over the whale site. The colonel wanted to inspect the ice conditions from the air. Not having seen a trace of man for over three hours, the colonel was incredulous when the pilot told him that the air space around the site was restricted due to heavy traffic. "Heavy traffic?" Carroll mused.

Flying westward, they descended rapidly from their cruising altitude over the frozen coast of Elson Lagoon. The aircraft banked steeply to the right, pinning Carroll and the crew deeper into their seats. In the split second it took the speeding plane to cross the narrow sandspit, they flew directly over the whales. From 2,000 feet in the air, the dozen or so people huddled around the small breathing holes looked like misplaced ants against a uniform, motionless backdrop of snowy white.

Carroll, mouth agape, stared wondrously at the remarkable site below him. He shook his head in amazement as the plane touched down at the Wiley Post Memorial Airport. From the ergonomic seat of his plush plane, the bitter, lifeless elements outside his window looked deceivingly like a fairytale wonderland as the plane taxied toward Randy Crosby's Search and Rescue hangar at the opposite end of the 7,000 foot runway.

Before the pilot could cut the engines, Carroll and Haller watched in bewilderment as the SAR hangar bays slid open, letting loose a stream of television cameramen and entangled technicians racing each other in a mad dash for position at the bottom of the airplane's steps. No longer did it seem like such a wonderland.

"This happens wherever I go," Carroll deadpanned.

Like a seasoned political campaigner, Carroll smiled broadly and briskly waved as he stepped off the plane. Nonplussed by the cluster of microphones stuck in front of his chest, Carroll warmly shook hands with a near panicked Ron Morris.

Like a protective father, the much larger Carroll put his arm around the beleaguered coordinator's shoulder. As they walked across the tarmac the cameras captured Colonel Carroll as he listened reassuringly to the animated Morris. They walked together into the "secured" part of the hangar, leaving Mike Haller to deal with the media.

Once inside, Colonel Carroll asked to meet the man in charge. He figured it was the big smiling man standing in a blue flight suit in the back of the room. His confident aura matched with his Grizzly Adams look gave Carroll the sense that this man was the boss. He was right. It was Randy Crosby, director and chief pilot of the North Slope Search and Rescue Command. When Carroll watched the burly rescue pilot pour him a generous mug of hot North Slope coffee, he knew they were distined to get along just fine.

Carroll boarded Randy's second chopper and flew out to the site. Carroll caught his first glimpse of the whales when the red, white and yellow helicopter prepared to touch down on the frozen surface of the Chukchi Sea. By mid-morning Sunday, Randy had already flown enough people out to the ice to know how excited they became the first time they saw the whales. Carroll was no exception.

When he stepped out of the chopper, Randy motioned to the colonel to duck his head until he was clear of the swirling blade. Although the ice seemed like it was rock solid, Crosby could not take any chances. He kept the chopper on half power. If the ice started to buckle beneath him, Crosby had just seconds to raise the helicopter into the safety of the air. Those on the ice would have to fend for themselves.

Carroll walked toward the whales while trying to listen to Arnold Brower, Jr., describe the ice conditions over the loud commotion of the television crews following them. He asked Brower how far it was to the ridge and if anyone had been out there yet. Brower said the closest paths through the ice were four to five miles away, twice as far as they were when the whales were first discovered nine days earlier.

Each day the whales were stuck beneath the ice, the farther they were from the safety of the lead's open water. But even that safety was rapidly vanishing. The open water lead that separated the growing formation of new ice from the encroaching polar ice pack was shrinking almost a mile a day. When Carroll and Crosby saw it Sunday morning, October 16, they figured it was less than 15 miles wide. If they couldn't free the whales before the two ice formations met and closed off the lead, the whales would die.

Brower walked with the colonel to the edge of the crowded hole. Not seeing any whales, Carroll tentatively leaned his tall frame to peer straight down into the bubbling dark gray sea. Just as his head broke the water's parallel plain, one of the whales burst out of the sea spraying water all over the startled colonel. That night's newscasts and the next morning's papers carried comical pictures of the decorated war veteran struggling to wipe crystallized whale breath off his face.

When they met him, Geoff and Craig had only one message for the colonel: Get that hoverbarge to Barrow as soon as he could. They told him that the whales he was fondly admiring didn't have much time. Although the chain saws could be counted on to help keep the hole open, the biologists didn't think it would be long before the whales started showing signs of fatigue. Carroll promised to do his best. Holding his hat so it wouldn't blow off, he offered the two biologists a customary salute and ran back to Randy Crosby's waiting whirlybird.

Crosby, Carroll and Brower flew west to inspect conditions at the ice's outermost edge. When Crosby lowered the 214 Lone Ranger into position for landing, the newest and most forbidding obstacle came towering into view. Powerful ocean currents had heaved up huge walls of ice. In some places, the pressure ridge rose as high as 30 feet above the ocean's surface. In the midst of all the shards, Crosby looked intently for a safe place to touch down.

Carroll and Ron Morris saw that the ice around the whales was not thick enough to challenge the hoverbarge's purported ice breaking ability. But the pressure ridge proved to be another story. There was no way the hoverbarge could break through it. Hoping to find weaknesses, the rescuers flew along the ridge to look for breaks in the ice wall where the barge might be able to sneak through.

The colonel could have cancelled the National Guard plan to tow the hovercraft. If the barge couldn't break the pressure ridge, why bring it from Prudhoe? Instead of giving up, Morris, Brower and Carroll agreed that the National Guard should proceed with the hovercraft operation. Brower was asked to help find Eskimos willing to scout the area for suitable routes the hovercraft could take through the pressure ridge.

After flying back to his waiting aircraft at the Search and Rescue Hangar, Carroll gathered his men, thanked Randy Crosby for his tour and told Ron Morris to keep those holes open.

"We'll see you in a couple of days," he said confidently to the cameras as he leapt up his King Air's aluminum stairs. He would be back, but not as a hero.

With Carroll gone, Morris had less than an hour to prepare for the arrival of the next contingent of VIP rescuers, the oilmen. The ARCO jet carrying Billy Bob Allen and Ben Odom followed Carroll's previous flight path. It made the same banking turn and was met at the hangar by the same chorus of reporters. For Randy Crosby, it was "deja vu all over again." Allen climbed aboard Crosby's helicopter promising Odom and Leathard he would be a good sport. He went along to show Pete he supported his efforts and would earnestly help him pull the rescue off.

The remarkable scenery of Barrow and the Arctic left Bill Allen unmoved. He had seen it hundreds of times in the past 20 years. This is where he made his fortune. He was sure he had seen all there was to see. But the impatient oilman and his patrician colleague were in for a sight that would change them forever.

Billy Bob stepped off the helicopter intent on concealing his lack of interest in the whales to the very end. He would tell the reporters how he hoped the three creatures could be freed. He would commend everybody who helped with the rescue, then return to the hangar, pour himself a cup of coffee into a styrofoam cup and fly off.

When the helicopter landed, it blew away the snow covering the foot thick floor of glaring, bluish-gray Arctic ice. Morris introduced Allen, Odom and Leathard to Arnold Brower, Jr., who had been busy at work with a crew of men trying to expand the whales' lone breathing hole. Allen and Brower conversed over the helicopter's loud roar. It was a few minutes before Billy Bob even realized he had not seen the whales. He did not know how long it would be before they appeared but he wasn't interested in hanging around in minus 25° weather to wait for them.

The first whale rose just as it had thousands of times before in the nine days since it was first discovered. But for Bill Allen it was in indescribable revelation, an epiphany. A look of youthful wonder swept across his face. Pete Leathard had never seen him so animated. The middle-aged oilman abandoned all his inhibitions and for a brief moment became young Billy Bob again.

He ran to the edge of the hole and quickly droped down to one knee. Eagerly reaching out across the open water, Billy Bob stroked his hand across the side of the battered whale's face. The whale moved still closer to Allen and jutted its head over the edge of the hole. In an irresistible appeal for more attention from its new friend, the whale knocked Billy Bob down when he playfully butted its huge but battered snout into his chest.

The whales worked their magic yet again. For Allen, as for most non-Eskimos, the whale's magnificence was a relatively recent discovery. Well into the 20th century, the only people ever to get so close to whales did so to kill them and at great personal risk. But man's transformation from whale killer to whale saver was so quick and so universal that by the end of that same century, hundreds of millions of people around the world would watch as great nations committed millions of dollars and hundreds of men to free three whales trapped at an isolated edge of the universe.

In the eyes of almost all seafaring cultures, the whale has always stood atop the pantheon of animal mythology. Throughout history the whale has played the part of legend, myth and allegory. From Jonah's punishment-cum-repentance in the mouth of the whale, to Ahab's battle of wills with Moby Dick, there has never been another creature quite like it. The Leviathan has run the gamut of human emotion while never falling from consciousness. The whale has been everything but ignored.

For most of human history, one word has best categorized man's relationship with a creature it barely knew: fear. Whales are the biggest creatures ever to inhabit the earth. The 100-foot blue whale is bigger than even the largest dinosaurs. Its gargantuan size convinced generations that the whale was evil. Ascribing evil powers that the whale did not possess, people avoided them at all costs. According to some legends, those who even saw them from a distance were marked for early death.

For so long, man knew so little about the whale, he thought it was a fish. But by the second half of the 19th century, the great beast was finally conquered. The once proud behemoth was no match for whaling fleets armed with harpoon guns. As man became more familiar with the animal he now relentlessly hunted, his conception of it began to change. The whale's long unknown attributes started to surface. Its remarkable intelligence, its grace, its unjustified trust of man confounded the age old stereotypes. But, more than anything else, the whale had a certain undeniable charm. A charm of remarkable gentleness. Old myths died silent deaths.

But only after slaughtering virtually every one of them did man first take note of the whale's greatness, a greatness he knew might vanish from the face of the earth. Perhaps out of guilt at having so long misunderstood and sought to undermine the creature now nicknamed the Gentle Giant, did man embrace the whale as a symbol of his own concern for a world he was destroying. Saving the whale was a first step toward saving ourselves.

After seeing the whales, Billy Bob Allen couldn't explain it in words any better than before. But he knew whales were special.

Chapter 10

From Kickers to Leads

News, by definition, is unpredictable. To people in Barrow, the stranding of the three California gray whales was an insignificant annual event. But to those on the Outside, it was an unprecedented chance to think of themselves as part of an effort to help rescue one of man's favorite animals. Once Oran Caudle's first pictures of the trapped whales reached Todd Pottinger's editing machine at KTUU-TV in Anchorage, it unleashed an outpouring of interest and concern rarely experienced in the human species.

In many ways, this was the story television was created to cover. It offered an abundance of spectacular natural imagery with almost no need for analysis. A picture of the rising, spouting and surging of desperate whales confined to a tiny hole in the middle of a frozen Arctic Ocean said infinitely more than the couched words of a television commentator. It captured the imagination of millions of people in a way network executives had rarely seen. Only the immediacy of television could convey the whales' almost hypnotic allure. Somewhat the same way that a cat stuck in a tree could mobilize an entire town, three gray whales stuck in Arctic ice mobilized an entire world.

Within hours of the first NBC broadcast on Thursday, October 13, six days after the whales were first discovered, the network's New York switchboard was jammed with hundreds of calls from ordinary citizens around the country. They wanted to know how they could help. Friday morning, Greenpeace's Washington office handled hundreds more from concerned members.

The people had spoken. What started out as an ideal story for NBC to use as a "kicker," a lighthearted piece used to close a news broadcast, for a brief time became almost a national obsession. Suddenly, America appeared desperate to learn and see more of the whales. Through jammed telephone switchboards and higher ratings points, the networks got the message. They rushed crews to Barrow to try to meet the growing demand.

The whales didn't stay "kickers" for long. By Sunday night, October 16, they were news "leads." Just three weeks before a Presidential election, and three days after they were first reported, the stranded whales became the top story on each network newscast. Among the estimated 30 million people who watched the whales gasp for air on Sunday's evening newscasts was President Ronald Reagan. He penned a note reminding himself to ask about the whales the following morning at his daily 9:00 AM briefing with senior White House staff members. Perhaps "helpless" was not the best word to describe the three whales. They clearly had done something that most other creatures could not do. Nine days after discovery, the whales compelled the most powerful man on earth to action.

Monday morning, October 17, the President told his Chief of Staff, Kenneth Duberstein, that he wanted regular reports on the rescue's progress. The daily written summary of the meeting circulated to every office in the West Wing, included a reference to the President's interest in the trapped whales.

The memo quickly made its way to White House Press Secretary Marlin Fitzwater, the President's spokesman. Almost instantly, Fitzwater saw an opportunity. Mentioning the whales at the President's morning briefing would demonstrate that Ronald Reagan was just as concerned about the stranded creatures as millions of other

Americans. Since no one wished the whales ill, the White House could not lose. After clearing the whales with the Chief of Staff's office, Fitzwater inserted a few words about them into the statement he was preparing to read to the White House press corps concerning the President's activities.

Ronald Reagan was preparing to leave office as one of the most popular Presidents in American history. Kenneth Duberstein had one mandate, to protect the legacy of the Reagan Administration in its final months. His job meant no last-minute missteps. The longest economic recovery, the friendly relations with the Soviet Union, and a renewed sense of American pride catapulted Reagan's approval rating to stratospheric heights. There were only a few areas where the President's image appeared slightly tarnished. Top among them was the environment.

Despite his widespread popularity, a vast majority of Americans still felt Reagan was a poor steward of the environment. George Bush, his heir apparent, all but acknowledged that shortcoming when he pledged to be "the Environmental President." If President Reagan intervened on behalf of three trapped whales in the waning days of his administration, maybe he could begin to heal one of the wounds that threatened to scar his otherwise glittering presidency.

Duberstein assigned a little known but critical White House department to take charge of the rescue. The Office of Cabinet Affairs (OCA) worked to iron out policy differences on issues ranging from acid rain to three whales trapped at the edge of the American dominion. The OCA tried to get all cabinet officers to arrive at a consensus before offering the President an option. Sometimes a consensus was impossible to reach. Not so with the whales. Everyone agreed: save them.

Bonnie Mersinger first heard about the whales at 7:00 AM, Friday, October 14. She was sitting in her small cubicle in the West Wing of the White House sipping on a thin straw pierced through the side of cardboard apple juice container. A few stolen minutes with Jane Pauley and Willard Scott were the only contact the attractive woman had with the outside world. Rarely did attractive 31-year-old women become Executive Assistants to the President of the United States by pursuing interests other than work.

Mersinger swung her tall athletic frame sharply around when she heard the word "whales" mentioned on her small Sony Watchman television. Bonnie Mersinger was jokingly referred to by her colleagues as the "resident White House environmentalist." Like millions of others, the instant she saw Oran Caudle's footage of the trapped whales, Mersinger had been hooked.

She didn't know what exactly, but there was something about whales that unleashed a strong feeling of empathy. Maybe it was her background. Before changing professions in the early 1980s Bonnie worked with animals, big graceful animals. She made her living breaking race horses, including Genuine Risk, the 1980 Kentucky Derby Winner. Until given the chance to work for Ronald Reagan, she loved more than anything else to train Thoroughbreds.

Mersinger was convinced Reagan would want to help the whales the instant he heard about them. Their plight played magically to two of his most profound emotions: his love of animals and his incorrigible soft spot for hard luck tales. She wrote him a memo about the stranding on Friday, October 14 but it was too late in the day. The President and Mrs. Reagan had already ascended Marine One, parked on the White House South Lawn, to spend the weekend at Camp David.

By 10:00 AM Monday the 17th, 10 days after the stranded whales were first discovered, the President of the United States was officially involved in the rescue and Bonnie Mersinger became his personal representative. She knew that protocol limited the President's direct authority to federal agencies. Since two of the rescue's four independent factions, NOAA and the National Guard, answered directly to him, Operation Breakout presented the President with a rare choice.

Everyone in the White House knew that when given a choice, President Reagan always liked to exercise his authority as Commander in Chief. Mersinger advised Ken Duberstein's office to route the White House involvement through the Alaska National Guard.

She collected newspaper articles about the whales on her computer. Skimming through them, Mersinger jotted down the names of key players: Cindy Lowry of Greenpeace, Ron Morris of NOAA, the oilmen, the Eskimos, and a National Guard Colonel named Tom Carroll.

A Guardsman herself, Bonnie called Frank O'Connor, an old friend in the Alaska National Guard to see what he could tell her about "Operation Breakout." O'Connor said that until the Guard entered the picture, there was no one in charge with the authority to set priorities. Now maybe a sensible command structure could emerge. O'Connor assured her that in Alaska, Tom Carroll was the most qualified person to deal with the problem.

Colonel Carroll was the man Bonnie needed. Through him she could convey the President's interest in the rescue and relay his offer of help. Together they could keep the Chief Executive completely informed on the well being of the whales. Around noon, Washington time, Bonnie called the National Guard's mobile command head-quarters at·Prudhoe Bay.

Although it was still an hour and a half before first light on Monday morning, Colonel Carroll had already stepped outside into the bitter cold to cross off checklists so the Sky Crane could start towing the barge. A civilian on loan from ARCO answered Bonnie's first call. He told Bonnie the colonel would soon be back. With the wind chill, it was close to 100° below zero on the frozen tundra.

If the Tom Carroll had been like other men, he would have returned in a few minutes. Colonel Carroll was obsessed. The colonel stayed outside, exposed to the life threatening cold for nearly 12 hours. He relentlessly barked orders over his walkie-talkie to the helicopter pilots and the crew on the barge. The men from ARCO and VECO who just met the colonel thought he was out of his mind.

Before the towing began, Carroll solved the key logistical problem: fuel. He estimated the helicopters would need at least 20,000 gallons of high octane Arctic aviation gasoline to pull the barge 270 miles from Prudhoe to Barrow. The colonel devised a self-contained operation to load the barge with enough fuel for itself and the helicopters. He sent for special refueling pumps from An-chorage. He also ordered his men to work with the VECO crews to load all 20,000 gallons aboard the hoverbarge in customized storage tanks.

Every item on Carroll's checklist was crossed off and ready by 11:00 AM, two hours earlier than he hoped. But when he gave the order to begin, and the powerful helicopter started to pull, the barge did not move. The downward thrust of air which lifted the 185-ton hovercraft broke the thick layer of ice that covered the shore. Carroll watched helplessly as his pilot, Chief Warrant Officer Gary Quar-rells, valiantly kept the Sky Crane from spinning wildly out of control and crashing into the frozen bay. After Quarrells safely landed his craft, Carroll went over to investigate.

The barge was mired in mud. A thick coat encrusted the rubber skirt needed to trap air so the barge could hover. Carroll had no choice but to call on the VECO crews, still recovering from the previous two days of backbreaking work, to don their Arctic gear, grab their pick axes and shovels and get back to work. They chipped off as much of the frozen mud as they could before collapsing in exhaustion.

Gary Quarrells tried again. He pulled his chopper with 22,500 pounds of thrust. After failing a second time, Carroll knew it was no use. The barge was just too heavy. He ordered the 20,000 gallons of fuel stored on the deck of the barge unloaded before trying yet again. Carroll arranged for the helicopter fuel to be prepositioned on the ice. Special Arctic tanker trucks drove all night hundreds of miles across the surface of a frozen sea placing 600-gallon refueling tanks every two miles along the route to Barrow.

The colonel pondered the latest setback while supervising the shutdown of the hoverbarge. His press aide, Lieutenant Mike Haller, handed him a message. The colonel wiped frozen mud from his numb face as he clumsily tried to unfold the note in a howling wind. It was from a woman in the White House named Bonnie Mersinger. Carroll didn't have time to be bothered. He told Haller to take care of it.

"But sir," Haller gently protested, raising his voice loud enough to be heard over the wind and engine noise. "She said she wanted to talk with you."

"Alright," the colonel relented. "Tell her I'll get back to her as soon as I finish out here."

Finally, around 10:00 PM, Alaska time, Carroll picked up the phone and dialed the number written on the message. He registered no surprise when Bonnie Mersinger answered. There were too many thoughts swirling through his restless mind for Carroll to realize that it was 2:00 AM, Washington time. He politely but professionally introduced himself to the female voice on the other end of the remarkably clear line.

Bonnie told the colonel that the President wanted to schedule a phone call to Prudhoe sometime on Tuesday afternoon. At first, Carroll thought it was a joke. He figured the whole thing was perpetrated by one of his buddies back east in retaliation for one of Carroll's famous pranks. He decided to play it cool. When she didn't seem amused, Carroll figured he should take her seriously.

He told her he would love nothing more than to talk with the President but he just couldn't commit to a time. The President of the United States, his Commander in Chief, wanted to talk to him and he wasn't sure he could take the call? What kind of a guy was this Carroll, Mersinger asked. Instead of becoming angry, she was intrigued. She wanted to find out more.

Bonnie asked the colonel what the Arctic was like. His answer sounded like a formal press statement. Bonnie thanked the colonel for his time and told him she would speak to him in the morning.

Her hand hadn't let go of the phone when something came over her. She had to call him back. At first no one answered. Without knowing why, she let the phone ring over a dozen times until someone finally picked up: "Guard-Prudhoe." She immediately recognized the voice. It was Tom Carroll.

"Are you always so formal?" she boldly asked the startled colonel. It was the first time anyone had spoken to him like a human being in what seemed like weeks since he left Anchorage. It was not yet two full days. Colonel Carroll was constantly under stress, but he never acknowledged it. When he heard Bonnie's friendly tone, he succumbed to an overwhelming wave of relief and collapsed into his chair. Suddenly the weight of all his worries vanished. He found himself opening up to a woman he barely knew, uncharacteristically confiding that so far at least, the operation was a disaster.

This frank admission broke down the barriers between them. Ignoring the fact that she called him, she jokingly asked permission to go home and get some sleep. After all, she reminded him, it was almost 2:30 in the morning and she had to be back in the White House in four and a half hours. He couldn't believe how open he was with a woman he had met over the telephone just a day before. "Just remember," he kept repeating to himself, referring to his pending divorce.

It had been almost three days since Tom Carroll last slept. Yet the highstrung colonel seemed immune to exhaustion. At 10:30 the night before another grueling day, the colonel had not finished. He looked around for someone to "spot" him while he worked out with free weights in the ARCO gym. Normally, to the dismay of the detail officer assigned to him, Carroll took his own weights with him wherever he went. But to everyone's relief, Carroll learned before leaving Anchorage that the ARCO exercise facility had their own. After working up a heavy sweat pumping iron, Carroll wrapped a white towel around his broad shoulders and walked back to his office through the heated hallways of ARCO's $300 million self-contained living complex. He wanted to talk to Ron Morris, the NOAA coordinator, to close the books on Monday, October 17, Day 2 of Operation Breakout.

Carroll was certain that a phone call from Prudhoe to Barrow, 270 miles away across the frozen tundra, would be expensive. But he didn't even have to dial "one." It was a local call, cheaper than a crosstown call in Manhattan. He called the Airport Inn and asked to be connected to Ron Morris's room. Ed Benson, the owner of the hotel, told Carroll that Morris was up on the Top of the World drinking with his new friends.

Throughout the day, Carroll checked on the whales and their rescuers by radio phone. By Monday afternoon, October 17, several Eskimos with their own chainsaws were on the ice helping Arnold Brower, Jr., keep the lone hole big enough for the whales to breathe. But the shifting winds and dropping temperatures iced it over almost as fast as the Eskimos could open it. The day's worst news came not from the failed helicopter tow in Prudhoe. Instead, it originated with the whales themselves. Their condition appeared to be rapidly deteriorating.

The night before, Sunday, October 16, Cindy Lowry lay awake in her tiny Barrow hotel room worrying about her first day on the ice. She tossed and turned anticipating what the whales would look like. She wanted to see them that very minute. But the pitch black darkness made doing so an impossibly dangerous risk. Anyone foolish enough to venture out on the ice became easy prey for hungry polar bears looking for their next meal.

Cindy resolved to wait for daylight. When she did fall asleep, it wasn't long before her phone rang unexpectedly. It was 5:30 AM and her initiation into a most unwelcome daily ritual. Instead of a standard wake up call, the hotel operator just let an Outside call through at around the time Cindy wanted to get up. Since she got so many phone calls, there was bound to be one at right about the time she wanted to be awakened. Whenever she picked up the phone, it was invariably a reporter from the Lower 48 asking about the whales.

Ron Morris wanted everyone to meet for breakfast at Pepe's before going out to the ice. Over six-egg omelettes, greasy home fries and soft Wonder Bread dripping in butter, the newly assembled rescue crew listened as Morris held forth. The biologists were startled when the man they were starting to trust glanced furtively around the dining room in a calculated attempt to excite the curiosity of nearby reporters. In a stage whisper, Morris told them, along with a roomful of competitive television and newspaper reporters, that he was carrying an official document issued by the United States Government.

Demonstratively tapping his left index finger against the right breast pocket of his faded red-checked flannel shirt, Morris said the mythical piece of paper gave him full and final authority over the whales. "I can kill them whenever and however I want," he said. Cindy was aghast. Geoff and Craig laughed in nervous shock. Who was this man, they thought. The reporters eagerly scribbled down the quote their editors would never use.

"Who is this bloke?" inquired Charles Lawrence, a Cockney-accented photographer from the *London Daily Telegraph*. "He must be out of his bloody mind."

Other reporters sitting close by looked Lawrence's way and nodded their silent approval. But that was all they could do. Unlike other stories where they thrived on the imperfections of their subjects, the reporters assigned to cover the whales were met with a most unusual reality. It was the whales people cared about, not the bizarre idiosyncracies of their rescuers.

Like him or not—and personally, I did not—Ron Morris was the only official source of rescue information. If reporters wanted continued access to Morris, which of course we all did, we had to stay on good terms with him. We laughed at his jokes and none of us reported his heavy drinking. Many of us invited him for meals, drinks and late night bull sessions. All of which he gladly partook. But what he seemed to love most was visiting the television edit suites where he would watch footage of himself for hours on end.

Whatever we thought about the biologist-turned-rescuer, none of us thought Ron Morris a fool. He possessed a remarkable, almost instinctive sense of how the media worked and how to use that knowledge to maximize and enhance his own personal celebrity. Just a day after his arrival, Morris cornered Geoff and Craig and told them not to talk with any members of the press unless he approved their doing so in advance. By blocking the press's access to rescuers other than himself, Morris felt his own stature would be enhanced.

He was quoted in every story and appeared on every newscast. Within days, he became a household name all over America. He masterfully created his own image of a gentle, tireless rescuer that the obsequious media passed on to an unwitting public.

For all of the private confessions of revulsion at Ron Morris and his growing delusions, we could not escape our own culpability. After all, we created him. We were the ones who rewrote the rules of journalism, allowing Morris to run a highly political operation free of the scrutiny or criticism we applied to everyone else examined under the microscope of American journalism.

Chapter 11

The President Watches TV Too

It was Monday morning, October 17. The three trapped whales had already survived 10 long days in a shrinking Arctic Ocean ice hole. What would have marked the end of a fatal ordeal for any other creature was, for this lucky trio, only the beginning.

Meanwhile, Cindy Lowry had arrived. The woman whose efforts to aid the helpless animals turned their plight into a national obsession was on her way to see them for the first time. Before driving out onto the ice with Geoff, Craig and Ron Morris at about 11:00 AM, Cindy checked with the hotel desk clerk for messages. She had no idea what to expect. It was her first morning in town. She thought maybe Kevin called to say hello.

As she walked toward the desk, she saw a frazzled bleached-blonde receptionist frantically trying to write messages while hunching her shoulders to hold a telephone to each ear. In one of the two-second intervals when the hotel phone stopped ringing, Cindy meekly tried to sneak in a request for her own messages.

"My name is Cindy Lowry," said the pretty, smiling whale saver, "Do I have any messages?"

"Do you have any messages?" the receptionist asked, her tone unmistakably accusatory, even through her thick Colombian accent. "You must be kidding," she then shoved a stack of 50 coffee stained messages directly into Cindy's startled face.

Nervously thumbing through them, Cindy was amazed at how quickly all these people found out who she was, and where she was staying. She counted about 30 reporters from newspapers, radio and television stations across the country who wanted to schedule interviews. But what really struck Cindy were the other messages. Like the one addressed to "the Greenpeace Lady" from a woman in Columbia, South Carolina. "Why don't you use dynamite to blast away the ice?" the message read. Another woman from Louisiana had a similar idea. "Why not drop napalm from helicopters to melt the ice around the whales? she asked.

A man from California asked Cindy why they didn't drop some bait into the water and pull them out like fish on a hook. People were spending their own money and time to track her down at the top of the world to offer their advice on how to save the three trapped whales. Cindy always knew whales were special, and now middle America did too.

Cindy didn't know until she read the paper the next day that even more calls were coming into Tom Carroll's command center in Prudhoe Bay. Hundreds of them came from the same kinds of people with similar ideas. The suggestions ranged from the impractical to the down right ludicrous. Nonetheless, Cindy could not help but be touched by the concerns of people so far away.

One person who called was a young businessman from Minneapolis named Greg Ferrian. On Monday, October 17, he heard Peter Jennings on "ABC World News Tonight" describe the Eskimos' losing battle to keep open the lone breathing hole. ABC correspondent Gary Shepard reported that, despite the Eskimos who worked around the clock, the falling temperatures made it almost impossible for them to keep sections of the hole from freezing over.

Greg Ferrian was familiar with the problem. His father-in-law owned a company called Kasco Marine that manufactured small water circulating pumps designed to keep ice from forming around boats in the winter. Kasco sold most of their $500 "de-icers" to marinas and duck pond owners throughout the Great Lakes region. Alaska was a vast new sales territory. Greg figured the de-icers would work just as well for whales as they did for ducks. The de-icers worked just fine in the dead of a Minnesota winter when temperatures regularly dropped below the minus 30° readings presently being recorded in Barrow.

True, Greg thought, the machines might not work well in the coldest Arctic weather, but this was only October. Relatively balmy Barrow was still several months from becoming that cold. Ferrian convinced himself the de-icers could do the job. They could help the three whales buy the time they needed to survive until the hover-barge arrived from Prudhoe Bay. And the de-icers could do so better and cheaper than anything else.

Greg wanted to help but he wasn't sure where to start. Finally he decided to call a local television station, KSTP-TV, ABC's Minneapolis affiliate. The KSTP newsroom told him to call ABC News in New York. After speaking with seemingly everyone else in the 212 area code, Ferrain finally reached someone nice enough to help him. She was a desk producer helping the ABC crew in Barrow cover the story.

Although she had taken dozens of other calls from like minded people trying to help, the woman was good enough to pass on Colonel Carroll's National Guard phone number. Ferrian was surprised that the connection to a place 300 miles above the Arctic Circle sounded so clear. Greg tried to describe the de-icers to Colonel Carroll's press aide, Mike Haller. He told Ferrian that the colonel would have to approve the plan, but, of course, he was out on the ice. Haller suggested if Greg really was serious, he should call back after dark, around 4:30 PM, Alaska time. By then, the colonel might be back at the ARCO/VECO command center.

When Greg Ferrian finally reached Colonel Carroll, his warm and personable manner seemed a welcome relief from the rude treatment he encountered en route to the top. The colonel listened patiently as Greg repeated his confident claims about the de-icers. Carroll told Greg the de-icers sounded like a great idea. They might be just the thing to keep the holes open and the whales alive, Carroll said. If it were up to him, he'd use them in a minute. But it wasn't. Ron Morris had to approve.

Ferrian cleared the line for a new dial tone to call Ron Morris. Remarkably, he got through on his first try. But Morris abruptly cut him off before he could explain his device.

"I've got to go," Morris barked. "I've got a helicopter waiting to take me to a press conference,"

Ferrian plaintively appealed one more time. "All I need is one word, a yes or a no. Can't we at least try?" he begged.

"One word?" Morris teasingly asked. "No," he snapped. Ferrian heard the click as Morris hung up.

But Greg didn't give up. Morris' response only further emboldened him. He called his brother-in-law, Rick Skluzacek, who ran Kasco Marine in his father's absence. Greg felt Rick should know something about his scheme to drag his company's de-icers all the way to the Arctic. Turning truth on its head, Greg told him that Operation Breakout wanted to use de-icers to help save the three stranded whales. Rick knew Greg had a penchant for crazy ideas, but this was definitely the craziest he ever heard. Experience taught him to beware. But Rick's initial suspicion gave way to the opportunity and challenge of demonstrating the de-icing machines to hundreds of millions of people around the world.

Now Greg had a real problem. Rick was actually interested. What would happen if Rick really did want to go to Barrow? How could Greg tell him the truth? That he lied to his own brother-in-law? Instead, Greg opted against panic and decided to worry about minor technicalities later. Greg Ferrian called Carroll back and lied again. This time he told him that he and Rick had already decided to help. They were booked on the next flight to Barrow with six de-icers.

Undaunted by the colonel's repeated reminder that their machines' use was not his decision to make, Greg asked the colonel if there were gas-powered electric generators they could use in Barrow. The colonel said he thought there were, but he wasn't sure. Before he could say that only Ron Morris could authorize their use, Greg had hung up.

"Damn," Carroll said impressed at the Minnesotan's tenacity. "This guy doesn't fool around."

Ferrian called his brother-in-law and lied yet again. It got easier each time. He told him that everything in Barrow was set. All they had to do was pack their de-icers and go. After a sleepless Sunday night, Rick called 3M, Control Data and other Minneapolis Fortune 500 companies. He tried to convince them to donate their private jets to fly the equipment to Barrow. The whales were such a great story and Ferrian such a great salesman, that three of the companies actually said yes. Each one had to back down however when they learned that none of their planes were available.

When Greg priced commercial flights to Barrow, he had a new reason to worry. There was no way he could lie about that. He knew Rick wasn't 100 percent sold on leaving merely chilly Minnesota for the already bitter cold Arctic. The $2,600 round trip airfare to Barrow might end the charade once and for all. Even Greg wondered whether the whole plan was too farfetched.

Greg knew the more time Rick was given to think about going to Barrow, the chances increased he would have to rule against it. Greg decided to give his brother-in-law no choice. He not only booked the seats, but he called KSTP-TV in Minneapolis and told them that he and Rick were going to Barrow to help the whales. Now, there was nothing Greg's brother-in-law could do. It was on the record. Jews called it Chutzpah. Minnesotans called it guts. Whatever it was, Greg Ferrian displayed it in abundance. He and Rick Skluzacek were on their way to Barrow.

Greg Ferrian hoped that KSTP-TV might mention the duo's trip to Barrow on the six o'clock news. The second he heard about the call, KSTP news director Mendes Napoli threw down his red pencil and dashed out the door to find his reporters. Napoli instantly knew he was onto the hottest story in the Twin Cities. The trapped whales, now leading all the network newscasts, had a local angle and KSTP was the only station that knew about it. Coming right before a critical ratings period, the news was almost too good to be true.

Napoli ran to the other side of the newsroom to use the radio phone. He desperately tried to reach Jason Davis, one of his top reporters who had left with a crew to prepare to do a live report for the upcoming six o'clock news. When Napoli found him in the microwave truck, he informed Davis there would be no live shot. He told him to go home and pack lots of warm clothing. Davis had a new story that would take him to Barrow, Alaska, with two local men who thought they could help free the three trapped whales.

Napoli read Greg Ferrian's home number to Davis over the cluttered radio. Davis pulled a portable cellular phone out of his nylon daypack and called Ferrian to introduce himself. "I'm Jason Davis, from Eyewitness News," the reporter said in his unmistakable Australian accent. Ferrian didn't need any introductions, he was a local news junkie and instantly recognized the voice of Jason Davis.

Ferrian's gamble paid off far more than he expected. He thought getting a mention on the news was a long shot. A crew was assigned to go with them to Alaska? He was ecstatic. Now there was finally something he could tell his brother-in-law that was true. There was no way Rick could back out. Hours later, Rick and Greg were standing in line at the Delta Airlines ticket counter for their flight to Fairbanks. The agents checking them in were so excited to hear they were going to help the whales, they shipped the six compact de-icers at no extra charge.

KSTP called the contractors remodeling their recently purchased corporate jet and told them the plane would be needed the next day to fly an Eyewitness News crew to Alaska. The contractors worked all night to get the Gulfstream ready for its new owners. They removed a gaudy double brass bed and ceiling mirrors from the plane and replaced it with a modest bar. The plane's previous owner, bankrupt television evangelist Jimmy Swaggert, thought drinking a sin.

Colonel Carroll didn't know what to make of the calls from Minnesota. He called Cindy in Barrow to ask her what she thought. But she had just left the hotel. Cindy was finally on her way to see the whales. Geoff and Craig tried to prepare her for the whales' worsening condition. Temperatures in Barrow were dropping by the day. The chainsaw crews could barely keep up with the new ice. The holes were freezing fast, and the barge was still at least three days away. As they drove their Chevy Suburban across the glassy smooth ice of Elson Lagoon, Cindy couldn't believe how isolated the three of them were. With all the reporters, whirling helicopters, and Eskimos with chainsaws, she expected a hubbub of activity.

Instead, she encountered an overwhelming, almost deafening solitude. From the time they crossed onto the frozen lagoon for the seven mile drive along the Point Barrow sandspit to the whales, she saw nothing but a barely discernible ski machine whining past far off in the distance. Even with the unblinking gaze of the world fixed upon it, the North Slope appeared no less hostile, no less alien, and no less inimical to life than at any other moment in its timeless existence.

They crossed over the sandbar that separated past from present. Their isolated world vanished in a sea of attention. The closer they got to the holes, the more people and activity they saw: ski "taxis" ferrying reporters to and from the whales, reporters conducting interviews at the water's edge. The contrast with the barren scenery on the rideout was surreal.

The Eskimos could tell instantly who belonged on the ice and who did not. Cindy did not. Those who did wore blood-stained walrus and seal skin parkas and carried high-powered rifles slung over their shoulders to guard against polar bears. Those who didn't, like Cindy, stood shivering in brightly-colored ski clothes, fashions better suited to alpine resorts than Arctic expeditions.

Geoff took Cindy to meet Arnold Brower, Jr. Brower had been out all night with his team of Eskimos cutting open several new holes in the ice. She was amazed that he showed no signs of fatigue. An Inuit hunter often spent days on end exposed to the harsh elements searching for game to feed and clothe his family. Millennia in the Arctic enabled the Eskimo to withstand conditions that the hardiest white man could not.

No one doubted the ruggedness of the VECO crews who broke the hoverbarge free of ice. But by watching them work, the white man soon learned that the Eskimos could have freed the barge faster with half the men and none of the suffering. They were a different kind of men. The Eskimos were built for the Arctic. It was their home.

The Eskimos cut ice at a feverish pace, oblivious to the minus 35° temperature. With no gloves or hats, and their coats unbuttoned, the Eskimos joked, laughed, and even performed traditional dances on floating slabs of ice. Cindy and her bundled but shivering fellow whites stood nearby, prime candidates for frostbite.

"Why would you come out to work in such cold?" this reporter naïvely asked a busy Eskimo.

"Cold?" the Eskimo responded with equal naïvete. "We're just out here enjoying the weather."

Arnold knew of Cindy and Greenpeace long before she set foot in Barrow. For years her organization fought against subsistence whaling. Under any other circumstance, these two people were enemies. To Arnold, Cindy was bent on ruination of his people and their ancient way of life. To Cindy, Arnold and his people continued to senselessly slaughter an endangered and magnificent creature with increasingly modern tools.

Brower realized this was a rare chance in the history of the Inupiat Eskimos. If he could win Cindy's friendship, maybe some way could be found to lessen the tensions dividing subsistence whaling villages and their environmentalist opponents. He eagerly extended a glove-less hand in a genuine desire to get things off to a good start.

Standing between them, Geoff could feel the tension and the opportunity. If Cindy accepted his hand warmly, great strides could be made. If she did so grudgingly, the damage might never heal. Cindy's pretty face instantly broke into a warm, radiant smile as she eagerly reached to grab Brower's hand for an emotional shake of friendship.

Brower looked at the woman and told her what she already knew. She needed warmer clothing. When Eskimos see a stranger freez-ing, they don't ask whether they want to borrow clothing, they just put it on them. Seeing that she was on the verge of frostbite, he grabbed the fur ruff dangling unused around his neck and leaned over to wrap it around her brightly reddened cheeks. When she saw the fur, Cindy instinctively backed away.

Brower did not understand. Did she want to be his friend or not? He didn't know why Cindy declined his hospitality. Was she recoiling under the touch of a blood-stained whale killer or was their another, less offensive reason?

Realizing her actions were being viewed as an affront, she profusely thanked Brower for his concern but told him she couldn't wear fur.

Why not?" Arnold asked. "Are you allergic?"

"No, no," Cindy said, laughing. "I just don't wear animal fur."

Brower never would understand these crazy whites from the Outside. He told her the ruff was hers when and if she changed her mind.

Cindy waited anxiously for one of the whales to surface. She still had not seen them. Two television cameramen jostled for position to get "good video" of the environmentalists first day on the ice. The strong willed Lowry was still a bit too unsure of her surroundings to tell the cameramen to back off.

As Cindy walked toward the empty holes with Arnold, the cameramen were too busy arguing with each other about who stepped into whose shot to notice Cindy's discomfort. They proba-bly wouldn't have listened to her anyway. Their job was to get the best video, not to win popularity contests. If that meant hurt or angry feelings, so be it. After the story ended and they were reprieved from this Arctic hell, they would never again see any of the people they were offending anyway.

Cindy could tell the whales apart before she even saw them. She absorbed every bit of information about the whales Geoff, Craig or Arnold could give her. The pictures in the paper and on the news gave Cindy as much perspective as anyone. Now, it was her turn to wait those first, long minutes until the whales finally surfaced.

When Geoff and Craig initially observed them five days earlier, the whales held their breath for six minutes at a time. But in the last few days, the two biologists noticed a change. With the dropping temperatures, increased human activity, and ice closing in overhead, the whales started surfacing more frequently. Instead of every six minutes, the whales popped up every three or four minutes. Geoff and Craig guessed that this was a sign of increased stress. The more strain the whales felt, the less time they would spend below the surface. The baby whale surfaced much more frequently than the other two, a further sign of its frailty.

Malik noticed the new behavior first, but he kept it to himself. He didn't want to upset the people working so hard to save the three whales. Perhaps the whales would resume a more normal diving pattern before anyone noticed anything was wrong. But after another day without improvement, Malik was no longer the only one who knew the whales were in trouble.

On Monday morning, the baby whale could barely lift its head out of the water to breathe. It was bloodied and battered from repeatedly banging against the razor sharp edges of the hole. Cindy leaned over to gently comfort the sickly whale with the touch of her hand. She murmured encouragement as it heaved ragged breaths. Her heart ached for the little whale she called "Bone" because all the skin had rubbed away from the whale's snout. The name immediately caught on.

The Eskimos used their own Inupiat language to name the baby "Kannick," or Snowflake. The two other whales would have their choice of several names, but none would stick. The Eskimos called the largest whale "Siku," one of the hundreds of words in the Inupiat language for ice. The rescuers from the Outside called it "Crossbeak," for its crooked jaw that never allowed the whale to properly close its mouth. The smaller of the two adolescent whales was given the Eskimo name "Poutu," a uniquely Inupiat word referring to a specific type of ice hole. Those English speakers who called it anything at all, called it "Bonnet."

Late Monday afternoon, word got to Arnold Brower that Colonel Carroll was making little progress with the hoverbarge in Prudhoe Bay. Brower and Malik urged Morris to start thinking of alternatives in the event the barge did not work. Up to that point, there were no other options. It was the hoverbarge or bust. Morris said waiting was the only thing they could do.

Morris' lack of Arctic experience limited his ability to think of new ways to help the whales. Instead, he continued to insist that Colonel Carroll would soon free the barge.

"But what if it doesn't come?" Arnold Brower asked impatiently. "Then what do we do?"

"You guys are the experts," Morris said defensively. "You tell me."

Malik suggested cutting new holes. Maybe the extra room at the surface would ease the whales' distress. Brower thought it was worth a try. He gathered three men with chain saws and instructed them to cut open a new hole 25' × 25' about a hundred feet west of the existing hole.

When they first expanded the original hole, Arnold and his men cut huge blocks of ice that they hitched to the back of a truck to pull them out of the water. Each new block they moved convinced them that they had created a most inefficient system.

When Geoff nearly fell into the icy waters while trying to lasso a rope around an ice block, Malik and Arnold realized they had seen enough. Malik started cutting much smaller chunks of ice, pushing them under the frozen ledge with the long aluminum shaft of a light harpoon used for seal hunting. Now, it took just minutes to open up a new hole. There were no trucks and no ropes, just a few Eskimos with chainsaws and poles.

The Eskimos walked a hundred feet further, ready to do it again. Malik paced off the dimensions of the new hole. He and Arnold sawed through the perimeter of the rectangle Malik had marked with the sole of his sealskin mukluks. Then they cut the floating island of ice into pieces small enough for one man to easily shove under the edge of surrounding rim. The Eskimos improved with practice. Each new hole took less time to cut than the one before.

But the whales would not move. They stayed in the first hole, the one they knew. Malik thought the activity at the original hole kept them from moving on. He asked people to move away from the old holes to see what the whales would do without any humans to lure them. None of the media moved. Like others, CBS cameraman Bob Dunn nodded his head agreeably and said, "Sure," but he didn't budge. Malik did not understand. Why did he say he would leave and then not move?

Even though each of the networks had hours of whale footage by Monday, October 17, the video of the whales was just too compelling. Reporters always had to chase their subjects. Now, their cameras, microphones and pens could take all the time in the world recording the magnificent, if not tragic images of three glorious whales trapped in tiny holes. After traveling so far to see them, it was impossible to get up and leave.

Everyone's footage was so equally spectacular, the cameraman joked they were on the fast track to the first collective Emmy Award for television news photography. The conditions were so perfect, nobody could lose. Even I took great pictures. As with the fully automatic 35 millimeter cameras sold since the start of the decade, all you had to do was "focus and shoot."

The pictures transmitted back to the Lower 48 were so consistently stunning, the networks could not get enough. The better the video, the more of it the networks aired. The more they aired, the more enthralled the public became. The more enthralled the public became, the more pressure was put on the rescuers to save the whales. Almost as fast as the story broke, the rescue was controlled by a force beyond anyone's control, the force of collective human fascination. Operation Breakout was on autopilot, the first "focus and shoot" story of the television era.

When the biggest event in Barrow's history broke, the town's top leader was nowhere to be found. The North Slope Mayor, George Ahmaogak, left town a week earlier, before the whales were national news, to attend an Alaska Federation of Natives meeting. But when the meeting ended and Barrow was the center of the world, the mayor didn't come back. For days, no one knew where he was, nor when he would return.

All the attention must have frightened the beleaguered mayor. George Ahmaogak was embroiled in controversy over more than the allegations of drinking and wife beating. Not only was the coverage of the whale story on autopilot during the rescue's early days, so was Barrow.

Barrow might not have had an official leader during those critical early days, but it still had its continued responsibilities. Arnold Brower called Dan Fauske, the North Slope Director of Finance. In the mayor's absence, Fauske was the only person authorized to tap the borough's treasury. He asked Fauske for money to feed his hungry men. Fauske planned the borough's $200 million annual budget. Surely the borough could afford a few hundred dollars for donuts and coffee. Fauske agreed.

Soon all the town's unexpected burdens fell into Fauske's shoulders. Randy Crosby called from Search and Rescue wanting more fuel for his helicopters. Since Saturday, October 15, the two SAR helicopters had been providing the media with non-stop shuttle service to and from the whale sight. Crosby had no idea what he was getting his department into when he agreed to give the NBC crew a free flight out to the whales. All the other reporters asked for equal treatment.

In 1975, Fauske traded in the verdant rolling hills of Iowa for the bleak white tundra of Barrow. He thought it would be a neat way to spend his summer before college. It was an exciting time. The Prudhoe Bay oil fields were starting to boom and so was Barrow. Fauske earned $30 an hour delivering water he drilled through 10 feet of ice in one of the thousands of frozen lakes on the tundra just outside Barrow. Things were so good, Fauske never showed up for freshman orientation.

The Eskimos saw Fauske as the one man who could help them make sense of their immense new oil wealth. He was white and smart and loved Barrow. In one of the best bargains they would ever strike, the Eskimos agreed to pay for Fauske's college degree in exchange for his promise to come back and run the borough's finances. When he returned from Gonzaga University, Fauske quickly whipped the North Slope Borough into financial shape. He not only raised more than a billion dollars to finance Barrow's massive capital improvements program, his strict management also earned Barrow the highest bond rating in the country.

Fauske agreed to reimburse Randy Crosby's excess fuel costs but saw a financial nightmare on the horizon if he failed to crack down

right away. Unable to reach him any other way, Fauske showed up at
Ron Morris' Tuesday morning meeting to tell him he did not have
the authority to spend Barrow money without his approval. Morris
told him all his costs would be reimbursed.

"By who?" Fauske demanded.

"The U.S. Government," Morris unconvincingly answered.
Fauske knew a vague answer when he heard one, and he knew of
nothing more vague than the "U.S. Government."

Randy Crosby almost wished Fauske refused him more fuel.
Maybe then he could get his hangar back from the television
cameramen and technicians who had taken it over. While waiting for
free flights out to the whales, the dozens of reporters and technicians lounging around drank his free coffee and ate his free donuts.
They looked like raffish students at a sit-in.

One of them spotted a basketball rim behind one of the parked
helicopters. They started playing pick-up games using a dirty
mechanics rag in place of a ball. Randy was glad to see them
occupied.

"Just be careful," Randy pleaded knowing he was at their mercy.

"Watch that rag," he told people who obviously weren't listening.
"Unless you all got $400,000 for a new engine, don't let it fall into
the intake vent."

"Sure," they said. "We're always careful."

Colonel Carroll thought he was being careful, too. He tried to
keep the media as far away from his Prudhoe Bay operation as he
could. The hoverbarge operation was going poorly, and he did not
want the hole rescue to bog down because of a few problems. He
knew that the media could kill the story just as quickly as they
created it. By Monday night, the 17th, the hoverbarge was only 300
yards further from where it started the day. What should he tell the
President the next day? Should he say that the operation was a
disaster? He needed someone to talk to.

At 5:00 AM, Tuesday morning, Bonnie Mersinger phoned from
the White House to start making arrangements for the President's
call. She was surprised to find the colonel wide awake. They had
spoken just a few hours earlier and she was exhausted. What could
possibly give the intriguing colonel so much energy, she asked
herself.

The slight breakthrough she thought she made with him the night
before no longer existed. Colonel Carroll was back to his formal

military self. He was anxious to continue their conversation but the activity around him and the operation's poor progress forbade it. Either it would happen some other time or not at all.

In just a few minutes, Bonnie told Carroll, Marlin Fitzwater would announce the President's schedule for the day. She asked him for four to six minutes around 3:00 PM, Washington time.

As the hour for the talk with his Commander-in-Chief drew near, the colonel displayed considerably less bravado than he had the night before. He was a nervous wreck and Bonnie loved it.

"Whenever you want me, why you just say so," he said, trying to draw on sapped confidence. She told him to stay in close touch. He would speak with several layers of White House bureaucracy before actually talking to "The Gipper." The first layer, the White House Communication Agency, was responsible for providing all the President's communication needs. The secretive office was manned by elite, highly-trained Army, Navy and Marine officers of the White House Signal Corps.

A Signal Corps officer asked the colonel whether the National Guard would need the phone line they were using. For every presidential call, the Signal Corps wanted to establish control over a line several hours in advance. The colonel checked with Mike Haller, his press officer, who jokingly offered his gracious assent to the Commander-in-Chief's use of it until lunch.

After "Signal" secured the line, Bonnie called back to verify information for a fact sheet the President would use during his conversation with the colonel. Bonnie asked Colonel Carroll what kinds of questions the President should ask him. It was important the President sound up to date since the press office would release an audio tape and transcript of the call.

At first the fuss over a simple phone call seemed absurd to Carroll. But respect soon took the place of amusement. He quickly learned that when it comes to the President's communications, no detail is too small. When he thought about the care the Signal Corps took, he found it reassuring. Besides, as long as the endless preparations gave him an excuse to talk to Bonnie, he had no objections. Bonnie asked the colonel about the principal characters in the rescue. She went through her list of people and organizations.

"What about the environmentalists?" she asked.

"It's Greenpeace," Carroll said.

When he didn't add any disparaging epithets, Bonnie sighed in audible relief. The last thing she wanted was to hear the colonel start shooting off his mouth against environmentalists just when the President was finally trying to act like one himself.

Bonnie had purposely not designed this phone call to appear overtly political. She didn't say anything directly. She just fervently prayed the colonel would not make her President look foolish. Bonnie had completed her advance work. She told Carroll that the next time they spoke would be after the President's call. Once the White House Signal Corps tapped into the phone line, they took control.

Colonel Carroll was in the cafeteria drinking coffee when the call came in from Washington. An ARCO secretary shouted his name.

"Colonel Carroll," she cried. "The White House is on the line!"

"I'll be right back, the President wants to have a word with me," the Colonel deadpanned to the nonplussed guardsman sitting next to him.

He picked up the receiver in his cubicle and said, "This is Colonel Tom Carroll speaking."

"This is White House Signal. Please hold for the President."

A few moments later, at 3:03 PM Washington time, an unmistakable voice came on the line.

"Colonel Carroll?"

For a brief second, the colonel froze. His heart stopped beating and his mouth turned cotton dry. Could it really be the Commander-in-Chief, the President of the United States, Ronald Reagan, that just asked for him by name?

"Yes, sir," said the colonel, now sitting ramrod straight in his chair.

"This is Ronald Reagan."

"It's a pleasure, sir."

"Well, I'm just calling to tell you how much I'm impressed by all that you are doing up there in this effort on the whales and to get an on-site report on the rescue effort."

"Very good, sir," the colonel responded. "There are a tremendous amount of people up here who appreciate the fact that you've taken time from your schedule to call."

The President politely asked Carroll to dispense with the obsequious supplications and get to the whales.

The colonel told the President about the bitter cold, but spared him the details of his problems with the barge. Carroll recited the names of everybody involved and their organizations, just as he had rehearsed with Bonnie.

Bonnie, listening in on a White House speaker phone, howled with laughter when the President deftly cut short the nervous, rambling colonel.

"Sir," the colonel continued, unmoved by the President's appeal for brevity. "I think this phone call will make a substantial difference in the morale of everyone involved. From the crews out there right now with the barge to the people working in Barrow. This is the kind of thing that makes it all worthwhile."

"Well," came the President's trademark utterance. "You can tell them all we're very proud of you and what you've done up there. And I'll let you get back to your rescue mission now. But just know that a great many people are praying for all of you."

Before he hung up, the President wished the colonel good luck.

But even Ronald Reagan's legendary luck wouldn't be enough to get the mired hoverbarge across 270 miles of frozen Arctic Ocean to Barrow.

Chapter 12

G'day, Australia

To journalists, the "story" of the three trapped whales showed more than just the miracle of modern telecommunications. It demonstrated just how powerful they had become. Never before had they propelled so many important people to act so quickly and decisively to affect an event of such marginal significance. In the hands of just a few people, a tiny hole in the middle of the Arctic Ocean was transformed into a place of global importance, at least for a few cold October weeks in 1988.

For the first time in the rapidly changing history of television news, a story of major international significance sprouted solely from the reaction of people removed from the scene. To people in Barrow it wasn't the whales that were newsworthy. It was the fact that Outsiders thought they were. The *real* news was how the helpless creatures became news.

The three stranded whales were transformed from Arctic routine to international headlines in three clearly defined stages. In the first stage, the whales were talked about among a few Barrow whalers anxious to harvest and sell them. Then biologists Geoff Carroll and

Craig George heard about them. They called the Coast Guard who told the *Anchorage Daily News*. Within 24 hours, the story became the "kicker" for Tom Brokaw's October 13, 1988, broadcast on the "NBC Nightly News." Six days after Roy Ahmaogak found them floundering in slushy arctic waters, the three whales were national news. Stage One.

The second stage lasted three days. From Thursday, October 13, through Sunday, October 16, the whales rose collectively through the half-hour network newscasts like an unheralded sprinter racing unexpectedly past all the favorites. In just 72 hours, the stranded whales went from "kickers" to "leads." It took that long only because the networks needed a few days to get their equipment and personnel to the top of the world. When they first appeared on network television, the whales ended newscasts. By Sunday night, October 13, 1988, they started them. Stage Two.

But it was Stage Three that eventually freed the whales. Once they led network newscasts, the world's attention gave the rescuers added impetus to draw on the superhuman effort and extravagant resources they would need to save the grays.

Early questions about how seriously the United States Government took Operation Breakout were answered when President Reagan made his October 18th phone call to Tom Carroll. The President's six-minute telephone chat with the Alaska National Guard Colonel convinced skeptics that America really had gone mad. Now, even the President of the United States was hypnotized by the plight of three marooned mammals on the North Slope of Alaska. With the imprimatur of a popular President, we could save our beloved whales in good conscience.

Soon, the American whale fever had spread round the world. The North Slope was going international. Foreign television crews began arriving in Barrow en masse, further crowding a town already about to burst its seams.

Shortly after news of the President's phone call ran on the wires, Ken Burslem answered a ringing phone in his Los Angeles office. Burslem was the Eastern Pacific Bureau Chief for Network Ten, one of Australia's three commercial television networks. His assignment editor in Melbourne wanted to know more about the whales. Burslem told him that the whales were fast becoming the biggest story in America. Bigger even than the presidential sweepstakes looming just three weeks away. He thought their plight would grip animal-loving Australians the same way it was mesmerizing the Americans. The Australian-based assignment editor gave Burslem the OK. Burslem booked himself and his crew on the next flight to Alaska. He wanted to be the first Australian to transmit pictures of the whales to the folks Down Under.

It took a few seconds for Burslem to recall what little he knew about the mystical frozen north. He confessed to his editors back home that his six years as Network Ten's U.S. correspondent did not begin to prepare him for an adventure on Alaska's North Slope. If Barrow seemed remote to a Yank, it was on the other side of Neptune to an Aussie.

Like most other globetrotting correspondents, Ken Burslem lived his life like a doctor on call. He kept two suitcases permanently packed for last minute story assignments. He kept one at his office and the other at home. When he got the call to Barrow, he figured his regular gear wouldn't be enough to keep him warm in the Arctic. It didn't take a genius to figure out it was cold in Barrow, but as an Australian journalist assigned to cover America from sunny Southern California, he was utterly unprepared for the bone-chilling experience that lay ahead. It would be one of the most unforgettable of his 25-year career.

He grabbed a lightweight ski parka in the mistaken belief that it would keep him warm during his short stay just 1,700 miles south of the North Pole. After all, he thought, how cold could it be? It was the second week of October. The temperature was in the mid-80's in Los Angeles, and back home the mild winter was stepping aside for another glorious Aussie spring.

The three-man crew from Network Ten boarded their flight at Los Angeles International Airport with the infectious smiles and pleasant demeanors native to mates from Down Under. When they stepped off the plane in Fairbanks, their jovial good humor was swept away in the subarctic wind. It was already minus 10° there. The coldest temperatures any of them had ever experienced. Burslem didn't know whether to panic or buy himself a case of beer.

They checked into their hotel on the banks of Chena River in downtown Fairbanks and called Melbourne to check for any new details. The news desk told him they were scheduled to do a "live cross" back to Australia in just over an hour. Burslem wished he'd opted for the case of beer. Instead, he panicked.

I'm glad I called," Burslem said. "Would have been a pretty boring live cross without me, huh?" he asked, laughing.

They gave him the number for KTVF, the local television station in Fairbanks. They were arranging live interviews between the anchors of Network Ten News in Melbourne and Sydney and the exhausted but still witty Burslem. Burslem called KTVF and asked for the person in charge of live crosses.

"Live what?" came the unsure response.

"Aw, hell," Burslem chided himself. He couldn't count how many times he had made that mistake. The rattled Aussie hardly needed reminding that Americans used the term "live shot" when referring to live satellite television interviews. How long had he been in America? he asked himself out loud.

"I'm so sorry, mate," he said to the confused man in the newsroom. "I mean the 'live shot' to Australia, do you know anything about it?" His eardrum nearly burst when the receiver at the other end of the line clattered to the floor.

"It's the Australian," screamed the excited KTVF employee. He asked Burslem where he was. When Burslem gave the man the name of his downtown motel, he was told to wait in the lobby and someone from the station would be there in five minutes to pick him up.

Burslem and his crew of three arrived at the KTVF studies dressed for a cool night at a Queensland "beach barbee." The folks at the station couldn't help but cackle. One of the men pulled Burslem aside and apologized for the laughter. Suppressing his own giggles, he told Burslem that if he went to Barrow dressed like that, he would die. Burslem stopped laughing himself when the man's friendly warning finally registered.

Burslem resolved to worry about the problem once the live interview was out of the way. Unlike American television, Australian television had few of the pretensions and none of the exaggerated self-importance so often associated with the American networks. Mistakes weren't ignored, they were often played up. Australian television reporters were allowed to show much more human emotion, particularly the light kind, than their American colleagues. For Ken Burslem, it would prove a good thing.

His instructions from Sydney were to stand outside in the frigid Alaska night so Australia's summer viewers could get a sense of how cold it really was. "Act cold," came the last word from Sydney. If there was one thing Burslem didn't need it was someone telling him to shiver while standing outside in minus 10° temperatures. What he didn't know, his flimsy red ski jacked would soon teach him.

The folks at KTVF were delighted to help this cheerful Aussie make television history. If it worked, it would be the most remote "live cross" ever broadcast in Australia, and the underdressed crew had not even reached Barrow. The Australians did not realize that Fairbanks, Alaska's second city, was a cosmopolitan mecca compared with the tiny Eskimo village. One of the studio cameras was rolled out the big back doors and onto the snow-covered parking lot to prepare for the outside shot.

Burslem stood between the camera and a large drift of plowed snow dwarfing him in the background. When someone from KTVF asked if that snowdrift was all right, Burslem howled loudly.

"Hell, we're Aussies," he said to the over attentive staff. "Most of those lucky bastards we'll be talking to don't even know what this stuff is. They're sure as hell are not going to know one heap of it from the next," he said, reassuring his nervous helpers.

If everything went off properly, the shot would work just like Oran Caudle's from Barrow. But instead of playing back pre-recorded tape, Burslem stood in front of a camera responding to live questions coming in over a phone line from Australia. The picture ran from the camera to a satellite dish in KTVF's parking lot. The dish would beam the video signal to the same satellite Oran used from Barrow, Aurora I, the geostationary orbiter parked 22,500 in space above Alaska. In Seattle, 3,000 miles to the south, the signal would be "looped" or relayed onto another satellite.

From there, the Network Ten crew in Los Angeles watched Burslem make his trademark funny faces on their test monitors. In Los Angeles, the signal was "looped" to its third satellite before being picked up simultaneously in Melbourne, Sydney and Canberra. In less than a second, the image of a Ken Burslem sticking out his frozen tongue started at the top of the world and traveled more than 125,000 miles before it ended up near the bottom of the world.

Moments before Burslem was scheduled to go live he pulled his favorite earpiece out of his pocket. It was the same one he took with him on all his stories. As he lifted it to his ear, the KTVF technician told him not to use it.

"Use one of ours," he said firmly. They were rubber and wouldn't freeze to his ear. His helpful protestations went unheeded.

Burslem thanked the man and told him not to worry. How could an earpiece freeze to my ear? he wondered. The interview would last only two or three minutes. The stations in Australia communicated with Burslem over a regular telephone line. He plugged one end of the earpiece into a phone and stuck the other in his ear. He couldn't watch it, but he listened to the program broadcast live in Australia like any viewer back home. When he heard the anchor announce his name and location, Burslem knew it was time to stop making the funny faces. He was on the air.

But as he got his cue, he felt a sharp sting in his left ear and tried inconspicuously to lift the hand not holding the microphone to fiddle with the sharp, unexplained pain. When he did, he was horrified. It wouldn't move. The man was right, the damned thing had frozen to his ear. Here was Ken Burslem, the American-based correspondent, reporting live in an historical broadcast to his native Australia with a tiny ear piece frozen to the side of his head. He just wanted it to end and when it did, he thanked God. Wrapping things up, he realized he couldn't quite remember what he had said.

But the people who saw it will remember it for a long time. Burslem knew something about his voice seemed funny, but he was too new to Alaska to realize what it was. He tried to coil one of his crews rubber cords only to find it stiff as uncooked pasta. When he reached his gloved hand to rub his itching chin, he could not feel a thing. The itch was nature's warning. His lower jaw was frozen. When he tried to speak his words came out slurred. Back home they thought he was drunk.

His producers thought so too. They did not make an issue because they just assumed their man got caught with his pants down. They knew he had just an hour warning before the live interview, not enough time to burn off the fire in his blood. If the same had happened to an American correspondent, warning or not, he would have been fired immediately. Luckily Ken Burslem was an Aussie. But in Barrow, Burslem's problem only got worse. As interest in the whales spread across Australia, Burslem was forced to stand outside Oran Caudle's frozen studio for longer and longer stretches in the middle of the bitter Arctic night. After just a few days in Barrow, Burslem actually found himself wishing he were back in Fairbanks. There it was warm; only 10° below zero.

By popular demand, Oran Caudle broadcast all the television transmissions from Barrow over the local cable channel. If the

Nielsen company had bothered to monitor the North Slope, Oran's ratings would have shot through the roof. Ken Burslem was an instant Arctic celebrity. Spontaneous crowds gathered around to watch their new hero do his nightly live broadcasts to Australia. As a joke, the Eskimos presented him a symbolic key to Barrow's new alcohol treatment center. Burslem loved it.

He swore to his producers that he was stone sober, but they didn't believe him. His slur was too real. Only a drunk could sound like that, they were convinced. "For Christ's sake," he exclaimed. "I wish there was liquor here to drink!"

It was impossible for Burslem's producers in balmy Australia to realize just how cold it was. With the wind chill the temperature difference between Barrow and Brisbane amounted to 140 degrees. When their own ratings started shooting through the roof, the Australian producers' dropped their concern. Their viewers couldn't get enough of Network Ten's man in Barrow. Soon, Ken Burslem was an Aussie legend. The whole nation tuned in each day to watch their heretofore temperate U.S. correspondent report live from outside the North Slope borough television studio in what looked to be a drunken stupor. Life played an ironic trick on Ken Burslem. He was one of the only reporters in Barrow who didn't drink.

It was a vicious circle for Burslem that ended only when the whales were free. The more drunk his frozen jaw made him sound, the more people Down Under clamored to see him. More and more stations across Australia tried to schedule their own live crosses with the jolly man at the top of the world. By the end of one of these long nights of chatter, Burslem could barely speak, almost unable to manage even the inebriated slur for which he had become so famous.

Not to be outdone, Ken Burslem's Australian rival, Network Nine, made their own quick tracks to Barrow. With Burslem's new found celebrity, Nine's mission was to stay close. They did an admirable job in the Australian whale sweepstakes. Their big coup came on one of the last nights of the saga when they put the staggering mayor of Barrow on live television. George Ahmaogak didn't need a frozen jaw to sound drunk, he was already. The folks Down Under fell instantly in love with their Inuit soulmate.

Chapter 13

The Arctic and the White House Joined by Love

The whales stranded 15,000 miles away became big news in Australia. While the American networks, caught up in their own self-importance, lost perspective of the relative insignificance of the story, the Australian reporters assigned to Barrow determined to let their viewers have fun. Measured against the scale of their own expectations, the Aussies came away clear winners. Ken Burslem would later win the Thorn Award, Australia's most prestigious television journalism award, for his distinguished reporting from the top of the world.

For those involved with the rescue, in the days immediately following the President's call there was little fun to be had. For National Guard Colonel Tom Carroll, the euphoria of the President's call wore off almost as soon as he put the phone down. He looked out his window and saw the sobering reality. He clung desperately to a plan whose problems grew more pronounced by the hour. Tuesday night, the second full day of the pull and the eleventh since the whales were first discovered, the barge that justified the rescue and was supposed to free the whales had become Operation Breakout's achilles heel. It was no closer to Barrow. Each time one problem seemed solved, another appeared.

The Sky Crane helicopters Colonel Carroll designated to transport the re-commissioned barge quickly showed their limits. The barge's massive tonnage combined with the brutal Arctic conditions proved more than the Sky Cranes could handle. After the helicopters finally ripped the barge free from its four-year frozen dry dock, its vast weight kept breaking through the newly formed shore ice. Each time a giant Praying Mantis pulled the barge out, it fell through the ice again after traveling only a few hundred yards. At this pace, it would have taken a week just to get out of the harbor.

By the night of Wednesday the 19th, 12 days after the whales were discovered, Tom Carroll's operation found itself in deep trouble. The barge was barely five miles from where it started. The rotors of the expensive helicopters were cracking under the strain, threatening the safety of their crews. As the rescuers in Barrow lost faith in the colonel's once proud operation, the press caught the scent of wounded prey.

Ron Morris's hidden delight at the colonel's sudden change in fortune was one of Barrow's worst kept secrets. Morris didn't mask his enmity. He was jealous the President called the colonel and not him. Morris constantly complained that Carroll never returned his phone calls. Morris wasn't alone in that criticism. By the middle of Operation Breakout's first week, some of the media thought the chastened colonel was dodging them. Now that his news was no longer so promising, Carroll was accused of trying to shield himself and his men from the questions of an increasingly anxious world.

By that Wednesday night, October 19, Tom Carroll was at the end of his rope. The press showed signs they were turning against him. ABC-TV producer Harry Chittick called him the "Keystone Colonel" for his inability to move the barge. A growing contingent of Eskimos tirelessly cut hole after hole while the barge lay listless just an hour's walk from its original berth. Why, if this wasn't a race, did the media make the colonel feel that he was losing?

He gathered his helicopter pilots to discuss plans for one last attempt to move the barge. If it didn't work, they would have to think of other options. If none were feasible, the colonel and his men would be forced to face the unfathomable prospect of returning to Anchorage in failure. The indignity of accepting his career's first operational defeat was bad enough. But being run out of his own state by carpetbagging media was more the hardened colonel could stand.

By Wednesday, October 19, the whales had been sloshing in the ice holes around Barrow for 12 days. The entire rescue mission, now five days old, was built around VECO's assurance that the hover-barge could easily make the trip from Prudhoe. Tom Carroll faced a crisis of his own confidence. His training told him to separate heart from mind. His job was to do, not to feel. But he couldn't help it. He felt plenty.

Colonel Carroll spent years carefully constructing sturdy walls of dispassion to protect his fragile heart. Now, a woman 7,000 miles away, a woman he had never even met before, was the force that unleashed his long pent up emotions. She was the only one he could turn to for comfort.

Bonnie and Tom talked constantly throughout Operation Break-out. In the first few days after the President's call, neither had yet mustered the courage to explore the other's marital status, but the game went on. The two grew remarkably close. After the disastrous Wednesday, the colonel and Bonnie spoke half a dozen times. The day's final call lasted four hours.

He didn't know why, but Carroll felt safe talking to Bonnie. Maybe it was because she was a National Guardsman herself, or because she worked for the President he so adored. Maybe she just evoked something that he suppressed far too long.

As much as Carroll was drawn to her, Bonnie was pulled even more toward him. But she had one critical advantage. For days, the colonel could only wonder what the woman he was quickly falling for looked like. Bonnie didn't have that problem. Every time she turned on a television, there he was. She saw a strikingly attractive, confident leader of men.

Wednesday night, Tom Carroll dropped his guard. He confessed that things weren't going well. He and his men just spent hours devising a last-ditch plan to get the barge on its way. While she needed to know the operation's progress so she could report to the

President, she found herself interested for Tom's sake. She desperately wanted the new plan to succeed, not so much for the whales, but for the colonel she knew only via the telephone.

Ever since they first tried freeing the barge, the National Guard rescue command used each of the helicopters to take turns pulling it across the ice-covered harbor. Carroll wondered what would happen if both helicopters pulled the barge at once. Would the effect of a double pull be twice as powerful? Would it be enough to get the barge out of its doldrums and on the way to Barrow?

Working with slide rules and pocket calculators, Carroll and his pilots stayed up until the early hours of Thursday, October 20, working through formulas and equations to determine whether the double pull was even a theoretical possibility. They put their mathematical skills to the test for hours until they finally got some answers. The helicopters would have to pull from a much lower altitude and with less than full power. The 800-foot tow lines had to be doubled in length. Too much pressure applied to either of the thick steel cables could send both helicopters spiraling to the ground in stereophonic explosions. If the colonel decided to try it, he would be the first. No one had ever attempted a double pull before. Regardless of the effect on the whales, Carroll figured the exercise would provide valuable lessons for more important missions in the future.

Carroll was worried about the media. He knew they had to be invited to cover the attempt, but he didn't want to make too much of the event because of the risk. If they sensed a hint of danger, they would be all over him, shaking the confidence of his men, increasing the chance of fulfilling their own naysaying prophecies. The kid gloves used to cover Ron Morris were thrown off in the media's treatment of Colonel Carroll. With Ron Morris off limits, Carroll was the only game the media could train their sights on.

At first light the next morning, the colonel and his men, putting up an optimistic front, walked out onto the Prudhoe Bay ice for one last try. The helicopters were gassed up and ready to go. The lengthened tow cables coupled their underbellies with the stagnant barge. Succeed or fail, military transport history was about to be made. The press pool circled overhead in a National Guard helicopter flown in from Barrow. Carroll double-checked that he could reach the pilots by radio. Before they took off, he gave them their final instructions.

"You're the pilots," he assured them. "It's your call. Any time you feel it's too dangerous, drop the cable and come on down."

His pilots knew the risks. They performed the calculations together the night before and reached the same conclusion. It was dangerous, but it just might work. The press hounded the colonel to do something. But if he wouldn't jeopardize the lives of his men for the sake of three stranded whales, he certainly wasn't about to do it for a press corps that had all but offered to make him their lynching party's guest of honor.

The choppers lifted off the ground at the same time and hovered a few hundred feet apart in front of the lopsided barge. The pilots went through their checklists and waited for the barge captain to signal that he was ready. When both helicopters and the barge were set, the Sky Cranes gradually eased forward in unison until the taut tow cables stopped them.

The helicopters increased power until, straining against the cables, the barge crept out of its last hole and started slowly sliding across the jumbled ice. The colonel and his men felt a brief flicker of hope. Maybe this would work. Their raised expectations were quickly dashed. No sooner had the barge started on its hopeful journey before it crashed back through the ice. It was the same old story, smooth sailing for 500 yards followed by another setback.

"It's no use," radioed pilot Gary Quarrells. "I'm begging off this one. It's just not going to work."

The colonel was disappointed but not surprised. In fact, he felt a certain relief. The heavy burden placed on his shoulders five days earlier was finally lifted. His men and the crews from VECO had done everything they could to move the barge. Nothing would work. The task was too daunting. General Schaeffer couldn't ask any more. No one could. He took risks, but limited them so that none of his men or equipment would be exposed to any unnecessary danger. Sure the media would point their fingers his way. But as the commanding officer, he was prepared to take the heat. He had no problem taking all the credit a few days earlier. Now the tables had turned.

When Ron Morris got word that the barge was a lost cause, he ordered Arnold Brower, Jr., and his Inuit crews to cut as many of their new holes as they could. It was too late to call off the rescue now. The whole world was watching. The whales had to be saved.

Cindy Lowry couldn't hold back her tears when she heard the

double pull had failed. She watched Bone grow weaker with each passing breath. The new holes were wide enough and long enough for the three whales, but for a reason no one understood, they would not use them.

By noon on Wednesday, October 19, Day Five of Operation Breakout, the Eskimos had cut a chain of 15 holes stretching a quarter mile toward the open water lead five miles away. The 30-foot-high pressure ridge separating the whales from the open water that meant freedom still loomed on the horizon. But for now, the rescuers concentrated on getting the whales moving in the right direction. They would worry about the pressure ridge when and if the whales ever got there.

The difference between the high-tech means used to move the barge and the low-tech means the Eskimos used to cut through the ice wasn't lost on Colonel Carroll. The barge was a failure while the chain-sawed holes seemed promising though still untested.

Cindy called Campbell Plowden at the Greenpeace office in Washington to discuss alternatives to the hoverbarge. Plowden was one of the foremost whale advocates in the world. Surely he would have a suggestion or two. At the beginning of the conversation Plowden apologized for the difficulty she had reaching him. Greenpeace had to hire eight temporary employees at the height of the Barrow rescue just to answer telephone calls from thousands of people around the world.

Plowden suggested Cindy get in touch with a person who had been calling the Greenpeace office for days with an unusual offer of help. He was a man named Jim Nollman and he called himself an "inter-species communicator." Nollman said he could coax the whales out of the original holes by playing back recordings of other whales with special underwater sound equipment.

Cindy had heard plenty about Jim Nollman and not much of it was good, but she figured she didn't have a choice. As far as she knew, Nollman was the only person in North America who had sound equipment capable of functioning in the Arctic. She accepted his offer of help and asked him to come to Barrow, promising to pay his expenses.

Thin-blooded to begin with, Cindy couldn't stay out on the ice for more than a few minutes before she started shivering uncontrollably. It took weeks for her teeth to stop aching from their relentless chattering. Her inadequate footwear held up so poorly she spent half her time lifting a leg off the bone-chilling ice and shaking it to circulate the blood in her numbed feet. Had she not refused to wear animal fur, most of Cindy's physical suffering could have been avoided. But the mental torment of abandoning a principle would have been worse.

She and Craig walked back to the meager warmth of a small portable hunting shack constructed at the tip of the sandbar to give the Barrow whale rescuers a respite from the inescapable cold of the windswept ice. The tiny hut stood like a beacon at the edge of North America, a hundred feet from where the continent slipped beneath the frozen Arctic Ocean.

When they pushed open the hut's flimsy door, Cindy and Craig were welcomed by several friendly Eskimos taking a break in the cramped but relatively warm quarters. They offered the two visitors styrofoam cups of piping hot coffee which they both gladly accepted. Cindy noticed the uncut chunks of Muktuk that the resting crew chewed on as high energy snacks. She wanted to ask them how they could eat whale meat at the same time they were working so hard to save the three whales stranded just a few hundred feet away.

For the Eskimos, the answer was simple. The creatures they were working so hard to save were not whales they depended on. The Inupiat Eskimos in Barrow ate Bowhead, not gray whales. It was their very dependence on the whale that led Malik, Arnold Jr. and now dozens of other Inuit volunteers to come out and help the troubled grays.

Inuit tradition revered the whales as the giver of life. Whales were not landed because Malik outsmarted them with his shrewd hunting skills. They gave themselves to him so that the Inupiat Eskimo people could live. The Eskimos now working to save the three Agvigluaq, or gray whales, were giving something back to the mighty creatures that for so long had given of themselves.

Before heading back to the ice, they asked Cindy if she wanted something to eat. In addition to whale meat, the shack was stocked with walrus, seal, even some polar bear meat. When she said she didn't eat meat, they offered her raw fish instead. After having stood out in the freezing cold all morning, she was so hungry that even that sounded tempting. As long as it wasn't meat, Cindy would gladly eat it.

"Here, dip it in some Eskimo butter," said the Inupiat worker who handed her a piece of frozen fish on a toothpick. She quickly plunked the fish into the yellow odorless liquid and popped into her mouth.

The instant her taste buds registered the unusually pungent flavor, she gagged and wretched uncontrollably. Cindy's unprepared palate was in violent revolt. When she regained control, she lamely looked up at the concerned workers and asked exactly what it was that stopped just short of making her vomit.

"Probably the butter," came one guess.

"What's wrong with butter?" Cindy asked to a chorus of laughs.

"You see," said one Eskimo, "it's not really butter."

"Well then, what the hell is it?" Cindy asked impatiently.

"It's seal oil," the man answered quietly. "We call it Eskimo butter."

That was all the explanation Cindy needed. She shuddered in disgust and walked back out into the cold.

In the 12 days since the three gray whales were first discovered, the scene on the ice changed dramatically. It was almost unrecognizable from the time Craig, Geoff and Billy Adams, their Inuit guide, first went to verify the reports that three whales were stranded off the end of the Point Barrow sandspit.

That cold October Tuesday, the three men saw three whales struggling aimlessly against the uncaring force of Arctic nature. The landscape was bleak and gray. There wasn't a soul within 10 miles of the six creatures. The three men never dreamed they could save the whales. The most they hoped to accomplish was to study them until they died. They had hoped to publish a study in a marine biology journal.

Now, the most distant edge of North America had become the center of the world. Heavy traffic travelled on the glassy smooth ice of the frozen lagoon whose western boundary was marked by the sandbar. A tiny corner of an endless, silent and motionless universe suddenly became an oasis of noise and activity. Speeding helicopters broke the hush by buzzing continuously over the increasingly crowded whale site. What started as three men visiting a like number of whales clinging to a lone hole, became hundreds of people surrounding dozens, and soon hundreds of freshly cut holes that would eventually stretch seven miles toward the western horizon.

Until the catastrophic oil spill of the *Exxon Valdez* six months later, the October whale rescue was the single biggest media event in the history of the state. The 150 journalists assigned to Barrow formed the largest press contingent ever to invade any part of Alaska for any reason. But of all the places in the Last Frontier, reporters chose to gather themselves and their expensive technology around a few tiny man made ice holes at the top of the world, the most remote edge of America's most remote state. At the rescue's height, there was one reporter for every 17 residents of Barrow.

Chapter 14

Barrow: Frostbite for the Big Time

Within a few days of the President's call to Colonel Tom Carroll, at least 26 broadcasting companies from four continents were transmitting their version of events from the overworked control room in Oran Caudle's studio. Less than a week earlier, the facility had never before been used to transmit. Its huge white satellite dishes stood as a powerful testament to money many Alaskans thought poorly spent.

Now Oran's facility transmitted footage of the whales almost 24 hours a day, to every corner of the globe. Suddenly, Barrow was the most glamorous byline in all the world. Vendors from across the state flew into Barrow to start hawking their wares. T-shirts of many different designs each proclaimed their own version of the same theme: "I'm saving the whales."

Pepe's Mexican restaurant had to open earlier in the morning and close later at night to accommodate the several hundred Outsiders with no place else to eat. Fran Tate, the owner, was no stranger to

174

national media exposure. She courted it at every opportunity. The mere fact that she owned a Mexican restaurant within striking distance of the North Pole landed her on the set of "The Tonight Show" with Johnny Carson and on the front page of the *Wall Street Journal* long before any reporters bothered to come to Barrow.

Fran Tate insisted the increased hours were for the convenience of the press, but the skeptical media suspected that she would stay open as long as she could to charge her customers what they considered outrageous prices.

Harry Chittick thought the fact that Pepe's successfuly charged $20 for their greasy version of a hamburger was a newsworthy as anything happening out on the ice. The ABC News producer wanted to get a sound "bite" from one of the out-of-town media while he was paying his oversized bill.

Chittick's cameraman readied himself right by the cashier. When CBS cameraman Pete Dunnegan paid his bill at the cash register, Chittick's videographer recorded Dunnegan turning to the camera, stuck a toothpick in his mouth and shrugged, "Twenty-one bucks for a cup of coffee, hmphhh," he said, scratching his head. "Must have been the extra sugar." That humorous bite closed that night's ABC's "World News Tonight" broadcast.

It was also the perfect close to Pepe's culinary career for Pete Dunnegan. Fran Tate was livid when she saw his quip on her TV. At dinnertime, she cut Dunnegan off at the door. In front of his colleagues, she told him never to set foot in her restaurant again. Dunnegan happily obliged. He was the envy of the press corps. The rest of us had no choice but to suffer Pepe's gastrointestinal consequences.

The more Barrow and the three whales made news in the United States, the more interest foreign broadcasters showed in reporting the story themselves. In the two days following the President's call to Colonel Carroll, British, Australian, and Canadian television crews arrived in Barrow, adding further bait to the fever-pitched frenzy at the top of the world.

But most intrigued by the whale story were the Japanese. By the time the rescue reached its crescendo, three of the four national networks had crews in Barrow. They marveled at America's latest bizarre obsession. They were less interested in Bone and its skinless nose than they were in people like Cindy Lowry, who cared so much about the tasty creatures. They wanted to explore what it was about three whales that could so completely unite almost everyone in a nation as huge and diverse as the United States.

Takao Sumii, the President of NTV, the oldest of Japan's four major television networks phoned my NY News Corp. offices that evening following the President's call. It was Wednesday, October 19, Day 12 for the stuck whales, and Day 5 for Operation Breakout. He tried to explain what it was about the American media his network sought to cover.

I may have been a journalist, but before I got to Barrow, I was also a viewer. I had the same emotions about the whales as almost everyone else. To me, from New Jersey, it sure seemed like the story from Barrow was about whales, not about the media. Only after I arrived in Barrow did I begin to understand that the whales were but one element in a fantastic tale.

On the MarkAir flight from Anchorage to Barrow, Masu Kawamura, the NTV correspondent, told me my job was to report on the media's coverage of the event, to give the Japanese viewer a sense the rescue's absurdity. I had to ask him what was so absurd about Eskimos working to save three trapped whales.

Like millions of other Americans, I wanted the whales saved. Not knowing any of the background or complexities that led up to the rescue, I was as mesmerized by the whales as anyone. It was that widespread attachment and fondness for the endangered animal that created the story in the first place. I watched anxiously as the whales slipped closer toward what looked to be an inevitable, pathetic death. Knowing nothing about the Arctic and its conditions, I cursed that damned colonel who the networks said was the one who couldn't get the barge to Barrow. I was exactly what the Japanese assigned me to analyze.

In Japan, whale meat was an age-old delicacy. The Japanese wondered what it was about the tasty mammals that seemed to so strongly touch the hearts of Westerners. They deeply resented the international pressure that forced them to pretend to have ceased commercial whaling. Far from stopping their slaughter of the great creatures, the Japanese just put a new, benign name on it and went right on whaling.

The 1986 International Whaling Commission convention banned all commercial whaling for five years. As signatories to the agreement, the Japanese faced a growing battery of economic sanctions if they didn't comply. The Japanese proposed a compromise. Norway, Iceland, Japan, and the Soviet Union would agree to give up commercial whaling if they could continue to hunt whales for "scientific purposes." Fearing no accord at all, other IWC members quickly agreed.

Before the ink had even dried on the new agreement, the demand for whales within the Japanese scientific community skyrocketed. Suddenly, Japanese "scientists" discovered they needed 1,100 "samples." But no one knew what it was these "scientists" wanted to "study." Nearly the same number of mammals the ostensibly defunct whaling industry killed the year before were now being slaughtered for scientific purposes. Japanese scientists bought whale carcasses from domestic sources as well as Norwegian and Icelandic whalers. When the scientists completed their "research," they sold the preserved carcasses back to the whalers who then re-sold the meat to Japanese consumers.

Now the whole world was coming to the aid of three whales. To the Japanese, they were nothing more than cows stuck in the mud. If the Americans were really serious about reducing the trade deficit, why not just sell the whales to Japan? To Japan, it was like spending millions of dollars to save livestock that were meant to be harvested and eaten in the first place.

We were met at the airport by Rod Benson, the man who housed us as well as reporters from the *Philadelphia Inquirer* and the *Chicago Tribune*. With our bags still in the snow-filled bed of his natural gas-powered Chevy pickup, the three of us joined Benson for an unexpected trip straight to the whales. We were several miles out to sea before I even realized we were on the ice, following lots of fresh tire tracks that seemed to lead all the way to the North Pole.

We met Geoff and Craig, who were busy calming Cindy after an unexplained altercation with Jim Nollman, the inter-species communicator. What I didn't know at the time was that Cindy was arguing with Nollman about his insistence on playing South African guitar music instead of the whale sounds he promised her from Seattle.

After traveling from New York, Toronto and Tokyo, the first thing any of us saw at the top of the world was a strange smiling man sitting in a canvas director's chair at the edge of an ice hole in the middle of the frozen Arctic Ocean. He was singing a strange chant he said was destined for the whales that were nowhere to be seen, deep underwater. Trying to escape his rhapsody, I started thinking maybe Masu Kawamura, our Tokyo correspondent, was right. Things certainly did seem absurd.

Then, standing on the edge of the ice hole, I was struck with an unexplained, striking pain. First in my left eye, and then, seconds later, in my right. It felt like a sharp object was cutting through my closed eyes. I knew it must have something to do with my contact lenses but I couldn't get at them. My eyelids were frozen shut. In the instant it takes to blink, the tiny droplets of condensation at the edge of my lashes froze my eyelids together, closing my eyes. My contact lenses had frozen to my eyeballs, my eyelids were stuck together and I hadn't been out on the ice for five minutes.

Sensing my disorientation and near panicked appeals for help, an Eskimo walked over and guided me to the relative warmth of a waiting car. A few minutes later, my eyes defrosted. I wore my glasses for the rest of the trip.

Rod Benson dropped us off at the Top of the World Hotel so we could check in with our NBC associates. They were NTV's American network partner. I introduced myself to NBC producer Jerry Hansen. With a wink and smile he assured me our trip to Barrow would be a memorable one. Delighted to get it off his hands, he playfully tossed me the keys to a battered old Chevy Suburban NBC rented earlier in the week. "It's all yours," he said with obvious relief.

No matter how bad it might have been, I said to myself, it certainly seemed more inviting than spending several hours a day hanging onto the back of a speeding dog sled in wind chill temperatures dipping to minus 150°.

Jerry gave me the standard instructions. "Never turn it off, and fill it up every night." There was only one gas station within a 100,000 square mile area. I made sure to remember where it was. What Jerry neglected to tell me was never to put the automatic transmission in the "park" position. On only our third day in Barrow, the truck's frozen transmission died halfway between town and the whales. Only after we collectively cursed the damned garage that charged us $200 a day for a truck that didn't work did we realize that the Chevy broke down because no one taught us how to operate it.

Left in "park," transmission fluid doesn't warm up with the rest of the car. Throwing the truck into gear with all the lubricants frozen destroyed our vehicle in less than 50 driven miles.

With a watchful eye out for polar bears, we removed our gear from the truck and lamely hitchhiked back to town. I reported the truck abandoned and passed by it for the next ten days on the way to and from the whales, wondering whether it would ever be claimed or just join the hundreds of other abandoned vehicles and garbage that clutter the sides of Barrow's few roads and alleyways.

By Thursday, October 20, Oran Caudle's studio was on the verge of a meltdown. The night before, despite the chaos that threatened to engulf him, Oran Caudle managed to pull off a live broadcast of the ABC News late night program, "Nightline."

Never before had "Nightline" broadcast from a more remote location. In New York, Ted Koppel wondered whether it was worth the risk to go live to Barrow. Only after Harry Chittick, the ABC producer on the scene, assured New York that they could pull it off did Koppel and his staff agree to give it a try.

Dressed in parkas and sweatshirts, Ron Morris and Arnold Brower, Jr., sat in aluminum folding chairs in the sparse setting of Oran Caudle's studio. The backdrop was cluttered with empty equipment boxes. The picture captured by the studio's one camera looked like it was shot by a 10th grader at a wealthy suburban high school somewhere in the Lower 48. Brower and Morris answered Ted Koppel's questions about the whales that were piped in over a conventional phone line from New York. Like millions of others, Koppel wanted to find out what it was about these three whales that turned whale hunters like Arnold Brower, Jr., into tireless whale savers.

When Arnold's answers fell short of what Koppel was looking for, Morris jumped to the aid of his Inuit colleague.

"They responded like any other community would," Morris said. "This is a humane effort. They were chagrined and felt sorry for these critters. It was the same kind of outpouring I see when other animals are trapped in Alaska." Brower breathed an audible sigh of relief.

ABC News correspondent, naturalist, and resident whale expert Roger Caras guaranteed Ted Koppel and his millions of viewers that the whales would never survive their ordeal.

"I hate to be a wet blanket," Caras said from the comfort of the

ABC Manhattan studio, "...they are exhausted, they are stressed and they've got a gamut to run. There will be polar bears on the lookout for any animal that's stressed or weak. Southeast Alaska, then British Columbia has many pods of killer whales, and the way these whales will be pumping with their flukes, will be very slow and will be detected as vibrations in the water by the killer whales who will close in. Then along the coast of Oregon, they'll pick up the white sharks. Then, if they have any energy left at all after running this gamut of teeth, they've got to move all the way down to central Mexico. All without eating.

"I don't think they will ever get to Mexico. They'll be lost from sight once they've cleared the ice and no one will ever know what happened to them. As much as I hate to say it, I don't think they are going to get there."

The once underused facility was now a madhouse. More than 20 domestic and international networks and local television stations, jostled, argued and threatened each other and a frazzled Oran Caudle for access to his studio and its transmission equipment. Oran didn't know where to turn. It got so bad that by midweek, reporters just barged into the studio and without pause abruptly threw Oran out of his own office. His adulation of the network "big boys" quickly turned to scorn. They were turning his fantasy into a nightmare. They were rude, drunk and had egos too huge to measure.

One night, a technician from one of the other Japanese networks scheduled a feed to Tokyo but never bothered to tell Oran. When the technician's time was approaching, he waltzed into the control room and, ignoring the crew using the room, turned on all his switches. But when he reached to adjust the audio level, he cranked it up so high that he blew out the fuses on the sound board. Fortunately, it was one of the last feeds of the day and the only one left to transmit was Ken Burslem, the cheerful Australian. Had the wayward technician fouled up an American network's transmission, they would have erected Barrow's first lamp post from which to hang him. Oran was up all night repairing the damage and getting ready for the next day's madness. The technician never apologized.

The producers from the three networks came to Oran and suggested he give them control of his studio until the story was over. They knew what they were doing, they assured him. Among them, the three producers had been in the business for more than 75 years. At what should have been the moment of his greatest professional triumph, Oran Caudle was being eased out of his own job.

Oran asked ABC's Harry Chittick why he and Jerry Hansen were so concerned about a meltdown. Chittick explained to Caudle that like any major story from a remote or foreign location, their number one worry was access to the satellite. In the news business, Chittick explained, competitors have two objectives. The first is dramatic footage and sound bites. The second is to deny the same to their competitors.

On stories in the Lower 48, it is hard to deny the competition the ability to cover a story, not like in a place like Barrow. As Oran knew, Aurora I was the only satellite that could "see" a signal from Barrow, and Oran's studio was the only facility that could access it in that remote part of the world.

A single broadcaster could easily gain a monopoly on the story by buying all the available time segments on Aurora I, a technique known as "bird-jamming." If one company could book all the time for itself, no one else could use the satellite. The Bird Jammer would face a pleasant dilemma. He could shut out all his competitors and keep the story for himself, making it an exclusive, or he could make a killing by selling segments of the time back to his competitors at enormous markup.

A "meltdown" was the last thing Caudle wanted. He checked with Alascom, the company that owned the Aurora I satellite, to see if anyone was trying to jam the bird. They told him that the unprecedented last-minute orders for time segments on Aurora I enabled Alascom to raise its prices past the point where even the networks could afford to corner the market. Adam Smith's invisible hand was so powerful it could even stretch to the heavens.

The American networks ended up with most of the time. After all, it was their story. Lucky foreign broadcasters like NTV and BBC had international affiliation agreements with American networks. Their footage was transmitted at times when their U.S. partners had excess inventory. The others scrambled for a few extra minutes here and there and paid exorbitantly for the privilege.

Caudle was not just frustrated, he was bitter. After all, it was his video that launched the story in the first place, and now he was being discarded like yesterday's garbage. Worse still, he heard rumors that some of the Outside media were making fun of him and the frontier town he came to help settle.

Suddenly, Oran had an unglossed look at the inner workings of network news. By comparison, the North Slope Borough Television Studio did not seem so bad after all. What struck Caudle were the endless arguments. ABC's Harry Chittick yelling at NBC's Don Oliver, the Japanese yelling at each other, and everybody yelling at CBS.

For two straight weeks, Caudle and his assistants worked from 4:00 AM until well past midnight. The day began with live shots for the American morning news programs. A steady stream of correspondents and camera crews pushed through his studio's revolving door for the next 20 hours. Finally, and fittingly, each day would end with the media's one true, unadulterated pleasure: Ken Burslem and his post-midnight "live cross" antics to Australia.

Caudle and his North Slope Television Studio staff were reduced to walking corpses. His apple juice and granola breakfasts were replaced by coffee, coffee and more coffee. Colonel Carroll would have been proud. Out on the ice, coffee was served by the barrelful. Cutting new holes while keeping the existing ones open was now a round the clock effort. The initial few hundred dollars authorized by North Slope budget director Dan Fauske to feed a half-dozen Eskimos grew at the same exponential rate as the rescue itself.

By the middle of Operation Breakout's first week, Fauske's costs had already ran into tens of thousands of dollars. It was turning into one of the coldest Octobers in Alaskan history. Temperatures were already reaching minus 40°. Just a few months later, in January 1989, North America would record its coldest-ever reading of 82° below zero just a few hundred miles south of Barrow. It was so cold, dozens more Barrowans were needed to keep the holes open.

With the mayor out of town and of touch, Fauske knew it was his call. Like never before, and almost certainly never again, the eyes of the world were on his tiny hamlet. Fauske knew that if the whales died, and he hadn't done all he could on his town's behalf, the world might blame him. The conservative Fauske was faced with the risk of his life.

He knew that if there was anyone who could save those whales it was Arnold Brower, Jr., and the Eskimos of Barrow. Brower knew it too. Just as soon as Fauske gave Arnold the OK for new expenses, Brower was back asking for more. He got it every time.

Except during whaling season, more than 70 percent of Barrow's workforce was unemployed. To help alleviate one of the modern era's most chronic by-products, Barrow created a local employment service called the Mayor's Jobs Program in the mid 1980s. To Fauske, helping the whales seemed like the perfect chance to put both the under-used program and Barrow's unemployed people to work. Brower posted a sign on the job board in the main hallway of the borough government building. Hundreds of out of work Barrowans, some more sober than others and a surprising number of whites, stood in line for a chance to earn $21 an hour cutting holes out on the ice. It would cost the borough more than $100,000.

The small rescue Cindy Lowry organized just five days earlier was now a massive, professional operation. It employed hundreds of highly paid laborers from the Mayor's Jobs Program, VECO, ARCO and the National Guard. But for all the added reinforcements, the whales wouldn't swim beyond their original hole. Ron Morris needed help. He summoned two top whale biologists from the National Marine Mammals Laboratory in Seattle. Maybe they knew a way to lure the whales away from the icy death that awaited them in the first hole.

That first hole was now one of many in a sea of ice stretching out to the open lead. But it was the only hole the whales would trust. They couldn't bring themselves to leave it. During the day, they could surely see the light from dozens of other new holes cut in front of them. No one, not even Malik, could figure out why the whales would not move. He thought that if they let the first hole freeze over, the whales would have no choice but to swim into the new ones. Cindy said it was just too risky. Malik wasn't convinced enough to argue.

The longer the whales lingered around their first hold, the less strong Bone became. The baby whale was so weak, Cindy wondered how long it could hold on. What would happen, she thought, if the other whales moved? Would Bone have the strength to move with them?

Watching Bone suffer tested Cindy to her core. But she found a reserve of strength that defied even her own explanations. Everyone on the ice admired Cindy's compassion. She was Operation Breakout's caring, selfless mother. She gave birth to it. If the whales belonged to anyone, they belonged to her, Ron Morris' "government document" notwithstanding.

Although she had no official role in the operation, she was the single most important force on the ice. She was beyond question and above reproach. No one, not even Ron Morris, dared take any action without first winning Cindy's consent.

People watched with fascination as Cindy stroked each of the tired whales with her soft, caring hands. But with Bone, it was special. Because it was the most vulnerable and least likely to survive, Cindy grew particularly close to it, and to everyone's amazement, Bone grew equally close to her. The baby whale seemed to respond to her encouragements. Remarkably, Bone always surfaced near Cindy no matter where she stood around the hole, like an infant instinctively able to locate its mother. Somehow the baby seemed to know that the tiny maternal presence on top of the ice was the key to its redemption.

But as close as the two appeared to grow, Bone drifted farther from the grasp of life. As it slipped away from Cindy's motherly hand, her once buoyant spirit sank with it. Nothing seemed to work, not the barge, not the President's phone call, not the new Eskimo holes, and certainly not the inter-species communicator. While the other two whales looked weak and unresponsive, the baby was down right listless.

Cindy and Ron were losing hope. By the night of Wednesday the 19th, 12 days after they were first discovered, the whales seemed doomed. No matter how precise their hole cutting technique had become, it seemed that as soon as the Eskimos could open up a new one, it would start to freeze over. Drifting snow blown by 30 mile an hour winds quickly turned the open holes to slush, threatening to entomb the whales before morning.

Chapter 15

Minneapolis Comes to the Rescue

Just as hope faded, help was on its way. After flying all night, Greg Ferrian and Rick Skluzacek, the Minnesotans bearing de-icers, finally arrived in Barrow. Throughout the trip from Minneapolis, Greg never told the truth to his brother-in-law Rick or Jason Davis from Eyewitness News. He did not inform them that Ron Morris refused to authorize the use of their de-icers. Greg told Rick that everything was set for their arrival at the top of the world.

When he first heard about it, KSTP's Jason Davis thought the idea of following two local boys trying to save three whales up near the North Pole sounded like a great adventure. But the instant he deplaned, Davis' enthusiasm evaporated. They were nearly blown over by a 30 mile an hour wind that made January in Minnesota seem balmy. Rick's first hint that things weren't going quite as smoothly as predicted came when Greg admitted the two had nowhere to stay. A minor detail, Ferrian promised.

They called the Top of the World Hotel from the airport. "Booked up," said the curt receptionist before cutting him off. It was the same story at the Airport Inn. Greg stood in line waiting to ask the Eskimo woman behind the MarkAir ticket counter if she knew of a place they could stay. He noticed a large cardboard sign written in magic marker and hung by a string at the head of the line.

"ALL RAW WHALE, SEAL, WALRUS and POLAR BEAR MEAT MUST BE STORED IN LEAK PROOF PACKAGES FOR SHIPMENT ON MARKAIR." When he turned around to point out the odd sign, Rick was already focusing his pocket camera to take his own shot.

When Greg reached the head of the line, he asked the overworked agent if she knew of any accommodations. He tried to joke that the trip from Minneapolis was a bit too arduous for a commute. Nonplussed by his poor attempt at humor, the agent suggested he call the Naval Arctic Research Laboratory (NARL) north of town.

"North of town?" asked a surprised Greg Ferrian. "I thought this was as far north as you can get."

"NARL is as far north as you can get," came the response. They loaded their six de-icers into the back of an Isuzu I-Mark taxi and climbed aboard for the five mile ride out to the northern tip of their native continent. When the driver told them the fare for the short ride was $50, they realized they had not only reached the edge of their continent but the edge of their means.

They arrived at NARL just in time to claim two of the last guest rooms in the remarkably tidy facility. The sterile smell of a hospital hung heavily in the air. In case either of them was burned with chemicals or acids while conducting one of their Arctic experiments, there was a red emergency shower nozzle in the hallway outside their room.

From the television report he had been watching before leaving Minneapolis, Greg immediately recognized the North Slope biologists Geoff Carroll and Craig George as they dragged their weary feet and aching bodies into their office across the hall. Ebulliently, he introduced himself to the exhausted duo, who had returned to their office to escape the whales, if only for a few minutes. Greg asked for just a moment of their time to explain the de-icers they had brought all the way from Minnesota at their own expense.

"These machines can keep your ice holes open," Greg assured Geoff, "That's our business."

Geoff thought it was worth trying the machines but he dreaded the idea of yet another sleepless night on the bitterly cold ice worrying about polar bears mauling him. He knew though that the whales needed help. The remarkable string of luck that had brought the whales this far seemed at an end. The dropping temperatures only deepened the whales' dire straits.

Craig told Greg and Rick they had to find Ron Morris. The biologists promised help, but they had to get away from Morris first, if only for a few hours. The coordinator had turned the whole rescue into a media circus and he was its ringmaster. For their own sanity, they needed a break.

Geoff told the two Minnesotans that the best way to catch Morris would be to wait for him at the Search and Rescue hangar. Craig drove them to the hangar at the end of the runway and introduced them to Randy Crosby. They waited two and a half hours before Morris landed in one of Crosby's helicopters.

With a slight wave of his hand, Morris tried to brush off Greg's insistent appeals. "All I'm asking is that you let us tell you about our machines." Greg pleaded. "You have to at least give us that much. After all, we just spent thousands of our own dollars to try and help."

"Alright," Morris relented, "I'll give you a minute and a half to explain them." He listened to Rick's short but plaintive explanation while carefully examining his fingernails in a conspicuous attempt to show his uninterest. Standing up to walk out of Crosby's office, Morris doubted the de-icers would work. Even if they did, he added, he thought they would make too much noise.

Rick pleaded with Morris to at least let them try the de-icers. After all, the Coast Guard successfully used them to keep open a 50 square yard hole in the middle of a frozen Lake Superior. Unimpressed, Morris told them to go back to NARL to await his decision. He said he would call them with a definitive answer.

Rick and Greg returned to their tiny room now cluttered with ice melting machines, and waited for Morris to call. After more than two anxious hours, they could wait no longer. Rick had to know whether his trip was a total waste of time and money and exactly how to kill his brother-in-law who dragged him into it. Around 6:30 that evening, they called Morris at the Airport Inn. His wife told them he could not be disturbed. He was preparing for his "Nightline" appearance.

A minute later, there was a commotion in the hallway. When Rick peered out the door to investigate, he saw Geoff and Craig frantically knocking on every closed door in the building. Craig spotted Rick and cried, "There you are. We've been looking all over for you."

The biologists just returned from the ice. Conditions were rapidly deteriorating. The holes were freezing back over. "The whales are losing it," Geoff told them. "I don't think they're going to make it through the night."

"Fuck Morris," Craig barked when Rick muttered something about waiting for the coordinator's call. "We've got to get those things on the ice."

They loaded two of the de-icers into the ice and snow covered bed of Craig's pick-up truck. They drove back to Search and Rescue to try and find a portable electric generator to power the de-icers. Randy Crosby told them the heavy crosswinds made the already risky proposition of flying at night too dangerous. As they waited for conditions to improve, Rick and Greg passed out sales brochures to the dozen or so nightshift journalists waiting for any news to report. Among those handed a brochure was Geoff and Craig's boss, Dr. Tom Albert, the director of the North Slope Borough Wildlife Management Office.

After his appearance on "Nightline," Ron Morris returned to the hangar. It was 10:00 PM, Wednesday, October 19, and Tom Albert was waiting for him. He angrily shoved the brochure in Morris' startled face. "Either we harvest those whales or you give these guys a chance." Albert stormed off before Morris could answer.

At around 11:00 PM, Randy finally found a portable Honda generator in the back of his hangar. After he replaced the spark plugs and cleaned the carburetor, the small Japanese generator smoothly purred to life. It was loaded, along with the de-icer, onto a SAR helicopter and flown off into the pitch black Arctic night. Hovering above the black void, Randy searched for the lone light of the hunting shed erected on the edge of the sandspit. When he was directly over it, he switched on his landing lights to look for a safe place to set his chopper down.

Cindy and Arnold Jr. had just about given up hope. That night was the worst weather yet. They were thinking about heading back to town for some sleep. All that kept them alone with the whales on this minus 40° night was their unspoken fear that the next time they returned, the holes, like the whales that depended on them, would have vanished without a trace beneath firmly frozen ice and windblown snow.

The arrival of the Minnesota brothers-in-law brought Cindy and Arnold back from the edge of despair. They expectantly gathered around the small silver and red generator while Randy tried to start it. But it was so cold, its components had frozen solid during the 12 minute flight from the hangar.

Craig suggested they try again with his own portable generator. That would require another trip back to town. As they all flew back to the hangar, Cindy knew they were leaving the vulnerable whales to their fate, if only for an hour. She wondered if they would survive. She wanted to stay out on the ice with them, but Arnold Brower, Jr., wouldn't let her. There were polar bears everywhere. If she stayed alone, the whales would have a better chance of surviving than she would.

Greg was exhausted. He pushed his tired body as far as it would go. He had to get some sleep. It was after midnight and he hadn't slept since before leaving Minneapolis 36 hours earlier. Since Rick was the expert on the de-icers, Greg was free to fall comatose on his cot at NARL. Rick stood shivering aimlessly in the dark Arctic night as Craig rummaged through his cluttered tool shed for the generator. How could he have lost it, he asked himself. He used it just a week earlier on his hunting trip with Geoff. When he found the generator, it started on the first pull. Treating it just like his truck, he left its engine running for the ride back to the SAR hangar where Randy and Cindy were waiting.

Randy thought the idea of flying his helicopter with a gas powered combustion motor running inside the cabin suicidal.

Crosby prayed that the FAA never found out what he was about to do.

Not only was flying a helicopter with a flammable engine running incredibly dangerous, it would also be incredibly cold. It was minus 60° just a few hundred feet off the ground and the on-board heater barely worked with all the windows shut. But with a running engine emitting deadly carbon monoxide fumes, they would have to fly with the windows *open* .

The trip out was the worst experience anyone of them could ever remember. Randy's arms were so numb from the cold, he could barely fly his aircraft. His left eye froze shut. Cindy broke down in tears that instantly froze to her stinging red cheeks. Rick wished he were dead, and Craig tried to take his mind off the excruciating cold by concentrating on a tune he was trying to hum.

Finally, the chopper touched down. Randy lowered his head onto the frozen vinyl dashboard, relieved that his dangerous mission was over. Craig and Geoff cradled the still purring generator like a fragile infant as he walked it out to the slush covered first hole.

Like panting dogs, the panicked whales were surfacing every few seconds. Craig figured the whales had reached the end. At any minute, the mammals could drown. Rick frantically plugged the power cord into the end of one of the compact de-icers and dropped it into the corner of the rapidly freezing hole. After bobbing up and down a few times, the buoyed device bounced into position. It was ready to be turned on. At the flick of a switch, it started to work. The slightly warmer water pulled up from a few feet below the waterline bubbled up at the surface. Instantly, the slush and ice around the buoy began to melt. The de-icers worked.

In its first ten minutes, the de-icers melted the slush and ice in half of the first hole. Almost as quickly, the whales started to calm down. Cindy, Randy, Craig and Greg were exuberant. Finally, they found a way to help the whales.

In his euphoria, Rick discovered a renewed source of energy that propelled him onward to the next hole. He set up his second de-icer and dropped it in the hole. Within seconds, it too worked. Soon, the next hole was ice free. Drunk with delirium, four lone souls danced on the surface of a frozen sea in the bitter cold black of an Arctic night.

They knew not to trust everything they felt and saw. Their exhausted consciousnesses crossed into a new realm. They stammered in disbelief. The next sight their eyes beheld was more than their weary minds could compute. The whales were in the second hole. Just a few minutes after it cleared of ice, the whales gave the first sign that they were interested in being rescued. The whales had moved.

The next move was man's.

Chapter 16

Saving Whales the Old Fashioned Way

Colonel Tom Carroll was frazzled. He tapped the sharpened tip of his pencil on the formica conference table provided for him by ARCO, his Prudhoe Bay hosts. His glazed eyes peered aimlessly through the frosted glass window and out to sea. In front of him lay a field of dirty styrofoam coffee cups that had accumulated since his National Guard unit hastily set up shot there five days earlier. All his mind could focus on was the prostrate, abandoned barge which lay listless on the ice.

The operation to save the three whales proved to be the strangest mission of his life. Called from his Anchorage home on a Saturday afternoon, Colonel Carroll was initially put in charge of a logistical aspect of a burgeoning whale rescue. His commanding officer, General John Schaeffer, assigned him a single straightforward task. General Schaeffer ordered him to move a 185 ton hoverbarge from its frozen dry dock at Prudhoe Bay to Barrow, 270 miles across of the ice covered surface of the Arctic Ocean.

Just 72 hours after arriving in the Arctic netherworld, Tom Carroll was briefing the President of the United States. If that wasn't enough, he was also falling in love with one of the President's assistants whom he had never seen. But just as the colonel's star began to rise, it fell back to earth with the force of a falling meteor. The colonel was back on the ground facing the bitter reality of Arctic logistics. His 15 minutes of fame were drawing to a close, at least for now.

By the night of Thursday, October 20, Day Five of Operation Breakout and Day 13 for the stranded whales, Colonel Tom Carroll found little comfort in the thought that his mission seemed a failure. He told his men they performed their duties with honor and distinction. They were assigned a difficult task with no more than an even chance of success. Despite mounting press recriminations, the colonel told his men they could hold their heads high.

Just as the colonel's emotional cycle entered the acceptance stage and his natural healing process began, General Schaeffer called and asked him what he was planning to do for an encore. Carroll thought Schaeffer was poking fun at him. After all, he thought, any more performances like the one he just directed and the entire Alaska National Guard might be the next endangered species.

General Schaeffer told Colonel Carroll if it were not for the National Guard, the whales would have long since perished. Carroll had much to be proud of. The general insisted that the Guard's participation and the colonel's command would continue as long as the rescue did. The Guard had invested too much time and money to back out now. If they did, the general said, the press would interpret it as a sign of weakness, a blow from which the Guard might not quickly recover.

It would also send the wrong signal to the rescue itself. If the Guard, with all its resources, gave up on the three whales, how would that play with the chainsaw-wielding Eskimos?

Schaeffer ordered Carroll to devise alternate plans to assist in the whale rescue. If no further logistics were available in Prudhoe, he wanted Colonel Carroll to redeploy most of his men and equipment to Barrow. That was where the action was. There was plenty the Guard could do there. Randy Crosby and his Barrow Search and Rescue helicopters were overworked. The Guard could help SAR run helicopter press tours of the whale site, and if necessary, they could coordinate press access to the rescue. Tom Carroll was back in business, though on a smaller scale. But as far as the press knew, he had never missed a beat.

Just a few hours earlier, the whales recorded their first hint of progress since the rescue began. At last they started to explore the new holes the Eskimos had cut for them on Wednesday. The Minnesota de-icers couldn't possibly have arrived at a more dramatic moment. They saved the whales when they were literally on their last breaths. Wednesday night's brittle cold completely sealed nearly every hole except the two kept open by the de-icers.

The colonel thought quietly for a moment about ways to help. His brief experience with the barge taught him many valuable lessons. Chief among them was the difficulty of performing even the Arctic's simplest jobs. Unlocking the barge from its four-year frozen berth was a feat in itself. Herculean efforts were required just to move it, some of which had never been tried before. While creative ingenuity was the only option available to many Arctic expeditions, the colonel detailed post mortem determined that an operation so fraught with unconquered obstacles could not depend entirely upon improvised solutions.

Carroll decided that Arctic innovations were better left to the innovators. If the National Guard was going to play a role of any significance in the whale rescue, the colonel resolved, it could only be done through tested, proven means.

Carroll called Ben Odom, the head of ARCO Alaska, and the rescue's chief financier. The two men had been in daily contact ever since the colonel and his unit arrived at Odom's expansive North Slope facility five days earlier. The barge disaster didn't change Odom's mind. He wanted those whales freed and his checkbook would stay open until they were.

Ben Odom's enthusiasm for the project was shared by nearly everyone at Atlantic Richfield. From the executive dining room to the canteens, the rescue was the chief topic of conversation throughout the ARCO Alaska tower. It united the company's 25,000 employees like almost no other event Ben Odom could remember in his 35 years with the company.

The $500,000 ARCO spent on Operation Breakout was one of the best investments it ever made. A $20 million public relations campaign couldn't have bought a tenth the goodwill ARCO earned helping free the three trapped whales. It seemed to be perfect timing. ARCO cashed in at a critical juncture in the history of the slumping Alaskan oil industry. No oil company in Alaska ever received more favorable press coverage than ARCO did during its two week investment in Operation Breakout. Usually the rich whipping boy of the environmentalists, ARCO now worked side by side with Cindy Lowry and Greenpeace. In the game of P.R. Pac-Man, ARCO swallowed any hint of criticism by pouring tremendous resources into a rescue destined to save three animals endangered by nature, not man's insatiable craving for fossil fuels.

Of course, ARCO's work on behalf of the three whales stranded in Barrow did nothing to clean up its share of the more than 11,000 acres of North Slope Arctic tundra the Environmental Protection Agency said were ruined by oil drilling. Nor did it change the industry's stance on exploratory drilling along the sensitive Arctic coastline.

Standard Oil Company was one of ARCO's chief competitors and a partner in the gigantic consortium of oil companies working the North Slope fields. Standard Oil wanted to share in ARCO's good fortune and it hastily donated three chainsaws to the rescue. The attempt quickly backfired. When Standard distributed press releases documenting their involvement in the rescue, the media immediately asked why they spent more money announcing their contribution than the combined worth of the three chainsaws they loaned to Arnold Brower.

Odom couldn't have been more encouraging to the colonel and his National Guard guests. The barge setback notwithstanding, the longer the rescue went on, the more ARCO could benefit from the goodwill generated by their efforts. Besides, Ben Odom wanted the whales freed for the same reasons everyone else did. They were innocent victims whose plight couldn't help but stir human compassion. He told Carroll that he and ARCO were at his service. Whatever the colonel wanted or needed, Odom would do his best to provide.

Carroll contacted Ron Morris in Barrow to find out what options, if any, the NOAA coordinator was considering. The colonel informed him the Guard had the mandate to help in whatever manner Morris saw appropriate. Morris told Carroll that he and Cindy had called upon experts at NOAA and Greenpeace to draw up a comprehensive list describing every plausible technique for breaking the ice or moving the whales.

Cindy Lowry was amazed by the extensive research her colleague, Compbell Plowden, had conducted from the besieged Greenpeace headquarters in Washington. Between asking and being asked questions of and by nearly everyone professing to be an ice or whale expert, Plowden had been on the phone for four days straight. He sent nightly faxes to Cindy in Barrow outlining what he had learned that day. She reviewed and edited the reports before passing them on to Morris.

The most promising alternative to the abandoned barge seemed to be "portable" water jet pumps. Originally designed to dislodge minerals imbedded in granite, they proved more than capable of blasting through thick Arctic ice deposits. The powerful pumps shot water pressurized at 35,000 pounds per square inch. Manufacturers assured Plowden they could blast through an eight foot wall of solid ice. But there were no pumps to be found in Alaska. Private contractors only brought them up to the North Slope on a per job basis. Like the Boeing Vertol helicopters Bill Allen wanted to use to tow the barge, the independent water jet operators fled the slim pickings of the North Slope in search of more promising pastures.

Every other option had too many drawbacks. Phosphorus burning powders were ruled out because of the potential destruction to other marine life, including free-swimming whales, that were in the area. The steel and glass cutting Particle Steam Erosion Laser was too heavy to transport from the Lower 48, and the mini icebreaker owned by the Amoco Oil company was busy protecting a drill ship in the Arctic Ocean 200 miles north of Prudhoe.

Earlier in the week when the barge was still expected, Cindy heard a rumor there was an icebreaker docked in Prudhoe Bay. The owners of the ship, the Arctic Challenger, turned down Plowden's request for help. It would be suicide, they argued, for their small ship to fight the Arctic ice so late in the year. The last time they tried to sail from Prudhoe to Barrow the voyage took three weeks, the ship was severely damaged, and that was in September. Luckily, no lives were lost. But this year the ice was even thicker and the owners were not about to risk their ship again for the sake of three whales. Plowden couldn't blame them.

About the only idea that seemed even remotely feasible, if

comparatively lame, came from the suddenly resurrected Tom Carroll. After hearing about the Eskimos cutting manual ice holes, Carroll asked Marvin King, VECO's top man in Prudhoe, if he knew of any readily available device that might cut holes even faster.

"Well, there's that ARCO ice bullet," he said in a tone lacking confidence.

"The *what* bullet?" asked Carroll, his curiosity piqued. King gently rubbed his tired ruddy face, sat down and let out an audible sigh. Their efforts to free the barge could have killed him and his men. It was the most difficult task any of them had ever performed.

Remembering all the frostbite, singed lungs, painful coughs, and frozen eyelids, the last thing King wanted was to get out there and start all over again with another one of the gung-ho colonel's crazy ideas.

Known by several other names, the "bullet" had one simple function. "Smasher," "ice crusher," "ice bomb," each described late 20th-century Arctic technology at its simplest. The five-ton concrete spike emblazoned with the light blue ARCO corporate logo looked like a giant toy spin-top. The bullet dangled on a steel cable beneath a helicopter. It was winched 100 feet up in the air and, in a reaffirmation of the laws of gravity, dropped to smash through the ice below. Sophisticated? No. Effective? Always.

The colonel wanted to know more about the bullet, but there wasn't much more King could tell him other than ARCO owned it and lent it regularly to VECO. Based on his incomplete understanding of ice conditions in Barrow, it didn't take much for Carroll to determine that the force of a five-ton shaft of concrete dropped from 100 feet would obliterate whatever lay beneath it. Colonel Carroll wanted to test it. Late Thursday evening, he called Bill Allen at his Anchorage home to see if he could smooth the way to getting ARCO's permission to use the bullet.

Ever since he touched the whales with his own bare hands five days earlier, Bill Allen was a changed man. His employees at VECO noticed it the morning after his trip to Barrow. He was more at ease, more attentive. Before his encounter with the giant whales, Allen could not fathom an animal as large and as graceful as the one he gently petted at the top of the world.

Unlike ARCO, his colleague Ben Odom's company, VECO had almost no contact with the general public. It sold its products within the oil industry. Except during a 1984 political scandal that rocked the state legislature, hardly anyone outside the "industry" had ever even heard of VECO. Its role in saving the whales would mean nothing to VECO's image while adding only red ink to its bottom line. Bill Allen contributed his company's time, energy and money for one reason. He wanted to save the whales.

Allen's secretary, Pearl Crouse, flung open the door to her boss's office, on Wednesday, October 19, sporting a bright grandmotherly smile. As she ushered in a bundle-laden postman, Crouse nearly burst with pride in the boss she adored. The mailman was carrying a canvas mailbag stuffed full of handwritten letters for the VECO chairman.

Hundreds of children from schools across the United States and Canada drafted letters to Bill Allen with salutations like "Dear Mr. Oilman," and "Dear Whalesaver." Many of the letters had no address, just "Whale Rescuers, Alaska." Within 72 hours of Operation Breakout's birth, the letters had found their way to VECO's Anchorage headquarters on Fairbanks Street.

Reading the heartwarmingly scribbled notes, Allen's mood turned jubilant. Carroll could not have picked a better time to ask him for his help in getting the bullet. In his ebullience, Allen would likely have agreed to almost any suggestion. The entire operation started when he authorized the use of the hoverbarge. But in the time it took for the barge to be rendered impotent, Operation Breakout had taken on a full-fledged life of its own, no longer dependent on any one man. Allen knew there was no stopping the rescue's momentum. Realizing it would proceed with or without him, he was determined to see it through, helping in any way he could.

The colonel had one more solo act to perform. If the bullet passed its test in Prudhoe, the National Guard would start punching its own path of holes out to the open lead, picking up where the Eskimos left off. Carroll briefed his Sky Crane pilots about the new plan. They were to test the concrete block to see if it worked. Waiting near the silent Sky Cranes for the test to begin, Chief Warrant Officer Gary Quarrells and his crew stared across the burnt orange horizon, mouths agape as they watched what looked like an extra-terrestrial vehicle with six-foot-wide treads slowly crunching its way across the barren landscape.

Arctic men called the odd truck carrying the heavy concrete

bullet a "Rollagon." The oil industry spent millions of dollars to design a machine that could carry heavy loads in the Arctic without damaging the sensitive environment. Since the wide treads dispersed the truck's massive weight over a broader surface area, it could cross fragile tundra and ocean ice without breaking through.

The bullet was attached to a recoilable high tension cable and hung from the middle of the Sky Crane's slender fuselage. Unlike the strain of towing the barge, this test was virtually risk-free. The high powered helicopter would have no trouble lifting the block and dropping it into the ice below. For once during their North Slope assignment, the pilots had it easy. No late night mathematical computations, no two way radios, no pep talks. Either the block would break the ice or it wouldn't.

Sitting next to his co-pilot, Gary Quarrells powered up the Sky Crane, locked in the bullet and prepared to head out to an open area of ice in the middle of Prudhoe Bay. At the last second, Colonel Carroll hopped on board for the ride. The pilots lowered the aircraft to just 100 feet above the surface of the ice. When it was properly positioned, Quarrells firmly gripped the joystick, anticipating the sudden upward thrust when the bullet was released. With a nod from Quarrells, the co-pilot released the winch holding the bullet in the chopper's cargo bay.

Like bomber pilots on a sortie, they pressed their helmets against the side windows for a better view. They peered down to see the effect of their non-explosive concrete bomb. They looked for the identifying buoy which was supposed to float in the newly opened water. When they spotted the bright orange buoy, it was bobbing up and down among the shattered shards of ice. The bullet worked. It broke clean through the two-foot-thick harbor ice. If the bullet could penetrate through that, it could easily smash the ice half as thick off the tip of Point Barrow.

Jabbing vigorously into the air, Colonel Carroll landed a loud congratulatory smack on Gary Quarrell's flight helmet. The co-pilot pushed the recoil button to raise the bullet back to its resting place under the fuselage. Maybe he wasn't dead weight after all, thought Carroll. Maybe his latest idea would help the Barrow rescue in its quest to free the whales. When they returned to base, Carroll called Morris and Bill Allen to tell them the bullet was on the way.

On Friday morning, the Sky Cranes were outfitted for the 270 mile flight to Barrow. The National Guard asked Randy Crosby and his Search and Rescue team to help them look for a local place to set up shop. There was only one place that could accommodate the National Guard and Randy Crosby's hangar was it. Not having much choice, Crosby reluctantly offered to house the Guardsmen and their workaholic colonel in his own facility. He sent one of his workers to restock the hangar with plenty of coffee.

Carroll and his men arrived in Barrow on Friday morning, October 21, exactly two weeks after the whales were first discovered and six days after making his first exploratory trip. Somehow, the whales had survived. Despite unimaginable stress, the whales managed to outmaneuver their own seemingly sealed fate for a fortnight.

With the exception of the still weak baby whale Bone, the mammals seemed as fit as at any time during their 350-hour ordeal. The middle-sized whale had been given the name Poutu, an Inupiat word roughly describing the icy hole it was trapped in. Poutu was breathing normally once again, its pneumonia overcome. The whale biologists Ron Morris summoned from the National Marine Mammal Laboratory in Seattle arrived to pronounce the animals in remarkably good condition.

Of all the problems they faced, food was never one of them. Several of the reporters, including me, asked why the whales weren't being fed during their confinement. The biologists told us that they wouldn't have eaten anyway. Like all other California grays, these three came to Alaska to take advantage of the rich deposits of amphopods that line hundreds of thousands of square miles of the Arctic Ocean's shallow seabed. They just finished spending the last five months fattening themselves up. Each put on several tons of extra blubber during the summer. Once they left on their 4,500 mile journey from the frozen Arctic to balmy Mexico, the whales wouldn't eat again until they returned in the spring.

Craig and Geoff were convinced that a marine miracle kept the whales alive in their tiny hole for two long weeks. The whales managed to balance their survival against a formidable assortment of obstacles. Each of the 5,000 breaths each whale had taken required a tricky maneuver against strong ocean currents through a small opening in the ice while fighting exhaustion and mental fatigue.

Malik didn't think it was a miracle. He knew it was the whales incomprehensible inner strength that compelled them to survive. If their Bowhead whale cousins could sustain his people for so many thousands of years, Malik knew the three grays could surely find a way to save themselves. Cindy didn't know what it was that pushed the whales onward in the face of certain death, but she thanked God for it.

During the two weeks of Operation Breakout, the Top of the World lobby was transformed from a modest hotel lounge into an international marketplace whose item of commerce was information about the whales and the effort to rescue them. The hotel was more than just the broadcast and print nucleus for media trying to cover the story. It also became Barrow's social hub. Self-proclaimed experts on just about everything from the Arctic to the whales purveyed their various theories to hordes of anxious newsmen clambering for any unreported angle. Here, rescuer and reporter commingled and cohabitated.

The smell of stale scotch cut through the smoke-filled air. Reporters and technicians clutched their overused and underwashed glasses. When glasses broke, the more determined connoisseurs had to make do with styrofoam cups, a tradition NBC producer Jerry Hansen started that was soon mimicked by others.

Climbing the sharp-edged iron steps of the world's northernmost hotel was an ascent into a rarefied atmosphere in American journalism. Nowhere else could the coordinator of a United States Government rescue constantly be seen drinking liquor in front of a passive, mesmerized press corps.

Affected by the numbing cold and the lengthening darkness, the mood in the lobby of the Top of the World changed noticeably on the morning of Thursday, October 20. News of the de-icers' success spread. Reporters hustled to phone in the report to their bureaus. Hours earlier, before going to sleep, their final prognosis could not have been worse. The bitter weather and howling winds threatened to entomb the whales before daybreak. A few reports predicted that the last person to leave the whales would be the last one to see them alive.

Ironically, there were no television cameras on the ice with Randy,

Cindy, Craig and the Minnesotan Rick Skluzacek to record the whales first move toward freedom. An unprecedented international obsession born out of the ability to capture the whales every move on film and video missed the first and only time when something specifically significant happened.

Not every reporter missed Wednesday night's miracle on ice. There were two lucky ones. As they arrived in Barrow on the same flight as Greg and Rick, *People* Magazine's Maria Wilhelm and Taro Yamasaki knew they were far behind in their effort to cover the rescue. Most other reporters arrived in Barrow days earlier. Maria figured they already knew where everything and who everyone was. Boarding the plane in Anchorage, she realized she desperately needed an edge to get back in the race. That edge was sitting right across the aisle in the form of two collapsed Minnesotans.

Aside from the Jason Davis' Eyewitness News team that wouldn't arrive in Barrow until a day later, Maria Wilhelm was the only reporter who could report Greg Ferrian and Rick Skluzacek's story. Maria was ecstatic. Someone answered her prayers. Just hours after stepping off their MarkAir flight, Taro and Maria had the only pictures of the de-icers thawing the hole and the whales moving into the new hole.

As if to make up for the previous night's blunder, reporters lined up early Thursday morning to get their first shots of the whales since they moved into the new hole. Each morning found ABC's Harry Chittick the first network man able to pull himself out of an irresistible Arctic slumber. 4:30 AM came early enough in the Lower 48, but after a day in the strength-sapping cold of the Arctic it was more than most people could bear. Throughout their millennia, the Eskimos always thought of themselves as hibernators. The only respite from the endless frigid night of winter was long deep sleep. In sleep, a body unprepared to function in the Arctic could slow its rapid-fire metabolism to a more normal rate.

Like the Eskimos themselves, reporters were overcome by the same indescribable exhaustion. No amount of sleep seemed enough. Traditionally light sleepers fell into unwakable comas. The lobby of the Top of the World was replete with people claiming they were sober falling asleep fully clothed, not to stir until 15 or 16 hours later. After eight hours on the ice with the whales, it was all I could do to stay awake past 9:00 PM.

Not everyone responded in the same way. Our cameraman, Steve Mongeau, stayed up drinking and laughing until all hours with our host Rod Benson, who markedly diverged from his brother Ed's puritanical temperance. After just a few hours of sleep, Mongeau was the first one to get up. Not only that, he worked harder and longer than anyone in Barrow. I slept at least 12 dreamless hours a night and still felt deprived.

But inexplicably, the mononucleosis which limited me to more than a few hours of daily activity back in New Jersey, vanished the moment my feet first touched tundra. Upon my return to the Lower 48, doctors were baffled. They had almost no history of such a case. Few of their patients sought refuge from chronic illness at the North Pole. Unable to proffer a better explanation, all they could surmise was that, unlikely as it sounded, the cold might have killed the virus. The lack of a logical explanation did little to temper the delight with which I cherished my restored health.

To the marvel of his colleagues, Harry Chittick managed to be not only awake but coherent for his 5:00 AM network conference call. The Vietnam vet and National Guard member claimed his secret came tumbling out of an $8 box of cereal he bought at Barrow's only supermarket. The dark Arctic stillness was broken only by the clattering radiator and the rhythmic crunching of Chittick's chewing. Pouring a measured portion from his $7 gallon of milk, he gazed wonderously at the surreal jagged ice mounds of the Chukchi Sea. They reminded him of the unforgettable images transmitted from the surface of Mars during the mission of the Viking space probe, stunning photos zapped across the 40-million-mile void of space. He marveled at the sea's curious and enduring luminance. There was no moon to light up the blackest of nights, yet the sculpted surface of the sea was limited only by the bounds of Chittick's imagination.

Comfortably wrapped in a tattered Army-issue green wool blanket, Chittick calmly waited for his phone to ring. Intermittently wiping drops of milk from his gray-flecked beard, he savored the solitude of the still, pre-morning Arctic. When he phone did ring, it would signal the beginning of yet another frantic, brutal day on the ice.

At first his superiors in New York tried talking him out of going to Barrow. It would look bad, they argued, for him to run off to the top of the world in an obvious attempt to play catch up with NBC, which broke the story. They soon changed their minds. Even though it took ABC 72 hours to transmit its first self-shot story from Barrow, they felt fortunate that Chittick was there to cover what had mushroomed into one of the biggest media events of the decade.

The indefatigable Chittick told his superiors that he ran into an exhausted but elated Cindy Lowry just a few hours earlier.

"The de-icers worked, the whales moved into the next hole!" she cried.

During his five days in Barrow, he had never seen Cindy so ebullient. He had watched her growing despair as she stood by helplessly as the whales' conditions rapidly deteriorated. He had seen no hint of the euphoric emotion she now displayed. Unable to imagine the agony of a single hour on the bone chilling ice, still less an entire day, ABC News executives could not understand why Chittick and his crew missed the whales' first big move.

Chittick tried to explain that, except for a lone light stationed to ward off curious Polar Bears, the whale site was pitch black. Besides, he could hardly order his videographers to drop their $100,000 cameras under water to film the whales swimming to the new hole. For that moment to be perfectly timed, the whales would have had to stick their heads out into the cold air long enough and speak English well enough to announce their impending move.

The misconceptions Chittick had to overcome were mild compared with the tales of other pressmen. British photographer Charles Lawrence, shooting for London's *Daily Telegraph*, was so hastily dispatched to Barrow he didn't have time to obtain American money. The first in a series of costly misjudgments the Briton made concerned his assumption that since Barrow was in the United States, its few commercial establishments would accept credit cards. When he wasn't dangling perilously from the back of a speeding dogsled hired by a more fortunate crew nice enough to let him hang on, he was screaming at his editors back in London to wire him the money he needed so he could properly cover the story.

His predicament grew worse when he discovered that no way existed to wire any kind of money to the tiny Eskimo hamlet. The nearest modern bank was in Fairbanks, 700 miles away. After enduring the humiliation of begging for cash, he eventually persuaded his office to authorize a paltry $500 wire transfer to

Fairbanks. Even if Lawrence could figure out how to get his hands on the money, $500 would barely last him two days in Barrow. He was livid, but desperate.

Lawrence spent most of his first few days in Barrow frantically trying to get the money tantalizing him from Fairbanks. Dozens of calls later, Lawrence found a courier willing to deliver the small sum to Barrow. After he paid the courier, the cash was half gone.

Moreover, the frustrated photographer had to put up with the incessant stream of absurd instructions he received from his desk in London. With no money, woefully inadequate clothing and nearly frost-bitten appendages, Lawrence was lambasted whenever one of his well-financed competitors managed to get a picture he didn't.

"Whatever you do," came the order from his superiors in the former capital of the English-speaking world, "make sure you get great pictures of the whales as they escape." Up to now, his English civility had enabled him to maintain a modicum of composure. But that was it.

"Ah, bloody hell. You've got to be joking," he shouted incredulously in his thick cockney accent. "Do you think the whales are actually going to flap their flukes and wave goodbye as they swim away?" he asked, unable to contain his fury.

Lawrence was so enraged at the request he stopped people passing by the wall phone at the Naval Arctic Researcch Laboratory. "Excuse me," he implored of a perfect stranger. Loud enough for London to hear, Lawrence asked of the passerby, "Can you believe this? These idiots want me to get pictures of the whales as they escape. I'm too upset to tell them. Can you please try and explain to them that we are talking about whales, not a trio of happy campers who wave goodbye at the end of their summer holidays?"

London got the message and backed off. Their man resented being overworked, underpaid and totally unappreciated. What he didn't get from London he more than got from those he entertained with his uproarious tales.

In analyzing our coverage, none of the estimated 150 reporters who flocked to the top of the world would have argued with one universal observation. No war, revolution or political campaign that any of us had ever observed proved more demanding or exhilarating than the story of the Barrow whale rescue. To some, like Charles Lawrence, it was a sign from heaven telling them to explore other lines of work. To others, like Harry Chittick and yours truly, it was the story of a lifetime, television journalism at its apex. There was no room for the usual hangers-on to interfere with coverage. We enjoyed unlimited access to all the key players in the drama without the retinue of press aides that attended most government operations.

After the whales made their first tentative move toward freedom, the rescue took on a new urgency. The whales had given new hope to an anxious world. An instinctive death wish was no longer a valid explanation for their poorly understood behavior. They had demonstrated the will to live and proved that they could and would work with their rescuers. Now that the whales were cooperating, there really was no turning back.

Chapter 17

Polar Bears Threaten to Steal the Show

Operation Breakout's command looked inward to the one group who had kept the whales alive since they were first discovered: the Eskimos. On Wednesday night, October 19, Arnold Brower's holes finally started to pay off. At the Thursday morning meeting with Ron Morris and Cindy, Brower offered to try to cut breathing holes clear out to the pressure ridge five or six miles away. In the meantime, village elders thoroughly versed in the ways of their native habitat would search for a way through it.

At Brower's suggestion, Morris tersely ordered Dan Fauske, Barrow's budget director, to authorize Eskimo search teams to target by land and air weak spots in the massive ice wall. Fauske was not accustomed to being treated like a supplicant. Morris' request sparked his ire. Who did this guy think he was? Fauske wondered. Only after Arnold Brower interceded, saying it was his idea, did Fauske relent. Eskimo hunters directed their helicopter pilots to promising routes through the ice ridge where they marked potential pathways by dropping plastic bags filled with red Kool Aid crystals. The red markings stood out clearly against the universal white backdrop.

The ways of the Inupiat Eskimos were alien to Morris. He did little to hide his feelings of superiority. Not surprisingly, his relationship with Brower and the Eskimos quickly unraveled. Not without reason, he felt the Eskimos and their supporters were anxious to show him up. In an effort to shore up support for his leadership, Morris hired two of his own ice experts to help him out.

As a coordinator from NOAA, he was in a position to tap the resources of the American government like few others. NOAA ran the National Weather Service, which employed many of the world's leading hydrometerologists, specialists on ocean ice. He called Gary Hufford, perhaps the foremost ice expert in the world. Morris ordered him and his associate, Bob Lewellen, to come immediately to Darrow. But much to Morris' chagrin, Hufford was the first to admit that, despite all his professional training and international reputation, Arnold Brower, Jr., knew far more about the local native ice conditions than he did.

Brower's promise to cut holes all the way to the pressure ridge pitted the intrepid Eskimos against the one force that even they could not master: the encroaching darkness. Resting near the top of the planet, Barrow experienced the most dramatic variances of daylight of any permanent human settlement on the globe. Between August 2 and November 17, Barrow goes from 84 days of total daylight to 67 days of total darkness. The four months in between are a headlong race toward endless night. In this four month period, Barrow loses up to 20 minutes of light every day. In the first five days of Operation Breakout alone, rescuers lost more than an hour of useable daylight.

The increased darkness brought not only Arctic depression, but rapidly plummeting temperatures. Thanks to the Minnesota de-icers, the Eskimos didn't have to worry about keeping the existing holes from freezing. Instead, they could concentrate on cutting new ones. The small pumps the press started calling "Arctic Jacuzzis" did that job for them.

By 9:00 AM Wednesday, Greg Ferrian and Rick Skluzacek were back on the ice. They were too busy to notice that every television and still camera north of the Arctic Circle was pointed right at them.

At that stage, they were still only heroes in the making. Because New York time is four hours ahead of Alaska, news of the late-night miracle on ice came too late for the network morning shows. But word of the Minnesotans' triumph dominated Thursday afternoon's satellite transmissions. By night time, their lionization was complete. Rick Skluzacek and Greg Ferrian were instant, if short-lived, American heroes.

Remarkably, the same Peter Jennings broadcast that propelled Skluzacek and Ferrian to Barrow caught the attention of another Samaritan businessman. This one manufactured chainsaw components in Portland, Oregon. Dudley Hollis of Omark Industries saw the Eskimos struggling to cut holes in the ice. He knew he had a product that could help. Less impetuous than the in-laws from Minneapolis, Dudley Hollis, a former logger from Australia, carefully assessed whether his product could actually help the Eskimos. His company made and sold chain for power saws to manufacturers around the world. At first Hollis wanted to send a 100 foot reel of extra chain. Hollis thought the Eskimos might need it to replace their chains when they snapped under the immense strain of sawing thick ice.

Just when they were about to send the reel of chain to Barrow, Hollis remembered the 11 Husqvarna chainsaws in Omark's test laboratory. He called Dan Fauske at the North Slope Borough to see if he wanted them. "How much is this going to cost?" asked Fauske warily.

His ears pricked up and his eyes opened wide when Hollis told him Omark would donate them. "Well, then," said Fauske jovially, "get your ass on up here."

Hollis' first day on the ice was almost his last. He fitted the adaptable saw with extra long blades enabling the operator to more easily cut through the ice. He explained the safety procedures as clearly as he could. But just in case, he snapped on a pair of thick steel mesh safety trousers.

Sure enough, the first Eskimo to fire up a Husqvarna carelessly spun around without looking, whacking Hollis' leg with the saw. If it weren't for the safety trousers, the chain, spinning at 50 miles an hour, would have sawed his leg right off, leaving him to bleed to death on the ice. For the rest of the day, even in this godforsaken place, Hollis couldn't believe how happy two legs could make a person.

That same morning, Harry Chittick convinced Randy Crosby of North Slope Search and Rescue to take an ABC camera crew on a polar bear hunt. After all, Chittick thought, when you covered any kind of a story from the Arctic, you had to show polar bears. All Crosby had done for the past five days was fly press missions to and from the whale site. As long as he wasn't needed for medical evacuations, he didn't object. In fact, he loved it. It was the most exciting thing he had ever done. Crosby relished the opportunity to take Chittick, a fellow pilot, on an aerial tour of his adopted Arctic home.

Crosby knew where to look for the bears he and his Eskimo neighbors called "Nanooks." He told Chittick that at 12 feet tall, they would be almost impossible to miss. Several Eskimos on hunting expeditions near the whale site saw bears only a thousand yards from all the human activity.

Polar bears are among the most fearless creatures on earth. They hadn't yet bothered the whales or their rescuers simply because they didn't want to. If they weren't frightened by Barrow, where they are regularly spotted roaming the streets, they would not be concerned about a few buzzing chainsaws and ski machines far out on the ice, the bears' home turf.

Chittick was surprised to learn that the polar bear was not a land animal. Since it lived primarily on ice and ate from the sea, it was classified as a marine mammal, just like the trapped whales. The bears only ventured onto land when migrating caribou were visible from the ice pack or when no food could be found in their normal habitat.

Polar bears were an endangered species protected by the federal government. While non-natives faced strict penalties including long jail sentences if they were convicted of killing a polar bear, Eskimos were allowed a limited hunt under Alaskan subsistence laws. The five or six times each year when an Eskimo was lucky enough to shoot a polar bear occasioned an elaborate local feast. Just as when a whale was killed, the news was broadcast on KBRW, Barrow's only radio station.

Oddly, the announcement on the radio made clear that only native Inupiat Eskimos were invited to take part. Non-Eskimos—even spouses, children and parents—were not permitted to attend. As the number of pure-blooded Eskimos declined throughout the 20th century, the feasts were shared among a shrinking and aging group of Arctic natives. Some feasts were even rumored to have hosted whites. However, those rumors could not be confirmed.

The hunter who killed the Nanook would host a traditional feast where the tasty meat would serve as thanks for his reprieve from great danger. Unlike the whale, the Nanook was greatly feared. Where the sight of a whale meant life, the appearance of a polar bear, naturally enough, presaged danger. Anyone who conquered the danger offered to share a portion of his deliverance with every native member of his community.

Sliding open the huge hangar bays, Randy Crosby hooked the tow tractor to the front end of the new Bell Long Ranger 214 whirlybird. According to Crosby's own regulations, one helicopter always had to be ready for an emergency. Since it was just over an hour before the first scheduled media flight out to the whales, they had less than that time in the air to spot a bear.

Crosby lifted off the Search and Rescue helipad dimly outlined by faint yellow lines obscured by the windswept snow. He swung the aircraft to the southeast and out to sea five miles due west of Barrow. The pressure ridge that Morris and the Eskimos were looking to cleave was the natural home to one of the world's most ferocious and endangered beasts.

As Crosby flew overhead hoping to find bears, Arnold Brower and his Eskimo scouts were down below armed with high-powered rifles to protect them from the animal they feared more than all others, the master of the Arctic.

In the most dangerous areas, the Eskimos walked back to back, guns drawn with arms and elbows locked as they scouted the towering ice walls of the pressure ridge looking for a place to cut a path for the whales. They hoped to avoid a confrontation with one of the huge and remarkably agile giants, but if they could not, they were ready to win it.

Crosby flew northeasterly toward the whale site from the open water side of the pressure ridge. He kept the helicopter less than 100 feet from the surface of the gray-black depths of the ice cold water. He told Chittick and his cameraman to keep their eyes intently focused out the right side of the aircraft. Polar bears liked to hunt along the edge of the ice pack where they could easily slip in and out of the food-rich sea.

Just as Crosby was about to lift his Lone Ranger to a higher altitude to head for another spot where he had seen polar bears, a mass of white fur leapt out from behind a slab of ice and bounded angrily toward the helicopter. Crosby swept the aircraft sharply around at a hard angle and dropped to just ten feet off the water to let the ABC cameraman get the best possible shot of the bear.

Exposing its huge teeth and swiping its deadly powerful claws, the massive bear started to rise on its hind legs in preparation for battle. Chittick was baffled. Did this bear really think it could attack a swirling helicopter ten feet off the ground?

But as his mind was framing an image of perplexity, Chittick's puzzled face fell expressionless. The bear stood fully erect. Chittick thought his once trustworthy eyes had finally betrayed him. He felt them tilting up in their sockets to stare the bear in the eye. He was flying in a hovering helicopter and looking up to see its head! He could hear the angry bear's deafening roar over the din of the chopper's spinning blades.

Unbelievably, the bear flailed its paws in an attempt to wage war with a helicopter. The ABC cameraman captured the entire dramatic sequence on video. It was not only the single most remarkable sight in Harry Chittick's career, it was also some of the best video to come out of Operation Breakout.

Because Eskimos were the only people allowed to kill a polar bear under state and federal law, they were the only armed scouts the networks could hire. Reporters covering the whales were told never to go more than a few hundred yards away from the whale site without an escort, except on the now heavily traveled ice paths.

But the reporters always thought they knew better. At least I thought I knew better. My hubris almost killed not only me but our unwitting Japanese correspondent, Masu Kawamura. On the way back from our first day covering the whales, we parked our balky truck on the side of the road and innocently strolled onto the ice pack. I was so enthralled with the prospect of walking on the ocean's surface I had to do it again. The idea seemed harmless enough at the time. Other than the minus 30° temperatures, what could possibly threaten us in such serene and placid looking surroundings?

In what should have served as more than adequate warning, our normally fearless cameraman, Steve Mongeau, displayed a determined reluctance to join in our little ice jaunt. A Canadian, Mongeau had reported from the Arctic before. He knew enough about polar bears to stay away from them. There was no way he would walk "out there" without a gun, he insisted. Masu and I knew better, we were reporters.

We walked blissfully onto the ice and rejoiced in our splendid and silent surroundings. As Mongeau and our truck receded farther into the dirty gray distance, we marveled at the fact we could stroll all the way to Norway, across the North Pole without ever touching land or seeing the water we walked on.

On the ice even the slightest breeze can cause whiteout, a blinding condition caused when swirling snow completely eliminates visibility and covers tracks. Like almost everything else in the Arctic, whiteout struck Masu and me without warning. Having no idea what hit me, I dropped to the ground to regain my balance and escape the biting wind. When I tried to look around for Masu I couldn't even see my own gloved hand. While prostrate, my face lay right on top of a pair of gargantuan fresh footprints. We knew we weren't far from the whales because we could hear both the helicopters and the faint sound of the saws. But because of the whiteout, we were totally disoriented.

As the wind howled in what we hoped would be just a momentary fit of Arctic rage, I first wondered what kind of an animal could leave such huge footprints and then I wondered how the tracks remained so fresh. Then, like a two by four, it hit me. The tracks still looked so new because they were just made. They couldn't be more than a few seconds old. Whatever monster made them couldn't be more than a few feet away. But I couldn't see him. I could only imagine. Even though I had expended my quota long ago, I prayed for yet one more reprieve from still another close call. Just as the wind died and the whiteout faded I could see the outline of a massive polar bear that seemed to be staring right at us.

In the shortest instant, it must have been frightened by the NBC helicopter hovering overhead. Startled, the bear raced off, fortunately not in our direction. Instead, it magically disappeared through a break in the ice. Whoever it is that dispenses reprieves, I owe him one. Afterwards, Masu and I were told that a favorite strategy of the Nanook is to wait for its victims to be blinded by whiteout before attacking.

Had the bear decided to come for us, we wouldn't have had a chance. We were hardly a match for a beast that can move at up to 40 miles an hour. Our ridiculously bright ski clothes and our virtual immobility made us easy prey for almost any predator. Had Masu perished and I survived, I would have had a lot of explaining to do to people in Tokyo. Even without the story of two mauled reporters, the video of the polar bear plunging into the water was good enough to make that evening's "NBC Nightly News" broadcast. If I didn't worship David Brinkley believe his observation that God looks out for fools, drunks and the United States before going out on the ice that day, I certainly did when I got back safely. My good fortune was enhanced by the fact that I fit nicely into all three categories.

Arnold Brower and his scouts came back from their pressure ridge expedition with bad news. They told Morris that while there were certain weak spots, none were shallow enough to be tackled by chainsaws. They could not be sure, but it seemed as though most of the ridge was grounded. That meant the huge ice towers reaching 30 feet in the air also reached more than 30 feet below the surface, firmly anchoring the ice to the ocean floor.

By Friday morning, October 21, Operation Breakout was back to square one. Although the whales had started to use the holes cut for them by the Eskimos, there still seemed no way through the pressure ridge. What could break the ridge? The question asked since day one had only one answer: an icebreaker. The rescue was right back to where it started a week earlier with Cindy Lowry back on the phone making calls to far away places. Many of them went to Campbell Plowden, her colleague in Washington.

Before the first Outside reporter arrived in Barrow to cover the fledging whale rescue, Plowden was already working behind the scenes to find a ship that could save the whales. Friday morning, October 14, the day after the first news of the stranded whales appeared on "NBC Nightly News," Plowden called his contacts in the U.S. Coast Guard which operated two world class icebreakers.

The flagship icebreaker, the *Polar Sea*, was making news of her own. She was mired in the ice-bound Northwest Passage on the way back from a ship rescue. A Canadian vessel was stuck near the western end of the Passage just a few hundred miles east of Barrow. The *Polar Sea* was trying to guide it to safety. Under normal conditions, Plowden was told, the ship would have sailed right past Barrow.

But because of the unusually bad weather in the Arctic, the ice at the Northwest Passage's western end was frozen too thick, even for the *Polar Sea*. Instead, both the icebreaker and the ship she came to save had to sail the other way, 1,500 miles across the top of the world and out into north Atlantic waters just a few hundred miles from Iceland. From there it was 12,000 miles back to Barrow through the Panama Canal. Plowden didn't need to ask any more questions. The *Polar Sea* was out.

"What about the other icebreaker?" he asked, knowing that the Coast Guard operated a second such vessel. The newer and sleeker *Polar Star* was in drydock at Seattle, undergoing extensive repairs. Neither American icebreaker could help in the cause that was uniting the world.

How could the United States have only two icebreakers? Plowden asked himself in exasperation. If he was in a position to approve the budget requests, he probably would have opposed shelling out $300 million for another icebreaker before the whale stranding. And the opponent of increased defense spending would have been right.

Except for Alaska, which consistently argued for more, the United States had little use for icebreakers. In the passion of the rescue, few people paused to reflect that, thankfully, we simply didn't need them. Unlike the Soviet Union, every single port in the United States was ice free, including those in Alaska. In fact, an argument could be made that we didn't even need the two we had. Most of the time they assisted Canadian vessels in the Northwest Passage: Canadian waters.

In his conversations about the U.S. icebreakers Plowden heard reports that there was a private 200-foot icebreaker in Juneau. His investigatory calls revealed she would be no use. At less than half the size of the *Polar Sea*, she was much too small to do the job. Designed to break the relatively thin ice in Southeast Alaska, she would have enough trouble just getting to Barrow, let alone contending with the huge ice blocks of the pressure ridge.

Plowden got the name of a marine services company in Seattle that reportedly worked closely with all the world's big icebreakers. The man at Croweling Maritime asked Plowden if he had spoken with anyone from the Soviet Merchant Marine office in New York. The Soviet Union operated the world's largest and most powerful fleet of icebreakers. With few warm water ports, they desperately needed them to assure passage of Soviet merchant and military vessels.

Right after he spoke with Croweling Maritime, the same anonymous woman who called Cindy Lowry in Anchorage earlier that morning with word of the VECO hoverbarge phoned Campbell Plowden in Washington. "Have you thought about the Soviets?" "Jane Whale" asked.

"Jane" told Plowden she just spoke to someone in Armand Hammer's Los Angeles office. Hammer is the nonagenarian capitalist who for decades proved himself most eager to supply the rope with which Lenin promised his triumphant Soviet society would one day hang the West.

"Jane's" request for Hammer's help met with an icy response. She told Plowden the woman she spoke with couldn't have been ruder. Enough with the gadfly industrialist, Hammer resolved.

Although Cindy told him not to bother, Plowden called Steve Ramser, from Alaska Governor Steve Cowper's office. He wanted to see if the governor could authorize the Coast Guard to request assistance from the Soviets. "Out of the question," came the predictable reply. If the state of Alaska didn't ask the United States Government to request Soviet assistance when an American ship got stuck or when seven Eskimo hunters were lost on the ice, Cowper wasn't going to ask the Soviets to help save three whales. End of discussion.

By Monday morning, October 17, the whales were already world news. Plowden woke up at 3:00 AM that day to call David McTaggert, the director of Greenpeace International who was in Rome. McTaggert was sick in bed but his assistant, Bryan Fitzgerald, listened as Plowden explained the problem. Plowden wanted McTaggert to persuade his contacts in the Soviet Academy of Sciences to send an icebreaker. Fitzgerald promised to convey Plowden's request to his bedridden director.

Plowden apologized for being unable to go into further details. In addition to the expensive international phone rates, he was in a rush. He had to be on the set of ABC's "World News This Morning" for an interview about the rescue. He told them he would be in touch as soon as he was finished with "Good Morning America," the second ABC News program on which he was scheduled to appear. Fitzgerald took Plowden's message directly to McTaggert. If he could send the Soviets a telegram, that might lubricate the interminably slow moving machinery of Soviet bureaucracy.

Before leaving ABC's Washington studios, Plowden called his

office to check for messages. Fitzgerald had just called from Rome. McTaggert agreed to send a telegram to the appropriate Soviet authority, Arthur Chilingarov at the State Committee for Hydro-meterology and Control of the Natural Environment, if Plowden would draft the text and find Chilingarov's telex number. Plowden spent the rest of Monday morning trying to get through on the constantly busy phone lines at the Soviet Embassy in Washington. When Plowden finally did get through, the clerk at the embassy gave him the telex number and address of the Moscow office.

Ironically, the man about to be asked to aid in the rescue of three helpless whales had his office on a street named after Pavlik Morozov, the small boy immortalized for doing his patriotic duty in the turbulent 1930s. He turned his dissident father over to Stalin's henchmen. His father was never heard from again, and Pavlik was made a shining star, a true Soviet hero.

Not ten minutes after Plowden got Chilingarov's number in Moscow, a reporter from the CNN capital bureau called asking about the Greenpeace request. Plowden was infuriated. Did someone betray him? How had the news media learned about his plans so quickly? CNN volunteered that the Soviet Embassy informed them of his call during their regular morning beat checks. Plowden had denied any knowledge. Now he would look like the one who leaked the story. If word leaked out before an official request was made, the plan would die aborning.

Plowden quickly drafted and faxed a copy of his proposed telegram to Greenpeace's Rome office for McTaggert to approve and forward to Moscow. Less than an hour after he sent the message to Rome, it was in Moscow. When Comrade Chilingarov arrived at work the following morning, Tuesday, October 18, Moscow time, the message from his old Greenpeace friend, David McTaggert, was waiting on his desk.

"Greenpeace urgently requests your assistance to help rescue three California gray whales trapped in ice holes less than a mile off shore from Point Barrow, Alaska," the message began.

The pressure ridge wasn't discovered until several days after that first telex. It continued, "A rescue operation is now underway but it will only succeed if the open lead, now six miles from the whales, does not freeze over. If this lead were to freeze over, would you be able to make an icebreaker available to help clear a path for the whales to escape? Please contact our Washington office which is in direct contact with our people in Alaska. Regards, David McTaggert."

As news of the whales spilled over into Europe, Chilingarov could hardly contain his glee. After suffering decades of the Western world's disdain for its persistent and brutal whaling practices, the Soviet Union was at the receiving end of a golden public relations windfall.

Even with the International Whaling Commission's 1986 moratorium on commercial whaling, the Soviet Union was still by far the world's single largest killer of gray whales. At the very moment that Chilingarov got the request to help-save the three grays stranded in Barrow, whalers on board rusty old Soviet whaling vessels were scrubbing their bloodstained decks after another productive season plying the waters of the Chukchi Sea hunting gray whales. The hunt was supposed to be limited to subsistence purposes only, but Glasnost had unshackled the Soviet media enough for it to report that most gray whale meat was fed to minks raised on Siberian farms.

The Soviet Union confessed to at least 169 gray whale kills in 1988 alone. Now, with no strings attached, the USSR was being handed a priceless opportunity to shed its image as one of the world's most relentless plunderers of endangered whales. Suddenly, by cutting a single path through the ice, the Soviet Union could transform itself into a great humanitarian power.

The Soviet Union was invited to save the very same whales its commercial whalers might just as easily have slaughtered. If they accepted the enviable challenge, the Soviet Union would reap one of the greatest public relations windfalls of the day. It would win the hearts and thanks of hundreds of millions of people the world over. Lenin would be proud.

Chapter 18

The Whales Nearly Bring a Government to Its Knees

David McTaggert's telex appealing for help was the first Arthur Chilingarov heard about the three trapped whales. Yet the Soviet minister immediately grasped the event's striking potential. It was a critical time in his leader's tenure. To date, Communist party chief Mikhail Gorbachev's extensive efforts to transform his empire's external image had proven a remarkable success.

But his domestic campaign to resuscitate the moribund Soviet economy was still unable to shed the shattered legacy of the 20th century's most anachronistic ideology. The only measurable index Gorbachev managed to increase in his brief reign as Soviet premier was the ever rising and unfulfilled level of his people's expectations.

Mikhail Gorbachev gave his subjects their first, if illusory, taste of freedom since Alexander Kerensky's ill-fated democratic experiment was crushed by the 1917 Bolshevik Revolution. But his subjects' patience remained uncertain and his domestic foes unyielding. To keep his fresh winds of change from turning into a fiery tempest of counter-revolution, Gorbachev's epochal reforms desperately needed time to work.

So far, he had masterfully won that time through a series of brilliantly paced measures aimed at winning the support of his Western adversaries. In three and a half years as Soviet General Secretary, Mikhail Gorbachev managed to convert even Ronald Reagan, his nation's most committed foe, one of the greatest diplomatic achievements in post-war Soviet history.

A seasoned diplomat, Chilingarov knew enough to avoid rejecting the Greenpeace request out of hand. But he didn't want to commit Soviet resources before his government could determine what was in it for them. He wanted to keep his options open. He immediately drafted a reply to Greenpeace dated October 18, the day after David McTaggert's initial cable.

"... Confirm receiving your telex of 17.10.88. We are trying to take measures for clarifying availability of spare icebreaker with Far East Shipping Company. We will inform you. Regards. Chilingarov. Gosgimet, Moscow, USSR ..."

Campbell Plowden read Chilingarov's telex on Wednesday morning, October 19, the day after President Reagan phoned Colonel Carroll in Prudhoe Bay. Plowden's ecstatic response was soon doused by sobering news. The Soviets were interested, but according to Cindy Lowry, the whales' prognosis was deteriorating. If they were to be saved, the Soviets would have to make up their minds to get to Barrow in a hurry.

After a perfunctory phone call to Rome to obtain permission to reply to Chilingarov, Plowden penned an urgent appeal for action: "Confirm receiving your telex of 18.10.88. A hovercraft barge is being towed to Barrow to attempt a rescue. It has been delayed several days. We don't know when it will arrive or how well it will work. Whales are very stressed. In case this rescue does not work, we urgently need to explore alternatives. Thank you for your efforts to check availability of spare icebreaker. Regards, Campbell Plowden Whale Campaign Coordinator; Greenpeace International."

The cable came over Chilingarov's telex machine just past midnight Moscow time on October 20, Day Six of Operation Breakout. A few hours after Chilingarov read Greenpeace's latest communication, the de-icers arrived from Minnesota to relieve the whales' late night deathwatch. Like the whales' condition, the chances of Soviet involvement would quickly improve.

By Thursday morning, October 20, news of the stranded whales had more than crossed the Atlantic, it had already begun to consume the people of Western Europe. With an ear pressed firmly against the Western heart, the Soviets knew the whales were big news. If they could save the icebound trio, they would collect the rescue's spoils. Campbell Plowden and Greenpeace knew this too and used it to great effect.

For years, Greenpeace International lobbied hard against continued commercial whaling by two of Europe's supposedly most progressive nations, Norway and Iceland. With news of the stranded whales now at the forefront of European public opinion, Plowden saw the same rare opportunity Chilingarov did, a chance to shape a small part of history.

The phones at every Greenpeace office in Europe were ringing off the hook. People from Italy to Ireland wanted to know how they could help save the three whales trapped in a place none of them had ever even heard of. European environmental activists were beating down Greenpeace's doors, waiting to be organized.

Of course, Plowden realized there was no way they could help the three whales in Barrow. But they could help other whales by putting pressure on governments doing business with nations that slaughtered them.

From Plowden's perspective, the three animals in Barrow stranded themselves at a most propitious moment. If ever there was a time to exert pressure on countries that still killed whales for commercial gain, this was it.

One of those countries was the Republic of Iceland, a tiny island nation in the North Atlantic whose quarter of a million people understandably believed that their geography was chosen by the hand of providence. Half an ocean separated them from the ancient, violent clashes of an old world and the titanic turbulent rise of a new one.

Iceland's people prided themselves on their model society. It was hard not to. They had the best of both worlds, a highly industrialized democratic society with virtually none of the social strains found in other Western countries. No crime, no drugs, and because they kept all non-Icelandic people out, no racial tensions. Just peaceful, hard-working people living an idyllic life on an enchanted island.

As much as Icelanders liked to think of themselves and their tiny island as an oasis of independence, their prosperity was wholly dependent on commerce with other nations. Iceland was one of the world's most successful exploiters of the sea. Its bountiful fish fetched a good price in Europe, and the whales killed by Icelandic harpoon ships earned fat profits from Japanese buyers.

But 1988 found Iceland tottering on the edge of recession. That year's European economic slowdown was drying up the market for Icelandic fish which amounted to more than 80 percent of its exports. To a prosperous nation unaccustomed to sluggish growth, 1988 was a year of crisis. That crisis peaked in September. Months of acrimony between the governing coalition's three parties lead Prime Minister Thorsteinn Palsson to quit the government and take his 20-member Independence Party with him. Within hours, Iceland had a new but considerably weaker left of center government ruled by Progressive party leader Strintrimur Hermannsson.

Once he moved into the Prime Minister's chair, Hermannsson's number one objective was to stay there. Keeping his country out of recession was the best way he knew to do that. But just weeks after taking office, he would be confronted by one of the most bizarre crises ever to rock his country. This crisis was triggered not by man, but by three whales trapped in ice on the other side of the world.

Campbell Plowden closely followed events in each of the few remaining whaling nations of which Iceland was one. He knew their strengths, and more importantly, their weaknesses. Like a bloodhound, Plowden smelled a vulnerable new government born out of crisis, not popular mandate.

The stranded whales gave Plowden more than an idea. They gave him the chance to strike his own blow against Icelandic whaling. The Barrow whales had mobilized a continent of activists and tens of millions of their supporters. Now they could join the more important battle to end the commercial pillage that pushed the magnificent creatures to the edge of extinction.

After clearing it with his superiors, Plowden sent a cable to Greenpeace's European offices telling them that the best way they could help save the three Barrow whales was to remind their members that the real threat facing whales were not Arctic ice floes, but rusting whaling vessels loaded with rocket propelled harpoons. It wasn't nature that threatened whales. It was man.

By Wednesday, October 19, West German activists seized on the publicity surrounding the three stranded whales and hoped to use it to widen a six month boycott against German companies that bought Icelandic fish. With news of the Barrow whale stranding, the boycott took off. Looking for a local angle to a remote story, German media started covering the previously obscure Iceland fish boycott. Pickets and protests that had gone on unnoticed for months were suddenly newsworthy. German fish importers were quickly forced to make a decision: stop buying Icelandic products or wait for consumers to stop buying theirs.

What was marginal business to West German companies was critical business to Icelandic companies. Tengelmann, the multi-billion-dollar West German supermarket conglomerate, owner of A&P, was the first to decide that it had enough. It ignored the boycott before just like everyone else. But once it burst into the national spotlight, substantial Tengelmann business was at stake. As news of the mounting Alaskan whale rescue spread throughout Europe, so too did the pressure on Tengelmann.

The negative image conveyed to the world was all too apparent to Tengelmann's public relations advisors. The world was banding together to save three whales while Tengelmann continued to conduct business as usual with a country that killed them. Tengelmann had passed the point of diminishing returns.

On Friday afternoon, October 21, Tengelmann announced that it was cancelling a $3 million contract with Icelandic suppliers to protest that country's whaling practices. Plowden's big gamble paid off. One of the largest importers of raw Icelandic shrimp, long a target of the Greenpeace boycott, finally relented. The boycott of the Republic of Iceland bore its first fruit.

News of the cancelled contract rocked Iceland and its nascent coalition. Prime Minister Hermannsson's new government was staring its first crisis squarely in the face. Three whales struggling for their lives in the frozen waters of Alaska's Arctic threatened to plunge a nation half a world away into economic and constitutional chaos.

The Tengelmann contract amounted to less than a quarter of a percent of Iceland's $1.1 billion annual fish exports, but that was just the beginning. Fish was to Iceland what oil was to Alaska: more than 80 percent of its commerce. Without the fishing industry, Iceland would crumble.

Almost immediately, other West German companies followed

suit. Aldi Supermarkets imposed its own boycott. So did NordSea. Adding the new cancellations to the cost of the ongoing American boycotts, Iceland's $7 million commercial whaling industry had already cost the tiny country $50 million, four percent of its 1988 Gross National Product. Hundreds of people lost their jobs within hours of the new cancellations.

Prime Minister Hermannsson's untested government had to act on a single, well-defined question. Was the revenue from 75 dead whales worth the price of international opprobrium and now, potential economic collapse?

To Arni Gunnarsson, a member of Iceland's parliament, the answer was a resounding no. Gunnarsson was a member of the ruling coalition's Social Democratic party. He came from a district in northern Iceland wholly dependent upon fishing. The cancelled contract had already put many of his constituents out of work.

Gunnarsson announced he would introduce a bill to disband Iceland's commercial whaling industry on Monday morning, October 24, 17 days after Roy Ahmaogak first discovered the Barrow whales and ten days after the U.S. government authorized their rescue. Word of Gunnarsson's plans sent shock waves through Iceland's new coalition government. Frantic cables were sent to two of the country's most important politicians, both of whom were out of the country presenting their credentials as representatives of the new government.

The Prime Minister offered Gunnarsson a deal. If Gunnarsson could hold off until Thursday, the Prime Minister would announce a ban on commercial whaling forever. The six-month-old boycott was on the verge of success. On Sunday, October 23, it looked as though one of the four remaining whaling nations was about to end the odious practice.

The astounding news was reported in all the Icelandic media and hailed as a great step forward. Since the International Whaling Commission's 1986 ban on commercial whaling, public opinion polls showed whatever their sponsors wanted them to show. Environmentalists brandished data showing an increasing majority favoring a ban on whaling. But opponents produced their own results showing an equally large number of Icelanders against an end to whaling if it meant capitulating to the "economic terrorism" of the boycotters.

The arms of the whaling lobby reached high into the government.

Next to the Prime Minister, the most important cabinet post was the Minister of Fisheries, a post held by a man named Halldor Asgrimmsen, Iceland's most ardent whaling advocate.

Asgrimmsen was in France when he heard about the Prime Minister's deal. He was livid. How could the Prime Minister unilaterally announce a ban on commercial whaling? National policy was determined by the cabinet, not by the Prime Minister alone. Asgrimmsen fired off an angry cable to the Prime Minister and returned immediately to Reykjavik, Iceland's capital. He promised to oppose the proposed ban with all the force he could muster. For Asgrimmsen, the issue wasn't Iceland's economy, it was his nation's sovereignty.

Asgrimmsen had powerful allies. Chief among them was Foreign Minister Jon Baldvin Hannibalsson. He was in the United States introducing Iceland's new government to senior American officials. Planned just days in advance, Hannibalsson's visit coincided with the height of Operation Breakout.

The Foreign Minister of a country that slaughtered whales for commercial gain was on a state visit to a nation spending millions of dollars to free them. Surveying the American political landscape the week of October 21-28, all he could do was lament the abysmal timing of his trip.

Foreign Minister Hannibalsson's most important meeting was with Secretary of State George P. Shultz. As his nation's top spokesman, the Foreign Minister was exposed to the concerns of allies like the United States. Whaling was invariably at the top of the list. With or without the Barrow stranding, he was sure to hear Secretary Shultz's appeal for Iceland to stop it. But now, it was likely to be the only item discussed during the 30-minute session.

Hannibalsson was acutely conscious of his uncomfortable situation, even before he was handed a telex from the Reykjavik Foreign Ministry. In it was the startling news of German boycotts and the Prime Minister's announcement that Iceland would halt whaling.

He knew the Fisheries Minister, Halldor Asgrimmsen, must be furious. Asgrimmsen said he would fight the decision and hoped Hannibalsson would join him. Just as the State Department was preparing a statement to laud Iceland's decision, the Embassy of Iceland urged State to delay congratulations until the reports could be confirmed.

Here rescue coordinator Ron Morris holds a press conference while photographers shoot from an angle that depicts the barren landscape of the frozen Arctic Ocean. Therefore, it appears that Morris is standing in remote isolation, not in back of the Top of the World Hotel. (Jeff Shultz for SIPA)

If Cindy Lowry of Greenpeace was the rescue's mother, then Bill Allen (center), president of VECO, was its father, and Ben Odom (right), senior vice president of ARCO Alaska, its rich uncle. Here the two men talk with MarkAir cargo sales director Ed Rogers from inside the belly of a U.S. Air Force C-5A transport aircraft that carried the prototype Archimedian Screw Tractor. (VECO)

When the hoverbarge failed, National Guard Colonel Tom Carroll came up with a new, less sophisticated way of breaking ice. Not even the mighty Arctic ice could withstand the force of a 10,000 pound concrete block dropped on it from 100 feet in the air. While the "bullet" had no trouble crushing the ice, it did nothing to remove the shattered ice shards which clogged the holes. (Micheal Echola, Alaska National Guard)

Before long, the once-isolated ice holes were wrapped in miles of frozen television cable and wire. (Tom Rose, NY News Corp.)

By Tuesday, October 25, eighteen days after the whales were discovered, two Soviet icebreakers arrived to break through the grounded pressure ridge of ice that was the last and greatest obstacle separating the whales from freedom. To the surprise of all but the Soviets, the vessels cut through the ridge easily. (Frank Baker for BP Exploration)

The world's largest aircraft, a C-5A Galaxy, landing at one of the world's smallest airports, Wiley Post Memorial. On board was Bill Allen's ice-cutting Archimedian Screw Tractor. (Frank Baker for BP Exploration)

Colonel Tom Carroll was the highest ranking United States military officer ever to step aboard a Soviet icebreaker. He spends a pensive moment looking out over the bleak frozen landscape from the aft deck of the *Admiral Makarov*. Bonnie Mersinger was convinced he was thinking about her. (Charles Mason for the *Fairbanks Daily Miner*)

The *Vladimir Arsenyev* was the smaller of the two Soviet ships. Its shallower bottom cut a quarter-mile-wide path through the ice, the path the whales would use to swim free. (Tom Rose, NY News Corp.)

Since he was unable to locate the only man trained to pilot the Archimedian Screw Tractor, Billy Bob Allen jumped in and drove the contraption himself. He planted the Stars and Stripes outside the cab to remind the Soviets just where they were. When he ran out of gas, he himself was reminded where he was: the middle of the Arctic Ocean. (Micheal Echola, Alaska National Guard)

And the whales swim free. (Tom Rose, NY News Corp.)

Hannibalsson met Shultz in the latter's Foggy Bottom office and in no uncertain terms told him that the Prime Minister's announcement, precipitated by the German boycotts, had catapulted his new government into a crisis the degree of which could not yet be determined. By Thursday, October 27, Operation Breakout's second to last day, the government of Iceland neared collapse.

The ferocious reaction of his two top ministers presented Prime Minister Strintrimur Hermannsson with an unwinnable situation. If he dug in his heels for a fight, his government would almost certainly topple. If he backed down, he could retain his post but would be left even weaker than before. To save his own neck, the Prime Minister backed down. The October 27 deadline came and went, his promise to Gunnarsson unfulfilled.

Iceland may have been back in the whaling business, but only at great domestic cost. For Campbell Plowden and the cause he fought for, it was a huge victory. A government was brought to its knees, all because of people's love of whales.

One of the saga's biggest stories went completely unreported in the U.S. press. Americans were so blinded by parochial interest in the three whales, they did not even notice their resounding impact on real people's lives halfway around the world.

Chapter 19

Desperate: Nothing Seems to Work

That the Icelandic crisis escaped notice in the country that touched it off was a remarkable and unreported story in and of itself. While Iceland's turmoil might not have been noticed by its allies, the Soviets paid close attention. The rarefied corridors of the Kremlin were abuzz with the astounding news from Reykjavik.

As the story of three trapped whales mushroomed into a worldwide media spectacular, so too did the pressure on the one man with the power to free them. Soviet Hydrometerology Minister Arthur Chilingarov. American environmentalists, long his opponents, had urgently requested his country's assistance. By the end of Operation Breakout's first week, Chilingarov was running out of time. He had to make a decision. Would he redirect Soviet icebreakers to Barrow or not? For the past three days, he had promised to try. By Friday, October 21, it was time for an answer.

Chilingarov had 72 hours to ask himself if there was any compelling reason for the Russians to assist in the rescue. In the three days since he first learned of the stranding, the story had taken on prominence far beyond its relative importance. He knew the western media was unpredictable, but he had never seen anything like this. He was at a loss to explain the Americans' passionate response to the trapped whales.

A fire of interest had consumed a nation in the midst of its quadrennial electorial trance. When this interest also engulfed Europe, Chilingarov knew there was no way he could lose. Thursday night, October 20, Moscow time, Operation Breakout's sixth day, Chilingarov instructed his ministry to seriously pursue the request. Within hours, word reached Chilingarov that one of the Soviet Union's largest icebreakers was finishing a six-month assignment deep inside the polar ice cap. It was building Northern Pole 31, a floating polar research station. The ship was only 300 miles north of Barrow.

Chilingarov's office transmitted new orders to Master Sergei Reshetov, captain of the massive 496-foot *Admiral Makarov*. Reshetov was told that once his float station duties were complete on Saturday, October 22, he must steer his Finnish built 20,241 ton vessel toward a thick grounded pressure ridge ten kilometers off the coast of Barrow, Alaska, U.S.A.

Reshetov received the news with resigned frustration. There was little he could do. To the diminutive captain with unkempt strawberry blonde hair, service in the Soviet Merchant Marine precluded dissent. An order was an order, Glasnost notwithstanding. Master Reshetov's job was to carry it out. Six months at sea made Reshetov and his crew more than anxious to return to their home port of Vladivostok. The Makarov left in March 1988 for a six-month tour. Northern Pole 31 took several weeks longer than expected to complete. But instead of heading back to the relative comforts of Siberia, the *Admiral Makarov* had a new assignment. On Saturday, October 22, she was to begin pulverizing 300 miles of thick Canadian and American ice en route to Barrow, Alaska.

At 9:11 PM October 21, 1988, Moscow time, Chilingarov sent Campbell Plowden the cable that would confirm Operation Breakout's coup de grace and presage the whales' eventual rescue. "...We are taking efforts on assisting in whale rescue operations. We are supposed to send for this purpose the icebreaker *Admiral Makarov.* Hope to receive your assistance for our icebreaker to enter U.S.

territorial waters and ice reconnaissance for its optimal routing in economic side of U.S. waters . . . We have sent required official note to U.S. State Department. We do not have complete assurance in this venture because of shallow waters for icebreaker in the area of the rescue . . . We are also in doubt about whales ability to pass through channel made by icebreakers. Regards, Cmde Arthur Chilingarov."

Anxious to get U.S. clearance for the Soviet vessels, Campbell Plowden called the Soviet Embassy's Merchant Marine office in New York. Surely, they know the procedures, Plowden thought. They must process requests like this all the time. The Soviet attaché told him that two environmental groups Plowden never heard of had already asked for help. Something about it reminded him of previously unknown Arab guerrilla groups tripping over themselves to claim responsibility for the most recent terrorist atrocity: the Sword of Islam, Guardians for Enlightened Martyrdom, and now the World Society for the Protection of Animals and the World Whale Federation based in, of all places, Arizona.

Plowden called Ben Miller, the desert whale saver, to inform him that Greenpeace was involved in getting Soviet support for the rescue. Miller told him his interest sprang from the television and newspaper coverage. A few days earlier, he started lobbying his own State Department contact to request Soviet assistance. Miller told Plowden he was dealing with a man in John Negraponty's office. Negraponty was the Assistant Secretary for Oceans and International Environmental and Scientific Affairs. He was the State Department's highest ranking environmental and scientific foreign service officer.

Friday afternoon, October 21, Campbell Plowden called Negraponty's office himself. He left a message urging someone in charge to get back to him as soon as possible. Propping the phone against his ear with his shoulder, he dialed the number for Jim Brange at the National Marine Fisheries Service. Brange wanted to help but told Plowden that the State Department could not issue the clearance without Pentagon approval. Brange and Plowden agreed to pursue different avenues. Brange would work Defense and Plowden could flex his clout at State.

At the end of the day, Plowden copied the correspondence between Greenpeace and the Soviets and bound them with an oversized paperclip. He asked his secretary to fax the bundle immediately to Cindy Lowry in Barrow. Two reporters were in the manager's office waiting to use the phone when a three bell signal alerted them to an incoming transmission. The glossy paper slowly emerged from the fax machine at the Top of the World Hotel. Unable and unwilling to restrain themselves, the unknown moles read the telexes exchanged between Moscow and Washington. Their eyes met in mutual delight. Rumors of Soviet involvement had abounded since early in the week, but the documents transmitted via satellite from 7,000 miles away could confirm it. They shouldn't have been snooping. Indignity of indignities, they would have to sit on their scoop.

Although the faxes went unreported, the Russian rumors spread through the Barrow press corps. The race was on. The first agency to report the Soviet decision would have the biggest exclusive since the story broke. But exclusives were hard to come by during Operation Breakout. Cramped quarters in the tiny town and its overwhelming isolation made the concept of confidentiality implausible. The instant one reporter learned something he or she thought consequential, it seemed like someone else was already reporting it.

Rescue Coordinator Ron Morris encountered what he saw as an insurmountable problem the minute he deplaned in Barrow a week earlier. He confronted a growing swarm of media all competing to cover a story that on the surface appeared to have only a few exploitable angles. There were only so many ways to photograph the whales. At first, the rescue was simple enough for every reporter to follow.

Colonel Carroll anticipated a media problem before he left Anchorage. Carroll and his press officer, Mike Haller, knew that the only way to bring order to a frenzied press was to restrict them without overtly trying to limit the flow of information. Prove to them it would be useless wasting energy looking for scoops by making information, pictures and access immediately available to everyone simultaneously.

When Carroll got to Barrow with the five-ton concrete bullet, he saw that Search and Rescue Director Randy Crosby had unwittingly created his own fledgling press pool. It started as just a trip or two a day, flying Barrow TV's Oran Caudle or Russ Weston of KTUU-TV out to the whales. The enterprise grew like the story itself. Crosby's operation swelled with unimagined activity. SAR went from flying three missions on Sunday, October 16, the rescue's second day, to more than 40 just four days later. His hastily filled out log sheets were scribbled with the names of more than 100 different passengers. His equipment and his men were being overworked. He wondered how long it would be before something gave.

To reporters, his free charter service proved a godsend. Regular and dependable access to the whale site for every reporter averted the battles often associated with heavily saturated media stories. Thanks to Randy Crosby, every media company that came to Barrow could get as close to whales as often as it wanted. Big or small, rich or poor, it made no difference. Operation Breakout was one of television's most succcessful equal access stories.

Ironically, the only thing that made coverage of the whale stranding possible in the first place was their propitious choice of location. The whales stranded themselves close to a village modern enough to boast a satellite television transmission facility. But once the story exploded, the value of the location was inverted. It wasn't Barrow's proximity that saved the whales, now, it was its remoteness. Had the stranding occurred in a location Outsiders thought even marginally accessible, a crushing tide of media would have overrun Barrow. Proper coverage of the story would have been all but impossible. Media relations personnel from every federal agency and news service coming to Barrow to help would only have gotten in the way.

Fortunately, for the whales, their rescuers and those reporters who did make the long journey northward, Barrow did not have the facilities to support the huge entourage that usually accompanies the networks on mega-stories. There were only so many hotel beds and only so many airline seats in and out of town each day. There were no alternatives. The instant Barrow hung out its "no vacancy" sign, the influx stopped dead. Barrow was full. By Thursday, October 20, Day Six of Operation Breakout, not even Colonel Tom Carroll could find a place to stay.

From the jungles of Southeast Asia to the untamed wilds of the Alaskan bush and seemingly everywhere in between, Colonel Tom Carroll thought he had seen and slept in it all. Then he got to Barrow, a place where he would spend 16 hours a day but never spend the night. At quitting time, he would hop on an Alaska Air National

Guard eight-passenger Otter aircraft and fly 270 miles across the tundra's numbing void to Prudhoe Bay. He slept in a tastefully decorated room in the ARCO compound now littered with empty coffee cups.

Since the day Ron Morris arrived, the rescue was recharged at daily early morning meetings. As the operation progressed in size and prominence, so too did the meetings' importance. By the end of Operation Breakout's first week, an invitation to attend was a symbol of access to the man with the operation's ultimate power. What started as an open breakfast at Pepe's became a mark of rank. Network producers assigned television crews to wait for the meeting to adjourn so they could pepper the departing participants with questions about the proceedings. But the rescuers were under strict instructions from Ron Morris to leave all media queries to him.

By Thursday night, October 20, six days after his arrival, Ron Morris wanted changes. He reshuffled his rescue command as if it were an executive cabinet. Those who didn't conform to his approach were none too gently pushed out. Morris' desire to direct a prominent inner circle increased in direct proportion to the growing coverage of his rescue. In came the Outsiders, biologists Dave Withrow and Jim Harvey from Seattle's National Marine Mammal Laboratory, ice experts Gary Hufford and Bob Lewellen from the National Weather Service, and on Saturday, October 22, NOAA's Pacific fleet Commander, Rear Admiral Sigmund Peterson.

As the Outsiders arrived, the original insiders were conspicuously left out, Craig George and Geoff Carroll among them. The North Slope Borough biologists who helped keep the whales alive for the five days before Operation Breakout began were no longer invited to the morning meetings, their knowledgeable counsel ignored, their pride hurt. Eskimo Arnold Brower, Jr., the man who kept open the whales' original holes and had successfully cut over 50 others, became no more than a "native" employee. They stored their resentments for another day.

The coordinator failed to learn the one critical lesson of Operation Breakout's first week. Simple technology and native knowledge kept the whales alive. Elaborate equipment did not. Even those involved in the ill-fated tow of the hoverbarge learned that in the Arctic the low-tech approach is often the best. Taking a clue from Arnold Brower and Malik, Colonel Carroll fell back on the simplicity of the concrete bullet, the most unadorned method yet found for freeing the whales.

By Friday morning, October 21, the two larger whales appeared in better shape than at any time since Roy Ahmaogak first discovered them. The de-icers brought from Minneapolis succeeded in keeping half a dozen breathing holes open during the rescue's most bitter night. The biting winds and encroaching darkness were no match for the compact water circulators. The more reliable the machines proved, the more calm the whales became.

By Friday morning, the three famous whales began displaying a remarkable attachment to the ever present massaging jets emitted by the machines. The two larger whales, Siku and Poutu, surfaced within inches of the de-icers, rolling playfully in the seductive flow of the "Arctic jacuzzis." Blissful, euphoric relaxation quickly replaced their fortnight of stress.

Arnold Brower and his crews tried in vain to get the whales to make significant moves toward the open lead, now almost five miles away. Brower made an ironic observation that quickly spread from rescuer to reporter and back again. Perhaps, he suggested, the de-icers were working too well. So well in fact that they had started to domesticate the once leery whales. What if the ultimate obstacle to the whales' freedom became the whales themselves?

That such an unmentionable observation was just now being examined proved that the rescuers had as much to learn as the whales. Of course the whales' chief obstacle was themselves. If the cetacean trio had properly interpreted the changing climatic conditions, they, like their fellow creatures, would be well on their way south, leaving the media to search for other spectacles.

The time of the morning meeting was moved back to 8:30 to allow the participants more time to prepare their presentations and make early morning phone calls. Some of the rescuers reported early at the Search and Rescue hangar for the morning briefing. When they arrived, they were met by several cameramen and their reporters desperate for a morsel of substantiation to confirm rumors of imminent Soviet involvement.

They gathered at the conference table in the hangar's L-shaped office area. Not unlike the colonel's command table at Prudhoe, it was strewn with stained plastic coffee mugs and tinfoil ash trays exuding the noxious smell of vaporized carcinogens. Cindy Lowry,

Tom Carroll, Randy Crosby and Arnold Brower, Jr., were determined to propel their unprepared leader toward decisive action. The coordinator, who had proven an adept media manipulator, had yet to offer tangible amelioration of the whales condition. After a week of public relations, substance was long overdue.

Ironically too, without Morris' preoccupation with the media there might not have been any rescue at all. Massaging the press was critical to the rescue's newly omnipotent hierarchy. Ideas that would have been unthinkable just a week before were now well within the realm of possibility: invoking the mayor's jobs programs, employing hundreds of Eskimos to cut open holes in the ice, the five-ton concrete bullet, and now, perhaps, Soviet icebreakers. They were all made possible by the masterful wooing of the press.

But this Friday morning saw an abrupt end to the atmosphere of good feeling. The irascible Morris trudged angrily up the thick rubber steps of the SAR hangar and in a particularly foul mood entered the presence of his waiting minions. The initiative and comity Morris brought to Barrow had regressed into bitter recriminations of almost everyone intimately involved in the rescue. His insecurity was manifest in Geoff and Craig's excommunication. If Morris sought to hide his antipathy toward the success of Arnold Brower, Jr., and his Eskimos, he didn't do a good job. His demeanor toward Brower and his tireless legions bespoke a resentment laced with what many felt was more than a touch of condescension.

The meeting proceeded with an icy chill. Morris reiterated his insistence that he alone deal with the media. His once reassuring control now fell on hostile ears. Cindy Lowry tried to convince others to give the beleaguered man the benefit of the doubt. He had an impossible task. There was no way everyone was going to agree with him. He was the only one empowered to make tough decisions that would inevitably upset those he overruled. Like him or not, Cindy said, Ron Morris kept the operation together and alive through some very trying times. The whales were about to be saved, she pleaded with her colleagues. Couldn't people try to keep their antipathies toward him in check for just a few more days?

After convincing her skeptical colleagues to give Ron Morris another chance, she spoke by phone with a reinvigorated Bill Allen. Allen and VECO still wanted to be part of the rescue. With delight, Cindy accepted help from anyone kind enough to offer it. Like

Colonel Carroll, Allen resolved to attempt less herculean methods to free the three trapped whales. Thursday night, the official abandonment of the hoverbarge all but complete, Allen lowered his sights but kept the freeing of the whales firmly in them.

In many ways, the voluntary acceptance of the humanitarian mantle was the biggest single boost to company morale that Billy Bob Allen could remember. The unexpected strength of his employees' will to help creatures in trouble filled him with pride. The rescue transcended industry, culture and language. His VECO laborers worked as hard to free the whales as anyone. They were trained in oil exploration and extraction, not wildlife management. But nevertheless they displayed a remarkable commitment to freeing distressed animals. The stranded whales changed not only Billy Bob Allen but also the empire he created.

Allen ordered his men to use more tested, less sophisticated equipment. Over a conference call, the North Slope operations manager, Marvin King, told Allen that another VECO device had been tested during the day and seemed up to the task. It was a custom-made amphibious vehicle built to tow the hoverbarge to and from offshore oil platforms.

To the delight of the humor-starved press in Barrow, VECO was serious when they named their machine the Archimedian Screw Tractor. Smaller than the hoverbarge, it was still too large to transport in one piece, even in the largest cargo aircraft. The tractor cut a 15-foot-wide swath of ice, slicing through it with the propellant force of its two long screw-shaped pontoons. Like the hoverbarge, it sat idle since the 1984 failure of the Mukluk Island oil well.

"Hell," Billy Bob exclaimed. "Let's get that son of a bitch on up there." When the euphoria subsided, Allen weighed the Screw Tractor option with tempered expectations. Allen was well aware that at best, his device would augment the rescue, not direct it.

Early Friday morning, Bill Allen told Colonel Carroll about the Screw Tractor. Pete Leathard couldn't get through on Cindy's interminably busy phone line. He left a message with the receptionist at the Top of the World Hotel asking Cindy to call him or Billy Bob as soon as she had a spare minute. They wanted to talk about the Screw Tractor. It was one of several calls Cindy would be unable to return.

The meeting on Friday morning, October 21, became a crucible for Operation Breakout. It was the first session without a master plan. The rescuers were on their own. All that carried the rescue forward was the momentum of Arnold Brower, Jr., the Minnesota de-icers, and rumors of the Russians. Just when the whales' condition appeared stable, the rescue's seemed terminal.

The rumor of Soviet involvement was not the only one bantered about in Barrow. So was word of the imminent collapse of Operation Breakout. If the Russians failed to come, Ron Morris would play his last card, wave his "government document," kill the whales and go home. After mobilizing hundreds of people and millions of dollars, the United States Government could not find a way to save three whales from the Arctic elements.

Unsubstantiated rumors of Soviet involvement abounded. They sent Ron Morris over the edge. If the rumors were true, why hadn't he, as project coordinator, been consulted? He confronted Cindy Lowry demanding to know whether she knew anything. Since Soviet participation was first discussed, Campbell Plowden had insisted on secrecy. Only if diplomatic channels failed to produce the desired results would going public become an option. At Plowden's insistence, Cindy kept her tongue.

Morris defiantly insisted on an answer from his one remaining friend. A moment of panic gripped him. What had he done to be stripped of his one chance at fame? His mind raced through the possibilities. He couldn't avoid the conclusion that if indeed the Soviets came, he would be swept away in the Arctic wind. But it wasn't as though he truly expected the adrenaline of the past week to continue unabated. In his heart he knew that one way or another the operation would end. The whales would either die or be freed.

His panic that Friday morning was perhaps a sharp reminder that he was a normal man with normal responsibilities.

As Morris' outburst came to an end, the room filled with silence. He leaned forward and slowly pushed back his chair. He wiped the beads of sweat from his face and uttered a slight harumph, as if to offer an apology. His colleagues were all too glad to accept. It was time to return to the matter at hand: freeing the whales.

In the first brainstorming session of the operation, Morris instructed everyone in the room to offer what they thought were feasible recommendations on how to free the whales. After each person listed his or her options, the group evaluated them.

Morris eagerly swept around the conference table collecting the papers. Options ranged from the concrete bullet Colonel Carroll was scheduled to test on the ice later that day, to the Archimedian Screw Tractor. Not surprisingly, the options most mentioned were the only ones that already worked: the Eskimos and the de-icers. The rescuers agreed to continue cutting holes toward the pressure ridge in the hope that the whales would use them.

In the week since Operation Breakout began, the average temperature out on the ice had already dropped to 25° below zero. The Arctic ice pack moved south nearly 20 miles and the shore ice grew farther out each day. The once 14-mile-wide lead had shrunk to barely a mile across at its narrowest point. If the whales could not be freed before the lead closed, no one could save them, not the Eskimo chainsaw gangs, not the National Guard, not the President of the United States, not even the mighty icebreakers from the Soviet Union.

If the Soviets did not offer their assistance, the rescue command would have to think of other alternatives or call it quits and leave the whales to their fate. Suggestions once laughed at were suddenly considered. Colonel Carroll offered to study the effects of detonating bombs of various destructive force to blast a path through the ridge. Knowing Cindy might object, he promised to clear his plans with her before trying anything on his own. Even if explosives could break the ridge, freeing the whales might not justify the risks to other Arctic life.

Chastened by their week-long wait for others, the Rescue Command went one step further. They began planning beyond the explosives. Assuming that they could never be used, Morris asked Cindy and others for other ideas on getting the whales past the 40-foot wall of ice.

"What about flying them over the ridge in nets?" she asked. Killer whales, though smaller than the grays, had been moved this way before, but the procedure was extremely dangerous. Luring a gray whale safely into a net under thick ice was one thing, lifting it safely out was quite another. Even the Sky Crane, the world's most powerful transport helicopter, might not have the power to pull the 50,000 pound whales out of the water and fly them the mile or so to open water. The whales would have to be tranquilized. Since a dose small enough for a man could kill a whale, administering drugs would prove tricky. Then there was the unknown effect of gravity. Would it split their huge girths wide open, splattering their entrails onto the ice below? That would surely make for morbidly fascinating video.

Dr. Tom Albert from the North Slope Borough contacted a friend in Norway who was an expert in drugging whales. He began preparing the serum. Sea World in San Diego, which had successfully airlifted Killer whales, began knitting a huge mesh net big enough for the much larger grays. It was an audacious scheme with little chance of success. But if all else failed, they would be ready to try.

With remarkable efficiency, Operation Breakout took on a mission all its own. While the upper echelons plotted to assault the pressure ridge, the Eskimos continued with their meticulous ice cutting. Arnold Brower and his crews had opened 55 new holes since they started cutting them earlier in the week.

As soon as the de-icers arrived two nights earlier, the three whales started using the new holes. But then, they stopped. Geoff, Craig and the National Marine Mammal Laboratory biologists couldn't figure out why. Maybe they were resting. After two grueling weeks, the whales were finally breathing normally again. They actually seemed to enjoy their bubbly new surroundings.

On Friday morning, Craig George suddenly changed his mind. Standing quietly with Cindy, he noticed Bone, the baby whale, still lagged behind Poutu and Siku the larger, more robust whales.

"Shit," Craig blurted out in sudden realization. "They aren't moving because of the baby."

Only when they were absolutely threatened by Wednesday night's freezing holes did the whales move. When they reached the relative security of the new holes, they stopped. It had to be for Bone. Craig's logic held up to Geoff's preliminary analysis. In a remarkable display of bonding, neither of the two adolescent whales, would abandon their helpless dependent. The only thing that could compel them to take such a radical step was a clear and present danger to their own well-being. The de-icers eliminated that threat.

By noon, the ice surrounding the whales had resumed an eery silence. As rumors of the Soviet icebreakers spread, most reporters fled back to town to tap their sources on the Outside. They finally had some legitimate reporting to do: real leads to follow, real people to talk to, real news. Best of all, they didn't have to stand outside in the minus 30° temperatures to do it.

Cindy wanted to make her own phone calls. When she last heard from Campbell Plowden, a Soviet decision, contingent upon U.S. approval, seemed imminent. The hundred-man round the clock rescue operation never really required Cindy's constant presence on the ice. Still she felt the whales were her domain. She had to be with them. But like everyone else, she was hungry, cold and wanted to go back to town.

Cindy ran to the SAR helicopter, gave Randy Crosby an affectionate pat on the helmet and climbed aboard. As Crosby gently lifted his aircraft and its human cargo off the surface of the ice, the chain of holes faded from view. The loud hum of the helicopter proved a welcome relief for Cindy. But the peace of the buzzing engines was short-lived.

A second string of reporters waited for Cindy and Ron to confirm the reports now being widely reported in the Lower 48: the Soviets had offered an icebreaker and support ship to help free the whales. The Russians were on the way. Not knowing what to say, Cindy elbowed nervously past the crowd to get to the nearest phone. She professed her ignorance several times before the reporters began to believe her. Later, when Cindy tried to tell the truth, she and Greenpeace would both appear a bit foolish.

When she walked into the lobby of the Top of the World, the press assumed a very different role. It was as though the lobby were a sanctuary where all who entered were "off the record." Once she went inside, the reporters no longer asked her any questions or stuck any microphones or cameras in her face.

It was then Cindy realized that reporters not only expected their subjects to act for them, they were actors themselves.

Chapter 20

The Russians Are Coming

Campbell Plowden, Cindy Lowry's comrade in Washington, plodded nervously ahead. While waiting to hear from the State Department, he followed up his two whale crises unfolding 15,000 miles apart. Even for a man whose job description included organizing boycotts and managing chaos, these were hectic times.

Lunch was long past when Tucker Scully called him. His frenzied pace prevented him taking even three minutes to wolf down the avocado and sprout sandwich he made for himself that morning. He had waited for Scully's call all morning. Tucker Scully was Assistant Secretary John Negraponty's top deputy at the State Department. He told Plowden that before State could officially authorize the Soviet vessels to enter U.S. waters, he would need answers to several technical questions.

Scully wanted specifics about the Soviet ships, their specifications and capabilities. He told Plowden it was standard State Department liability procedure. If the ships ran aground or a Soviet crewman were injured in U.S. waters, the Americans didn't want to be responsible. Scully didn't know how long it would take for him to get back to Plowden. Counseling patience, he promised to call back as soon as he could, but advised Plowden not to get his hopes up.

Until then, he told Plowden, "Keep a lid on it. We don't want word of this leaking out before its time," he said.

When the time was right, the State Department wanted to break the story themselves. Plowden wondered why people at State spent more time worrying about protocol than about policy. Why were they so insistent about "handling" the announcement? It could only make Plowden wonder. Did they want to steal all the credit? Or did they want to create the proper conditions to spurn the Russians' help?

"How can you possibly read something sinister into this?" Plowden asked the dumbfounded foreign service officer. "The whole world wants action and all you can do is stall!" Plowden had exhausted his patience. "What is it with you people?" he asked, not expecting an answer.

During those fateful October days, Plowden was hardly alone in his demand for immediate action. After almost a week of gripping but frustrating drama, the world's passion for the whales' safety was reaching a climax. Everyone longed for resolution, and Soviet participation seemed certain to provide an answer. The sooner their ships were permitted to enter U.S. waters, the sooner the world would know whether the whales could be saved. Unless the icebreakers could crush the pressure ridge, hope was lost.

Plowden called Cindy. Stymied by the State Department's terminal caution, he had nothing new to report. Instead he listened to his near exhausted colleague. For the past week Cindy had slept only a few hours a day. Between boisterous reporters making noise at all hours and never ending calls from quote-hungry jounalists on the Outside, it was all she could manage.

She took Plowden's call on the phone in the lobby. A long line formed behind her. All the private room lines were jammed. Cindy was lucky to find it free. That was rare. Most reporters had to wait over an hour that confusing Friday for a chance to be filled in on the story's rapidly unfolding developments taking place a world away.

"Is there anyone there who can help us?" Plowden pleaded. "What about the guy the President called, the colonel? Maybe he has some connections."

Cindy didn't know how to react to her desperate co-worker. For reasons she was never able to acknowledge, she didn't want to ask Colonel Carroll. She had only met him a few times. She wasn't in a position to complain about his treatment of her. Every time they spoke, he was perfectly pleasant. She just didn't like the idea of getting him involved.

Plowden instantly detected her reluctance, but he insisted she approach the colonel anyway. "You're the one who claims we don't have any time," he reminded her. "Just ask him to help us."

Plowden, Cindy Lowry, and everyone else for that matter, knew that Tom Carroll must have impressive connections. After all, the President called him, not Ron Morris. Cindy's reluctance was quickly overcome by her concern for the whales. Besides, she had worked with Bill Allen, Ben Odom and the other oil people, and the National Guard never drilled oil wells or polluted the oceans. For the first time, Cindy let her preconceptions interfere with the rescue. Dismissing her wayward thoughts, she raced to locate the colonel.

Cindy found the colonel reviewing flight logs in the Search and Rescue hangar, impervious to the pandemonium all around him. She was taken aback by the warmth of his greeting. Subconsciously she hoped he would show some visible sign of resentment to justify her negative feelings. Without knowing it, the amiable colonel stirred her guilt.

"If there is a way I can help, I'd be delighted," he told her in what sounded like a genuine tone.

"In fact there is." Cindy answered. "We are trying to expedite the State Department clearance of the Soviet icebreakers and we were wondering if you could help us out."

Carroll froze. His eyes darting about the room, he looked as if someone just shot him in the larynx. "The Soviets?" he asked not knowing whether he actually restated the two words. He was stunned. The question took him completely by surprise. He was flustered and could not hide it. Since no one from headquarters in Anchorage mentioned anything about the Russians really coming, he never believed it. He thought it was just another rumor. He started to panic. If Cindy realized the question had shocked him, she might tell the media that he opposed the idea. They would really let him have it.

His mind raced, but it spun in circles. He glanced frantically around the room looking for something, anything, to distract him long enough to regain his equilibrium.

For once, everyone in the room was occupied and no one was calling his name. He was alone. How could he possibly be expected to help clear the Soviets to sail in American waters? He was a colonel in the National Guard, not a diplomat or a freelance peacenik. Operation Breakout notwithstanding, Tom Carroll's duty was to the Guard, to his country.

"The Soviets," he confidently began, "Well, you see it's just not that..." Losing some luster, he stammered on, "I'm just not sure exactly how to...there are things you probably don't, I mean you can't...The Soviets, huh?"

The composure that brought Tom Carroll this far was gone. Vanished in the Arctic chill.

His reaction to the word "Soviet" was as instinctively visceral as Cindy's reaction to the word "military." He groped for a lifeline to pull him to safety. "Soviet" was one of the most despised words in an American soldier's vocabulary. For the sake of the security of the United States, it should have been. Gorbachev notwithstanding, the Russians still had more than 1,000 ICBMs aimed at American cities and three million troops poised to pierce the heart of Europe.

This was the morning for emotional overload. First Ron Morris, then for a brief instant Cindy Lowry, and now the very model of control, Tom Carroll himself. His head throbbed with confusion. He had no orders or indications from his superiors on how to handle this one. God forbid he appear to aid and abet the enemy. He tried to convince himself that he was blowing the whole thing out of proportion. He was getting only an hour of sleep each night, and the coffee he was forced to drink amounted to little more than muddy water. Still, he had his career and the integrity of his superiors to consider.

It was time for a decision. Cindy had pushed his button.

"NO, NO NO!!" he barked. "Why on earth would you want the Soviets? There is nothing they can do that we can't. Besides," he insisted, now the center of attention in the stunned silence of the SAR operations room, "the ice is too thick and the water is too shallow."

Cindy's hunch proved right. The colonel's aversion to all things Soviet might have jeopardized the whales had it gone undetected. But now it had been brought to light for all to see. The colonel had been neutralized. His opposition was effectively removed from the icebreaker's path. Cindy was too stunned to gloat. At 5'4", little Cindy Lowry was the undisputed champion and there were a roomful of witnesses to prove it.

Her restraint further highlighted the colonel's anguish. He showed desperation, she, composure. He wanted to keep the Russians out, yet his irrational reaction only eased their way. Cindy politely asked Randy Crosby if she could borrow his phone to call Plowden in Washington. Out of deference to his new friend, Crosby silently nodded his assent. It was a painful moment for the colonel and he didn't want to make it any worse. She entered Crosby's office, leaving the door open. She didn't want the colonel to think that she would further humiliate him behind closed doors. Her refusal to engage in vengeful behavior only aggravated his defeat.

Surprisingly, she had no trouble getting through to her Washington office. Plowden was awaiting her call. "Tell your people at the State Department that we all want the Soviets to come. We need them here."

Colonel Carroll draped his fatigued frame over a metal folding chair. A pane of glass separated him from Cindy as he lowered his head resignedly into his hands. He would have to cooperate. He would try one contact: Bonnie Mersinger in the White House.

Plowden got the details on the two Russian vessels from the Soviet Consulate's merchant marine office in New York and passed them on to Tucker Scully at the State Department. The news was everywhere. Plowden could not possibly contain it. His contacts at the National Marine Fisheries Service appealed to their superiors to expedite State Department authorization. The wheels were well in motion. The stage was set for an official announcement later that afternoon.

Cindy told Randy she wanted to go back to the ice. She wanted to be with the whales. Politics and international negotiations she would leave to others. But just in case, she phoned Ron Morris who was making calls from his room at the Airport Inn. His wife had just arrived from Anchorage and not a moment too soon. Her presence had an almost immediate calming effect on the high-strung coordinator. Cindy asked Ron if he knew anything about the pending announcement. He told her he did not. He promised to tell her when and if he did, a promise he couldn't keep.

Cindy flew out to the whale site on the first press pool flight. At Colonel Carroll's direction, Crosby and SAR were to fly a single crew from each medium: print, radio and television. There was one flight in the morning and one in the afternoon. Whatever the pools gathered would be available to everyone. Crews wanting their own material had to find their own way out to the ice. For major stories the video consisted mainly of pool footage. Unless one of the networks had a scoop or some kind of exclusive, most of the original footage was ancillary.

Unsure of when she would have another chance to eat anything other than raw fish dipped in sea oil, Cindy consumed a cold Pepe's greaseburger she saved from the night before on the 12-minute flight out. The cloudless skies glowed burnt orange over the timeless Arctic landscape. From the protective cocoon of the cabin, she looked out at an austere yet magnificent sight.

While Cindy spent the late afternoon on the ice, Ron Morris received an urgent call from the office of William Evans, the Undersecretary of Commerce in Washington. It was time for a decision. The faceless State Department pinstripes had finally decided to permit the Soviets to enter U.S. waters. Their analysis determined that the cost of rejecting the Soviet offer would be greater than accepting it. The Russians were coming.

But like most other facets of international diplomacy, the mechanics of making the announcement were far more complicated than the announcement itself. The State Department called the shots. To de-emphasize its importance, the State Department wanted the lowest ranking person they could find to make the announcement. They wanted to built as large a buffer between the upper echelons of American government and the whale rescue as they could. State wanted to distance itself from potential failure. Ron Morris was their man.

They told Morris to call a press conference with a strong Arctic backdrop, a setting no one could possibly confuse with the Doric columns of Washington. He eagerly agreed. Morris chose the reporters' favorite spot, across the street from the Top of the World Hotel. He would stand with his back to the jagged ice of the sea. The very picture of isolation was in fact just a stone's throw from the hotel's warm lobby.

They gave him an "official" version of events leading up to the announcement that he was told to recite to the hastily gathered press, a version few would question. He hung up immediately and went to the Top of The World. As he briskly walked alone up Momegana street, Morris' heart raced with excitement. He was about to make the most significant announcement of his professional life. The United States Government asked him to inform an anxious world that the Soviets were on the way to help save the three stranded whales. His stature was certain to skyrocket. A nameless mid-level biologist from an obscure federal agency had become an international policymaker, or so he might have thought.

Unversed in diplomatic protocol, he did not realize that he was merely a pawn in the State Department's scheme to downgrade the rescue he headed. He was an unwitting participant in his own dethronement. Now that the Soviets were on the way, the U.S. Government began a frantic attempt to disengage itself. The further the government could extricate itself when the Soviet ships arrived, the less damage to American prestige if the Soviets managed to steal the show. Gorbachev had stung the State Department too many times in the past. They weren't about to take any chances over three lousy whales.

Morris pushed open the hotel's thick steel door, brandishing a broad, knowing smile. His obsequious friends in the press corps instantly saw that something was up. "What is it?" asked Harry Chittick of ABC. "Have you heard something about the Soviets? We're getting a lot of flak from New York. They needed confirmation. The Washington bureau is ready to back me up, but I need something to go on."

Morris gave his friend Chittick an exaggerated wink as if to say, "You guessed it." Morris stood on his tiptoes and shouted, "Everybody listen up. How soon can you all be ready to do an important press conference?" He knew full well the effect his question would have.

The reporters and their cameramen answered with their feet. Everyone within earshot of Morris dashed to their edit suites to fetch their equipment and ran outside to claim the best camera positions. As soon as the major networks were set up, Morris would make his announcement. But because of the time difference, it was too late for the evening news. Morris thought that a great shame.

It was no shame to the State Department. That was exactly the way they wanted it. It was a widely known secret around media-conscious Washington that Friday nights were the best time to release the worst news. Conventional wisdom dictated that it would be Monday before most people would take the time to digest it. In the case of the three whales, it would prove a gross miscalculation. It never occurred to the Foggy Bottom spin doctors that they were dealing with a situation that was anything *but* conventional.

Morris carefully positioned himself atop a mound of ice silhouetted against the bleak horizon to read his proclamation. He told the shivering but intent group of two dozen reporters what the Commerce and State Departments told him to say. Namely that it was they who worked to get the Soviet icebreaker, not Cindy Lowry, Campbell Plowden, or Greenpeace.

Morris' account was accepted with blind faith. Reporters in Barrow were so far removed from the story in Washington, we really had no choice. Ironically, when Cindy publicly objected to being totally left out of the official version, several reporters roundly criticized her for trying to "steal" the credit. All she could do was laugh. Greenpeace couldn't win for losing.

As the news spread to the handful of reporters watching the infuriatingly nonchalant whales, they hurriedly made their way back to town. By dusk, only a small core remained, just those who opted to stay with the whales rather than chase down a talking head recounting events happening thousands of miles away. For the second time in three days, the media missed the news they came for. While they covered Ron Morris' moment of glory in town, they missed the single most dramatic episode of the entire rescue.

Later that afternoon, Cindy had returned to the ice. She stood alone at the edge of the third hole. Several layers of clothing, green down pants and a heavy white parka provided scant warmth. She marveled at the mastery of her body. It adjusted to the Arctic long before her mind did. Mysteriously, she stopped shivering days earlier. Once her body became acclimated to its new environment, it began conserving her precious energy. For the first time since she got the call from Geoff and Craig a week before, Cindy Lowry was at peace, her mind and body as one.

As she looked out toward the white horizon, she wondered what the whales must be thinking. Did they know how serious their predicament was? She wondered whether they could reach Baja, even if they could be redeemed from their Arctic catacombs. She asked Craig the same questions during a break at the Eskimo shack. His reluctance said it all. His limited expertise could hold out little hope for their survival.

How could Cindy disagree? Until Wednesday night, their condition collectively deteriorated until they almost died. Then they adopted the attitude that they were on a spa vacation, lounging in the jacuzzi bubbles as though their troubles had magically disappeared. Did they know they were the darlings of an adoring world? Did they know that close to a billion people, 20 percent of the human species, knew about them? Did they realize they were bringing down a government across the North Pole? Did they know the Russians were on the way to save them?

She was overcome by a rare moment of peace. Knowing her anxiety would return any minute, she relished it. Closing her eyes, Cindy sat down on the ice. She concentrated intently on the silence of the Arctic dusk, broken every few minutes by the reassuringly warm sound of a whale surfacing just a few feet away. Never had she been involved in a more stressful project, but neither had she experienced such a moment of total peace. The irony enveloped her.

She had tried meditating before, but it never worked. She wasn't the type. Why, she wondered, was it suddenly working on the of the frozen surface of the Arctic Ocean just inches from three gigantic but helpless whales? She imagined her spirit hovering a few feet above her body. Through her closed eyes whe watched the whales perform their ghostly dance. Her fears, like her sensation of cold, vanished. She feared neither for herself nor, oddly, for the whales.

Somehow, they would manage. With this revelation, Cindy's hovering soul reunited with her body. She gradually awoke refreshed to her Arctic reality. She opened her eyes, radiating a smile lit by an inner tranquility. The sight of a group of Eskimos laughing heartily in the distance entered her newly recharged consciousness. Cindy slowly walked over to say hi, and maybe even join in the fun.

A block of ice, cut from the edge of the hole, floated on the ocean surface. She saw Malik and Arnold Brower nearly doubled over in laughter. They watched Johnny Brower hamming it up as he balanced himself on the floating slab. The other Eskimos joined him in an Inupiat version of the Beach Boys' song, "Surfin' USA." Johnny Brower was hanging ten on the Arctic Ocean!

It was no small feat. The slab bobbed up and down in the angry current. Staying upright required intricate balance and control. Unlike a tumble from a wave off Malibu, a wipe-out here had dire consequences. If he slipped when the ice block was tipped up on its edge, he would fall through and become trapped under the ice. Mercifully, he would have only seconds of consciousness. Half a minute later, Johnny Brower would be dead, his surfing career cut tragically short.

Surely, they must know this, Cindy reassured herself. Yet they were products of the Arctic. If they could have such fun watching Johnny Brower doing his best Duke Kohanamoku imitation, she could too.

When the silliness subsided and Johnny jumped off the slab onto the safety of solid ice, the crew finished cutting the hole. They started dismantling their equipment only to be distracted by the distant sounds of unexplained excitement coming from back near the whales. A look of terror swept across Cindy's face. She appealed to Arnold and Malik for an explanation. Neither knew any more than she did, but the steady look in their eyes calmed her to the point where she could run with them to investigate the commotion.

Jogging across the flat ice in heavy clothes, Arnold consoled Cindy. "Everything is all right," he assured her.

"God, what's happened?" she cried. "Just let them be all right."

Sure to his prediction, the two big whales seemed fine. As they approached the darkness of their 14th trapped night, the whales suddenly started exhibiting an unusual, robust urgency. The change in their behavior was clear for all to see. It was as if the whales knew something was about to happen. Without warning or explanation, the whales started surfacing more forcefully. Instead of lounging comfortably at the surface, they powerfully cleared their lungs. The mist exhaled from each of the whales pair of blowholes formed thick V-shaped clouds that hung in the air.

It wasn't panic. It was controlled, determined energy, the building up of momentum, the starting of mighty engines. The whales were about to move.

After a last surging lunge for air, the whales dove deep into the dark cold water. Instinctively, Cindy and Craig raced to the next hole. They knew the whales would move. Waiting for them to surface, they heard their unmistakable sounds. But the sounds were distant. Excitedly they turned their heads in the noise's direction and found themselves looking toward the lead. The whales had skipped the hole where Craig and Cindy waited, surfacing unexpectedly in the next one.

Seconds later they dove again, popping up two holes closer still to the lead. Suddenly, the whales were using the holes with abandon. The Eskimos had been on the right track. The whales understood. For the first time since their stranding the whales were at last ready to resume their annual journey southward.

Cindy leapt with joy. Her whales wanted to live. She could hardly keep up with them as they hurriedly moved down the Eskimo-carved ice path. At this rate, they would reach the end of the mile-long chain in no time. While Cindy and Craig chased them, Arnold Brower and Rick Skluzacek rushed to move the de-icers to each new hole the whales used. They kept one de-icer going in the old hole but let the others freeze over. There was no turning back. The whales would have to put aside any second thoughts. If they tried turning around, they would find their old holes sealed within a matter of hours.

It was the high point of the rescue. For the first time since they were discovered exactly two weeks earlier, the whales moved decisively toward the open lead. Cindy could hardly contain her exultation. Tears of joy welled in her eyes, only to freeze before they could make their way down her glowing cheeks. In all her years of rescuing whales, this was the most glorious moment of all. After a week of bitter frustration, acrimony and resignation, these whales proved to the world that they were determined to survive their brazen tryst with fate.

Fittingly there were hardly any media on hand for the event. When during the course of the rescue had they covered the truly newsworthy developments? Most were back in Pepe's recovering from their coverage of the other news item, Ron Morris announcing the Russian's pending arrival.

Cindy hugged nearly everyone she saw. The ice was awash in emotional embrace. Everyone was so caught up in the heady moment it took several frantic shrieks for attention from a lone Eskimo woman to cut short the euphoric pandemonium.

"The baby, the baby!" she shrieked. "Where's the baby?"

It struck Cindy like a dagger. Where *was* the baby? How could she not have noticed that since they began celebrating she had seen only the two larger whales? She screamed in panic as she sprinted toward Arnold, the whales' protector.

"Bone, Bone," she wailed. "Has anyone seen Bone?"

Craig George was right. The whales were protecting the baby whale. That was why the whales moved. When the baby gently slipped beneath the surface never to be seen again, the survivors readied themselves for freedom.

Bone was gone. Now there were only two whales left to save.

Chapter 21

Risking Lives for a Six-Second Scoop

Arnold Brower was indignant. "Don't scare me like that," he admonished Cindy. "Just watch what you say." He shook his head in aggravated annoyance and insisted that he had just seen the baby whale seconds earlier. Instead Brower retreated into his own well-known dispassion. He focused intently on the hole he was trying to keep clear of ice. Suddenly, he paused before lifting his seal pole out of the water. In a brief moment of uncertainty, he dropped the hollow aluminum shaft and let it float on the water's surface.

Throughout the unbridled emotion of the past several minutes, the seasoned· Arctic hunter had remained a pillar of stoicism. He preached to other subsistence hunters the need for practiced discipline in the bitter elements. Now he scolded Cindy, desperately hoping she was wrong. In the Arctic, he lectured her, there was no room for misplaced emotion. Survival depended on the facts, not the unfounded whims of the heart.

"We're out here killing ourselves and you go and panic over Bone. Just watch," he said, trying to restore their composure. "Just watch."

For the next frightful moments they did. Silently, they stood just inches apart waiting for the baby whale to return. Cindy trusted Arnold. His angry rebuttal reassured her. But this time, Arnold Brower was wrong. Bone was dead. After several moments, acknowledgment of Bone's fate became inevitable. Cindy broke down, consumed in grief. It was the most irrational week of her life. Her strength was shattered. Bone's death marked the nadir. The tragic but unavoidable conclusion came just after the elation of watching the two surviving whales move to the new holes.

Craig and Arnold, in a desperate attempt to calm her down, tried to coax Cindy off the ice and into a waiting truck to drive her back to town. The sooner she left, they thought, the sooner she might recover from the trauma of Bone's death. They were right. She calmed down the minute she sat down. Her hysteria behind her, Cindy insisted on taking another, last look for the baby whale and its scraped snout. She closely inspected the first holes waiting for a sign of Bone. After a moment, she knew it was not to be.

A week of intense proximity enabled Craig and Cindy to grow close enough for him to clutch her with his down-covered arm. "You did all you could," Craig comforted her. "Cin, if it weren't for you, they'd all be dead and you know it."

He was right. But Cindy didn't feel she deserved special commendation. The whales needed help and she offered it. That was her job. Contrary to Craig's well meaning intention, Cindy felt Operation Breakout became what it was not because of her, but because of the way people responded to her appeals.

Fran Tate, the owner of Pepe's, put up notices in the Top of the World to alert all the media and rescuers that her restaurant was closing early. The past few nights, Tate and her glassy-eyed employees had been manning the skillets and the deep fryers past midnight only to open again at 7:00 the next morning. Although she had been threatening to close at 9:00 PM since the rescue began, this time Craig believed her. Frankly, he was looking for any excuse to leave. Bone was dead and the melancholy on the ice was getting him down. Besides, he was hungry, cold and tired. The more energy people expended bewailing Bone, the less they would have for the two living whales, who were still quite desperate themselves.

As soon as Cindy was in the running truck, Craig jammed the transmission into drive, expertly spun his wheels on the ice, turned the vehicle sharply around and started the 17-mile return trip to Barrow. Rounding the northernmost tip of North America, Craig drove around the edge of the narrow sandspit to the smoother and safer ice of Elson's Lagoon.

Cindy looked out her pitch black window and marveled at the totality of Arctic nothingness.

She consoled herself by putting things in perspective. The rescue was just a momentary flash. Millions of people from around the globe were following the events of the three whales so closely that none of the hundred or so reporters had the time, energy or inclination to focus on the Arctic itself. The story would come and go. The drama would end, but the Arctic would remain. The rescue activity seemed significant when experienced in person or watched on television, but when compared to the vastness surrounding it, it was nothing. Hours after the last rescuer left, the Arctic would envelop the site, leaving no trace of human presence.

While Cindy stared intently into the night, Craig focused on the lone light that shined just over the horizon. It shone distinctly through a thin bank of low lying fog. It must be the temporary light put up by the borough to help guide vehicles on and off the ice, Craig thought. He was startled at its remarkable luminance. Even through the fog, it showed the way for miles. Craig couldn't understand why the lights didn't get brighter the closer he got. Perhaps he had lost his way. At the instant Craig contemplated panic, the gravel road that marked the beginning of the continent came into view. He thanked the light that led him there. He thanked the Arctic moon.

When Cindy checked for messages, she hoped to see one from Kevin. Suddenly she missed him terribly. She couldn't bear to be alone in her grief. She wanted to share it. The receptionist could read the disappointment on Cindy's face when she broke the news that no one had called. The first time Cindy wanted messages, there were none.

She ran upstairs to phone him. It was just after 8:00 PM, Friday night, October 21, two weeks to the day after the whales were discovered and one week since Cindy first started orchestrating their rescue. Until now, she never had the time or reason to miss her boyfriend. Bone's death changed all that. She hurriedly called his office. As she was about to hang up, she remembered that the election was just two weeks away and that Kevin was probably busy at work. Next to Cindy, elections were the most important thing to Kevin Bruce, who was one of Alaska's most prominent political consultants. Surely he couldn't have gone home yet, she told herself. Maybe he was screening his calls.

"Honey?" she asked lamely at the sound of the beep. "Are you there?" Before she could finish, Kevin dashed across the room to pick it up.

"Hi" he exclaimed with delight. "I'm really sorry about the baby whale."

"How do you know about that?" Cindy was puzzled. "You're the first person I've talked to since I've been back and I haven't told anybody."

"Oh really?" said Kevin. "It's all over the news. I just saw it on CNN."

Cindy was amazed. It wasn't an hour since Bone was first discovered missing and there were few reporters on the ice to cover it. But in less time than it took Cindy to drive back to Barrow, pick up the phone and dial Kevin's number, reports of Bone's all but certain death were already big news, bigger news than the Russians. She marveled at how the revolution in telecommunications had shrunk the world. News, even from one of the most remote regions on Earth, crossed the planet in an instant. Viewers in the Lower 48 learned about Bone's death before most reporters in Barrow.

Friday, October 21, was a day of double headlines: Soviet participation and Bone's drowning. By emphasizing the bad news, the media might well have sounded the operation's death knell. Unlike most news events which portray negative aspects of the world in which we live, Operation Breakout proved an international sensation because it described humans following a noble impulse to save helpless animals. If the coverage that Friday continued to focus on Bone's death, the story's good feeling might end. News executives didn't want their reports to provoke despair. If it turned as negative as every other story, their audience would lose interest.

Newsmen knew that this was different from almost any other story they had ever covered. It was the ultimate perversion of the "cat up a tree" story, a redux of the media frenzy surrounding Jessica McLune's 1986 rescue from a Midland, Texas, well. People's only interest in the whales was to see them saved. People were tired of politics, economics and war. They looked to the whales to help them escape, if only for a little while.

Notwithstanding the State Department "spin" doctors, news that the Russians were on the way led Saturday morning papers across the United States and Canada. Many editions carried banner headlines befitting a major story. Weekends are usually slow news periods. But papers need headlines on weekends just as on any other day. Television newscasts still need top stories. That weekend of October 22 and 23 belonged almost solely to the whales.

What worked against the State Department worked for Operation Breakout. Bone's death was not reported in the Lower 48 until after midnight Eastern time, much too late to run in the Saturday papers. By the time Sunday rolled around, Bone's passing was already old news, yet another ironic stroke of luck.

But Cindy wouldn't have known it by the constant ringing of her phone. Through the night, reporters from the Lower 48 and around the world called to verify that Bone had died. Even though it was all but apparent that the baby whale had drowned she didn't want to confirm it until first light Saturday morning. She and the rescuers could search the area once again for the missing whale and then let Ron Morris make whatever pronouncement he saw fit.

Around 10:00 PM, Bill Allen and Bed Odom returned to Barrow to help prepare for the arrival of the giant Archimedian Screw tractor. Allen and Odom's men at Prudhoe Bay were scheduled to work all night breaking down the pontoon ice crusher into sections small enough to fit on board an airplane that would fly it to Barrow, 270 miles away. After a day of round-the-clock maneuverings, Alaska Senator Ted Stevens convinced both the White House and the Pentagon to authorize the U.S. Air Force to deploy the tractor to Barrow. VECO faxed the screw tractor's dimensions from Prudhoe Bay to the Pentagon. The only plane big enough for the massive load was the biggest one in the American fleet, the Lockheed C-5A Galaxy cargo transport aircraft.

Bill Allen was busy until late at night using the phone in Ed Benson's apartment. Benson, who owned the jammed Airport Inn, wanted the big oilman out of his kitchen so his family could get some sleep. Benson won a reprieve when Chuck Baker, another VECO representative, gave up his room for Allen and Leathard in exchange for permission to return to Anchorage. It was a no-lose proposition for Baker. He was the envy of most of us who had to stay in Barrow.

By Saturday morning, Allen and Leathard were famished. They hadn't eaten since leaving Anchorage the day before. The hungry oilmen were first in line at Pepe's on Saturday morning. Cindy Lowry was in the same predicament. Unsure who was standing next to her while she waited for a table, Cindy immediately recognized Bill Allen's unmistakable Texas drawl. Allen was too busy talking with Pete about details of the Screw Tractor to notice the tiny woman who orchestrated the massive international rescue. When Craig and Geoff came in, two of Operation Breakout's biggest players were introduced.

Allen politely tipped his ten gallon Stetson hat as if being introduced to royalty. He broke into a thin sympathetic smile and quietly said, "Ma'am, it's awful damn nice to meetcha. People all over the world owe you a lot of thanks, me included." Cindy warmly accepted the good graces and asked Allen and Pete Leathard to join her for breakfast. They happily obliged.

Before they sat down, Allen whispered in Cindy's ear. "Can I see you over there," he whispered pointing to a quiet corner of the dining room. "I'd like to talk with you in private." Cindy was repulsed at the thought that the gangly oilman might be about to make a pre-breakfast pass at her. Allen walked ten paces to the corner while Cindy followed warily behind. When they both stood in front of the kitchen door, Allen leaned against the overhanging doorframe and took on a look of sympathy and understanding.

"Hell, I know how much you wanted to save that baby," he said to Cindy's vanishing smile of curiosity. "I just want you to know that you have done all that you can and that you have my word that we're going to do our damnedest to save them last two critters. I ain't never seen no whales until I came up here last week, and let me tell ya something, they are incredible animals. We're gonna save 'em, ma'am. I promise you."

Before Operation Breakout, Cindy felt nothing but hostility for oil companies and the people who ran them. They were the bad guys. Their business was pumping oil. If that meant wreaking environmental havoc, so be it. Now suddenly here was the quintessential oilman expressing his love for whales. In the moment it took him to convey his genuine empathy, Cindy realized how muddled her perceptions had become. She was a professional environmentalist. Bill Allen was an oilman. Without hesitation, she gave an unprepared Bill Allen an impromptu hug. They laughed, and Cindy walked back to the table sporting her infectious smile that returned for the first time since Bone's death.

While Cindy, Geoff, Craig and Arnold were getting ready to go back on the ice to continue to search for the missing whale, Ron Morris was trying to find out when the Russian ships would arrive. Acccording to the State Department, the Soviet vessels were due in Barrow the next night, Sunday, October 23, a week to the day after Operation Breakout began, 16 days after the whales were found. When the two Soviet vessels finished their work on the Northern Pole 31 float station, they faced a 300-mile journey to the southwest.

When the announcement was first made the day before, on Friday, October 21, Captain Sergei Reshetov's best analysis indicated that it would take two days to reach Barrow. But soon after their departure from the floating ice station, he found conditions much worse than expected. The shifting ice pack made navigation treacherous His artful dodges and traverses would add hours to the trip.

Reshetov was worried. Rarely had he seen such dangerous ice conditions so early in the year. He could only imagine what kind of winter lay in store. He sent a cable to Vladivostok asking officials for aerial ice reconnaissance. Having spent a career in the Soviet Merchant Marine, Reshetov knew not to get his hopes up. U.S. reconnaissance capabilities were light-years ahead of his own country's and Reshetov knew it. If ever there was time to demand quid pro quo, this was it. It was the Americans who asked the Soviets for help. Now the Soviets could ask the Americans for help of their own. The Soviet Merchant Marine forwarded their request to the U.S. State Department. Saturday morning, the State Department passed it on to Glenn Rutledge at the Navy/NOAA Joint Ice Center in Suitland, Maryland.

Rutledge assembled Arctic ice data compiled daily by the National Ocean Service, an arm of NOAA. He put together large maps detailing ice thickness and openings in the polar pack. The data proved invaluable to Master Reshetov and the Soviet icebreakers. But as good as the data proved to be, Rutledge knew it could be better. Aside from stranding themselves in the first place, the whales had been carried by an uncanny streak of luck since the very beginning. It was luck that led Roy Ahmaogak to find them in a tiny hole in the ice, luck that caused the whole world to pull for them and spend millions to free them. And now, as that same luck would have it, American satellite imaging was on the verge of a major leap forward.

On September 24, 1988, just two weeks before the whales were discovered, the U.S. Air Force deployed the most sophisticated weather satellite ever built, launched into orbit aboard an unmanned Atlas rocket. The state-of-the-art $100 million satellite, called NOAA-11, could produce much more sharply defined images than earlier U.S. satellites. But NOAA-11 was not scheduled to start operating until December 1988, too late to help whales. The media firestorm over the whales proved as much a NOAA emergency as any life-threarening hurricane.

The agency had received more publicity in Operation Breakout's first week than it had in the 18 years of its existence. The previously obscure federal agency, unknown to most Americans, was on the front page of every newspaper in the country. That included the *Washington Post*, the newspaper read by the people who approved NOAA's annual budget. For people inside the Beltway, it was NOAA's coming of age. For the agency, the whole affair was a godsend. NOAA ordered its special satellite turned on immediately.

By Monday, October 24, eight days after Operation Breakout began, the newest and most sophisticated weather satellite ever deployed had its first assignment: freeing the whales. Suddenly, the two whales sputtering in the waters off Barrow had entered the space age.

But while a $100 million geosynchronous satellite compiled ice analysis, Eskimo crews under the direction of Arnold Brower continued the task of cutting open holes so the whales could breathe. When Cindy returned to the ice Saturday morning, the whales were energetically popping in and out of the last of the 55 holes. They swam under more than a mile of frozen sea in one night. Now, there was no doubt, the whales were on their way. If the Russians could cut through the pressure ridge, they would soon be free.

After a week's practice, the Eskimos were cutting new holes at a furious pace. That Friday night, Ron Morris pushed them all to work even faster. "The Russians will be here in two days," he told a skeptical Brower. "They told us they can work only one day. I want the whales as close to that damned ridge as we can get them."

Brower took his order and ran. Saturday, Brower's men cut 15 new holes before noon. The two whales were keeping right with them. Morris wanted all his guns firing. He pressed Colonel Carroll to get his concrete bullet into the arsenal.

On Saturday morning, the colonel managed to stave off yet another near disaster, potentially the worst yet. Just hours before, Colonel Carroll's National Guard contingent completed the last of its redeployment from Prudhoe. All 12 Guardsmen landed safely in Barrow aboard two Bell Huey helicopters, the workhorse of the Alaska National Guard. The Guard unit prided itself on its ability to operate in America's most hostile weather.

But that Friday night, Colonel Carroll's unit displayed just the opposite foresight. After shutting down their engines, the guardsmen left the expensive helicopters outside the hangar. Moments later, they were frozen solid. Discovering the lapse, Colonel Carroll was outraged. He opened the huge bay doors to roll the helicopters inside. Thankfully, Randy Crosby was there to stop him. Crosby was shocked to see the Guard about to break one of the first rules of Arctic aviation: *never let frozen equipment thaw too quickly.*

"What the hell are you guys doing?" Crosby shouted in disbelief. He explained that if the frozen helicopters were brought inside, vital parts of the aircraft would crack. Crosby told Carroll and his men that his helicopters had to be defrosted slowly. If he wanted the Hueys to fly again, Carroll would have to leave them outside wrapped in nylon parachutes and let the feeble Arctic sun do the rest.

Saturday, October 22, was the warmest day of the past two weeks. While it was still 15° below zero on the ice, the temperature in town almost reached the double digits. Scantily clad Eskimos made the conditions seem almost balmy. The heaviest garb to be seen was a light, unbuttoned windbreaker. Even they were scarce. Few wore hats and almost no one wore gloves. Teenagers strutted through the frozen streets in sneakers and tee shirts.

I actually saw one kid in a brightly colored bathing suit riding through the icy streets on a bicycle. Reporters stuck out plainly among the locals. To us it was more than cold. It was downright bitter, even in our expensive designer ski clothes. Eskimos never donned hats and gloves in weather warmer than 20° or 30° below. We always wore them.

Later that Saturday morning, the Colonel unveiled the Arco ice crusher, his latest scheme for freeing the whales, Operation Breakout's next media spectacular. For the insatiable press and their whale crazed audience, the fifth and sixth days of Operation Breakout, Friday and Saturday, October 21 and 22, were a news bonanza. The Russian icebreakers, Bone's death, and the ice smasher added up to the rescue's climax: the Super Bowl of whale-saving.

After traveling to the end of the world to cover what started as a nature story, reporters soon found themselves facing the same inveterate media manipulation they dealt with every day down in the Lower 48. Early Saturday morning, Mike Haller, Tom Carroll's media relations officer, posted a schedule for the day's events at the entrance to Pepe's, in the Top of the World Hotel, and at NARL, where the international and late arriving press stayed. Activities began at 8:00 AM, several hours before daybreak, at the old Navy hangar south of NARL. Colonel Carroll's men hitched Arco's five-ton concrete block to the CH-54 Sky Crane helicopter.

Some reporters faced a dilemma. They could go to the ice with Cindy or watch the bullet. Having each invested up to $10,000 a day in covering the event, the fiercely competitive American television networks weren't going to take the chance of being beaten. By Saturday morning, each network had at least two camera crews, enabling them to cover more than one event at a time. While one crew could film Arco's bullet, the other could be on the ice with the two whales.

Amid a modicum of fanfare, half a dozen cameras watched the Sky Crane lift the five-ton battering ram off the frozen tarmac. Since the event was designed with the media in mind, Gary Quarrells landed the helicopter after a quick circle around the hangar. He took off again to give the cameras a second chance. On the ground, cameramen ran around the helipad to photograph the Sky Crane from different angles. The helicopter flew slowly so the camera crews would have plenty of time to board the three SAR helicopters and film the Sky Crane while still in flight. Taking a page from Jesse Jackson's 1988 presidential campaign, Haller knew that the longer the Sky Crane flew, the more chance every cameraman would have to take the perfect picture of it.

Carroll agreed with Morris' order not to frighten the whales. He would test the bullet several miles from the Eskimo holes. But by Saturday morning, it seemed that nothing could startle the freedom-starved leviathans. The deafening clatter of the helicopters didn't appear to have any effect. The chances of the five-ton concrete block spooking them seemed remote. While the three press helicopters formed a mile-wide triangle around it, the Sky Crane hovered 50 feet above the frozen sea awaiting final orders from Colonel Carroll.

Once again, the colonel was on the line. He was getting used to it. During that time his world underwent a remarkable transformation, from quiet anonymity to the turbulent center of an absurd operation. Whatever Tom Carroll said or did was reported around the world. Tom Carroll was headline news, a center of one of the decade's biggest media events.

But the height of his great adventure wasn't played out on the ice or in the air. It took place each night on the telephone with a woman 7,000 miles away. There was one constant. Her name was Bonnie Mersinger. Their bond was instant. This faceless woman in Washington was suddenly the center of his frazzled life. Carroll was convinced that the three whales he was summoned to rescue stranded themselves so he could meet the woman of his dreams. They spoke every day. Officially, it was a chance for the colonel to brief the White House on the progress of the rescue. But unofficially, it was the chance for Tom and Bonnie to grow closer. With each conversation, their relationship intensified.

After wishing Bonnie the "top of the morning," the colonel gave the order for Quarrells to "drop the bomb." Just as it had two days earlier, the free-falling battering ram easily broke through the ice. Quarrells punched ten more holes before Arnold Brower and his Eskimo scouts arrived to examine the results. The Eskimos immediately saw a problem. The bullet broke the ice, but it didn't remove it. The heavily broken blocks still floated in place. Brower knew that the only way the gray whales would use a hole was if it had been meticulously combed free of even the smallest pieces of ice.

The bullet was retired after just one run. Operation Breakout had taken yet another of its many ironic twists. The distinguished colonel met with more logistical setbacks in the first week of the whales rescue than he had in 20 years. Yet Tom Carroll was a national figure. Next to a 41-year-old junior Senator from Indiana who was about to become Vice President, Tom Carroll was the person most Americans associated with the National Guard. And like his Hoosier comrade, the colonel would rise above the cacophony of hostile critics crying foul at every turn.

Colonel Carroll learned of the whales' latest crisis when he returned to the Navy hangar. The high-priced NOAA biologists flown in from Seattle were baffled. The two whales stopped dead in their tracks. They seemed stuck, as if something was preventing them from moving on. The whales' eagerness to forge ahead was as strong as ever. The walkie-talkies crackled with activity. Anybody with suggestions was urged to help.

But the sophisticated technology was of little use. Malik went to the Eskimo warm-up shack without his radio. The rescuers were eager for him to return so Craig raced to fetch him. He waited while Malik finished chewing a piece of smoked walrus meat. On his way out the door, he picked up a chunk of muktuk from the whale he and his crew killed a few weeks earlier and popped it into his mouth.

They jumped on the back of Craig's waiting ski machine. The loud roar of the fast machine made conversation en route impossible. Instead, Malik savored the particularly tasty piece of whale blubber. As the crowded holes came into view, Malik wiped his mouth with satisfaction and prepared to get back to the task of saving the dead bowhead's two stranded cousins.

The "little big man" jumped off the machine and lifted up his red baseball cap, now a trademark. It was emblazoned with an oval black and white patch bearing the name of the trade group to which every subsistence whaler belonged: "Alaska Eskimo Whaling Commission." Malik knew the contours of the frozen ocean he was standing atop better than anyone. Before he even saw them, Malik had a strong suspicion what held the whales back. The instant he peered into the hole they wouldn't enter, his suspicions were confirmed.

Unlike the other 70 holes the whales used in the past 24 hours, this one wasn't black. Light reflected from the ocean bottom cast a distinctly gray hue. The whales were stuck at the edge of an underwater sand shoal only 12 feet deep. That was dangerously shallow, even for shore-dwelling grays. The whales had hit a roadblock and, like their rescuers, were unsure how to proceed. Saving whales was new to Malik. Normally, he killed them.

Suddenly, the answer hit him. "A detour," Malik exclaimed. "Would a whale swim if he thought he might get stuck?" he asked no one in particular. "Let's cut holes around the shoal."

During the hour the whales were blocked by the sand bar, Arnold Brower and his Eskimos cut 14 new holes. Bill Allen was impressed.

"Well, look at that Archie Bowers work," he said, mistakenly referring to the Eskimo leader.

But the holes would never be used. Malik and Arnold Jr. turned their back on the errant path and probed the area for deeper water. As soon as an alternate path was marked and new holes cut, the whales followed. The 14 misdirected holes froze without a trace.

The rush was on to get the whales through the last four miles of ice and out to the pressure ridge. Supposedly, the Russians were only a day away. The rescuers counted on having but one chance to get the whales through any openings the Russians could cut through the pressure ridge. No one knew what kind of a problem the ridge would present, or if the Soviet ships could even surmount it. Ever since Bone vanished, the whales lived up to their end of the bargain. They burst into the new holes before they were fully cut. Now more than ever, the rescue's success depended on the Eskimos.

When the Soviets agreed to join the party, the media scrambled for the first pictures of the Russian ships plowing through thick polar ice en route. But NBC was the only network with an independent means to win the race: a helicopter. It was a widely known secret in the prefab corridors of the Top of the World Hotel that NBC would start its chase through the menacing Arctic skies as soon as the Russian ships were within 200 miles of Barrow.

No one was more aware of the looming scoop than ABC News producer Harry Chittick. Chittick had been griping to Ron Morris for days about NBC's helicopter and the unfair advantage he thought it gave his competition. Jerry Hansen, Chittick's NBC counterpart reminded Morris that there was no law against renting a helicopter and that, to date, there were no restrictions on flights that prevented the NBC chopper from getting the rescue's best and most reliable aerial video.

Chittick knew NBC had the edge, but he thought there might be a way to steal the scoop right from under Hansen's nose. Chittick spent Saturday morning trying to rent his own aircraft. The airplane he found would enable him to slip right past the slow-flying NBC helicopter and out to the icebreakers. He didn't even need a pilot. He was licensed to fly himself.

Researchers in his Los Angeles office looked up the icebreakers in the maritime bible, "Jane's All the World's Ships." Figuring out the icebreakers' speed, the ABC researchers calculated when the vessels would come within range. But by the time Chittick finally rented an airplane, it seemed too late. NBC appeared to have won again.

On Saturday afternoon, NBC's Don Oliver checked in with the international information exchange that connected the Soviet Merchant Marine, the U.S. Government and the Russian ships. Almost everyone knew where the center was located, Randy Crosby's office at the SAR hangar. SAR easily adapted to its new role. It was already headquarters for Tom Carroll's National Guard unit and the transit terminal for the media. In all but name, SAR was Operation Breakout's official headquarters.

U.S. Government reports placed the Russians about 170 miles northeast of Barrow where the icebreakers encountered unexpectedly thick ice. The ships had to reduce their speed to less than three knots, much slower than originally predicted. Moreover, the satellite photographs and computer-enhanced charts transmitted to the bridge of the *Admiral Makarov* revealed that a large ice floe lay directly across the planned route to Barrow. Master Reshetov had no choice but to chart a lengthy detour. The revised schedule estimated the icebreakers would arrive in Barrow 24 to 36 hours late.

Though still too far away to help the whales, the icebreakers were within striking distance of making it on the evening news. The NBC helicopter had a standard range of about 350 miles under "favorable conditions," a term which could not be applied to the Arctic. The "no return point" was 175 miles. Flying outbound any further than that meant there would not be enough fuel to make it back. The weather threatened to make the trip even more dangerous.

Dense ice fog hugged the ground, hiding a thick layer of cloud cover just overhead. By the end of October 1988, Barrow was already so cold that even the tiniest particles of water vapor froze into ice crystals so small they escaped even the force of gravity. The ice fog enveloped everything. In settled areas like Barrow, ice fog reduced visibility to absolute zero. By mid-afternoon, Randy Crosby grounded all his helicopters and advised others to do the same. NBC was not about to let the weather get in the way of a good story.

The safety of the freelance crew was a minor impediment to obtaining the first video of the icebreakers, pictures that would run at most for five to eight seconds on the evening news. Viewers would never know the risks taken to get them. The pressure to fly was never explicit. It didn't have to be. News doesn't wait for the timid and it doesn't give second chances. Since NTV, the network my company was hired to represent, was paying for half the helicopter, I insisted we get in on the action. Earlier that morning, over Pepe's greasy home fries and soft, butter-soaked Wonder Bread, I asked Jerry Hansen, the NBC producer, what he thought about using our chopper to find the approaching ships. Hansen swallowed nervously as if I had divulged a state secret. His wary eyes looked around to see if anyone had heard, motioning for me to keep quiet. "Everything is being taken care of," he told me. He was right. It was.

My cameraman, Steve Mongeau, and I went to NARL where our helicopter was based. For several hours we waited inconspicuously for the pilots to give the "go." By late afternoon, it was apparent that the ice fog wasn't going to lift. The two pilots showed little enthusiasm for the Saturday night death run, but they had most demanding clients. They had long since quit reminding us to keep our seatbelts on while hanging out the hovering helicopter's open doors.

The weather was as uncertain as the precise position of the Soviet ships. All that was certain was our intent to look for them. If the icebreakers were exactly 170 miles away, they were five miles inside the "no return point," just ten miles short of the helicopter's maximum range. There was precious little margin for error. NBC cameraman Bruce Gray remarked that finding the ships in the thick fog with so little room to maneuver would be like finding a needle in a haystack. Long stretches of silence marked the eerie journey out. But as the fuel gauge neared half empty, there was still no sign of the Russians.

Encroaching darkness threatened to spoil more than the photography. As night fell so too did the chances of survival should anything go awry. As it turned out, no one would have survived in an emergency landing anyway. We later learned there were no flotation devices on board the aircraft.

As the helicopter came perilously close to the "no return point," the pilots turned off the inner cabin intercom so they could talk among themselves without alarming the unkowing passengers. If they didn't turn the helicopter around within the next 90 seconds, it would not have enough fuel to get back. There would be no choice but to land on an iceberg and pray to be saved. Because of the safety violations, the pilots didn't want to take the chance of radioing for rescue for fear of losing their licenses.

When they turned around to announce their ominous dilemma, Gray was excitedly preparing his camera to shoot. At almost the exact point of no return, the eery silhouette of the 496-foot *Admiral Makarov,* the pride of the Soviet ice-breaking fleet, loomed menacingly into view. The satellite tracking proved stunningly accurate. It was within yards of the pilots' projections. Spinning his finger in the air to signal a flight around the ship, Gray pleaded for the chance to at least get some decent pictures of the immense Soviet ice-breakers. He furiously readied his camera for the difficult task of shooting under such rushed conditions. It was now or never.

The chopper dove within just a few hundred feet of the ships towering deck. Curious sailors clambered on deck to inspect the unidentified visitor. Gray told the pilots to slow their air speed so he could make the special adjustments his camera needed to work in the near dark. When the chopper's nose pulled away on its uncertain flight back to Barrow, the only footage of the Soviet icebreakers sat on Gray's lap. He had a marginally important scoop. But as his own life hung perilously in the balance, he wondered whether what he had just done was courageous or stupid.

Flying across the pitch black Arctic, no one was sure what lay below: water or ice. Worry quickly degenerated into panic. The fuel gauge continued to plummet. With the heat turned off to conserve fuel, the temperature in the cabin dropped below zero. The minutes stretched long and uncertain. Thankfully, a fortuitous shift in the wind cut the helicopter's drag, giving it just enough fuel to allow a safe landing at the NARL helipad. The footage everyone had risked their lives for didn't even air until 24 hours later on NBC's "Sunday Night News." By the time the precious pictures had run, ABC had already aired their own footage shot 16 hours after NBC's. NBC won the battle but lost the war, a war that, like the rescue itself, was created and fought by and for the media.

Chapter 22

Sergei Reshetov: "Let's Cut Ice"

Like the whales they were diverted to save, the Russians were running very late. By the time the massive ships broke across Barrow's horizon at around noon on Tuesday, October 25, the two icebreakers were almost two days behind schedule. The 440-foot *Admiral Arsenyev*, the smaller of the two ships, led the way. Eighteen days after the stranded whales were first found, two of the mightiest ships in the Soviet Merchant Navy arrived to complete the trapped animals' improbable route to freedom. The ships were so large, and the terrain so flat, they were easily visible from town, some 25 miles away. Parked at a safe distance from the Pressure Ridge, the massive icebreakers were less than ten miles from the whales they came to redeem.

Crowds of reporters busily jockeyed for position in the line outside the SAR hangar. They were desperate to see the day's press pool assignment. Master Reshetov cabled Ron Morris to tell him that the American pool reporters were welcome on his ship. After all, the Russians had dispatched the icebreakers with an eye to favorable publicity. Pool coverage rotated on a daily basis among the four American networks: ABC, CBS, CNN and NBC. Because of our own rented helicopter, we rarely had to rely on the pool. The exception was for access to the Soviet ships.

CNN correspondent Greg LeFebre and his two man crew were the first non-Soviet television reporters scheduled to board the massive *Admiral Makarov*. They joined coordinator Ron Morris and his overseer Admiral Sigmund Peterson, the Pacific NOAA fleet commander. Randy Crosby flew them out. We trailed just a few hundred yards behind in our own helicopter. The only difference was that they were allowed to land and we were not. We did the next best thing, augmenting the pool material with our own exclusive aerials. Big deal

Listening to heavily accented instructions from the *Arsenyev*, Crosby eased back the throttle and touched down squarely on the landing pad at the stern of the 496-foot ship. The engine idled while Crosby waited for the signal to power down. His eyes darted about in fascination.

As he waited, Crosby couldn't help but think what a far cry this was from a normal day's work. Ten days before, he was just the director of the North Slope Borough's Search and Rescue Department, a peculiar emergency services division established to aid subsistence Eskimos. His primary job was rescuing stranded native hunters stuck on the tundra or a floating block of ice in the middle of the Arctic Ocean. Now he was piloting a U.S. admiral and a CNN television crew, but VIP's were nothing new. Just a year before, Crosby flew novelist James Michener around the Arctic to research his bestselling book, *Alaska*.

But landing on Soviet icebreakers? That was new. The huge hammer and sickle painted on the smokestack dispelled any doubt about where he was. By convention of international maritime law, Randy Crosby, father of four, had just landed in the Union of Soviet Socialist Republics.

Crosby saw a heavy metal hatch slowly open at the base of the ship's superstructure. It was the first sign of life. A few seconds later, a small, heavily bundled man tentatively emerged. He walked to the helipad, stopped, and stared. After giving the American visitors the once-over, the unidentified man turned back toward the open door and nodded.

Brandishing warm smiles and effusive greetings, several more of the ship's crew appeared. Ron Morris waved the CNN camera crew out of the chopper first so they could capture every bit of the official welcome on film. A Soviet television crew was already on deck. With both cameras rolling Morris jumped down from behind the helicopter's plastic door to bask in the attention of Master Sergei Reshetov and his next in command, First Officer Alexander Patsevich. Behind him came NOAA's Admiral Sigmund Peterson.

"Ron Morris, U.S. Government," the NOAA coordinator introduced himself to his Soviet counterparts. His rank grew more impressive each time he mentioned it. By week's end, Morris would reportedly tell journalists and rescuers alike that he was the Reagan Administration's official representative. The White House was furious. Bonnie Mersinger's line was bombarded by White House and Commerce Department higher-ups demanding that someone "put a muzzle" on the coordinator.

"Who the hell is this guy?" a senior White House official demanded of Mersinger, the administration's whale rescue liaison. It was her job to find out. Just ten days from obscurity, Ron Morris was on record as saying he was an official representative of the President of the United States. Assistant Commerce Secretary William Evans saw the low-level Ron Morris on television speaking to reporters as if he were sent to coordinate the rescue by Ronald Reagan himself. Angry and dismayed, Secretary Evans sent Morris a stern confidential memo of rebuke:

"I have been contacted by the White House via the Secretary of Commerce's Chief of Staff with reports that you have represented yourself to the press as an official representative of the President and/or the Administration," the memo began. "This is incorrect behavior and you will cease all contact with the press on the subject of any fisheries program without first clearance from the Assistant Administrator of NOAA for Fisheries. You do not represent the administration. You have either been grossly misquoted or have not made your role clear to the media as a federal employee."

After introductions and a short pose for the rolling cameras, CNN's Greg LeFebre asked the first question. He was surprised to hear the Soviet captain answer him in excellent English. NOAA interpreter Svetlana Andreeva, brought specially from Washington, was delighted to learn she wasn't needed. Maybe now she could go home. Reshetov invited the Americans to his quarters for an obligatory shot of vodka. Even Randy Crosby pounded one back.

When they reached the captain's cabin, Morris opened up a weathered leather satchel and pulled out the most recent satellite image analysis, charts and other data compiled by federal agencies for presentation to the Soviets. Morris and Admiral Peterson briefed Reshetov on Operation Breakout and the last remaining obstacle to the whale's freedom, the massive pressure ridge. After hearing Morris' summation, Master Reshetov opened his arms, clearly relishing the challenge. He turned to the cameras and said, "Let's cut ice."

But before work came a little more pleasure: a second toast of vodka, a tour of the ship, and a chance for the Americans to meet its sea-weary crew. Although anxious to be reunited with family and friends, the Soviet sailors seemed eager to help the trapped whales. Together, the Americans and their Soviet counterparts walked to the dreary officers' mess where a Soviet-style lunch of borscht, potatoes and a tasteless meat stew awaited them.

Before Crosby boarded the helicopter for the return flight to the United States, a few gregarious Soviet crew members rushed to give him an assortment of pins and buttons. They also gave him a fur hat emblazoned with a gold-rimmed scarlet star of the Soviet Red Army.

"Christ," he chortled as he prepared to lift off from the Russian vessel. "I sure as hell never thought I'd be so damned proud to wear a Commie hat."

Moments later, the American chopper was back in the United States.

Immediately after the Americans departed, Reshetov consulted with his crew to devise a strategy for attacking the pressure ridge. The Americans doubted whether the Soviet ships could break through. Bridling at the implied American insult, Reshetov determined to prove them wrong. He had to decide which of his two ships should attempt the first assault.

The crew combined the remarkably clear American satellite imagery and its own estimations of ocean depth and ice thickness. It recommended that Reshetov deploy the *Admiral Arsenyev* to see if she could find any exploitable weaknesses. Since the smaller ship had a shallower keel, she could more safely break ice over the dangerous shoals and sandbars off Point Barrow. Because Reshetov was unfamiliar with the American waters, he didn't want to take any chances. If the *Arsenyev* wasn't up to the task, he could always call in his big gun, the *Admiral Makarov*, which was anchored just a few hundred meters off the ridge.

A trio of pesky helicopters buzzing like mosquitoes swirled overhead as the *Arsenyev* engaged new powerful engines and belched a huge plume of black smoke. The big ship easily cut a channel to the ice wall, preparing to strike it head on. The *Arsenyev* was ready for her first assault on the pinnacled pressure ridge. Just as the American rescuers fit the stereotype of a country excessively reliant on technology, the Soviets were about to epitomize the world's image of their own nation: brute strength and size.

The helmsman threw the powerful engines into reverse. The Finnish-made ship needed room to build up speed before hitting the outer edge of the ridge. The crew braced itself for the first contact. For several minutes, the men waited expectantly, unsure of the impact. The double hull of reinforced steel was designed to withstand tremendous strain, but Reshetov was uncertain whether the grounded ice would give. He expected the worst and ordered the crew to do the same. The *Arsenyev's* bow met the glacial blue wall in a thunderous collision. The deafening sound of 24 million pounds of grinding steel crushing the thick ice was audible for miles.

But the wrenching noise belied the remarkable ease with which the *Arsenyev's* bow parted the ice. As his ship plowed ahead undaunted, Reshetov broke into hearty laughter. The crew joined him, breaking the tense silence. The last remaining obstacle to the whales' freedom was falling beneath the mighty bow of the Soviet icebreaker. For the first time since the whales were discovered 18 days earlier, Operation Breakout, suddenly and inexplicably re-named "Operation Breakthrough" by the U.S. Government, was on the verge of success.

At sea for the past six months, the crew had no comprehension of the dimensions of the rescue it was instructed to assist. Since they received their orders from the highest levels of Soviet government, the crew naturally assumed it was being asked to perform a daring, critical task, perhaps vital to its nation's security. What the Russians just figured out was that the ice they spent the past four days traversing was much more treacherous than that which they were summoned to cut. The ship's massive bow crushed its way ever closer to the curious crowd of onlookers and the whales they came to liberate.

No one, not even the Eskimos, had any idea the Soviet ships could so effortlessly cut through the ridge of grounded ice. Just minutes before, Gary Hufford, the NOAA ice expert brought specially to Barrow to help in the rescue, told reporters he thought the wall might well be impenetrable.

After several hundred yards, the pressure of the ridge ground the icebreaker to a halt, a normal occurrence that Master Reshetov expected to happen much sooner. The helmsman backed ship for another run at the ice wall. A huge cheer erupted as news of the icebreaker's success reached the crowd of rescuers and journalists gathered a few miles away. After ten days of setbacks, something finally worked.

Operation Breakout was reaching a crescendo. The pressure ridge, thought to be the last great obstacle to the whale's freedom, was no match for the *Admiral Arsenyev*. As soon as the Eskimos could finish their path of ice holes, the whales and the world could get on with their lives.

Bill Allen's last chance to help save the whales was fast approaching. Three days earlier, on Saturday, October 22, a Galaxy C5-A, the free world's largest aircraft, landed at Barrow's Wiley Post Memorial Airport. Barrow's Budget Director Dan Fauske, who lived across the street from the runway, was outside shoveling snow from his sidewalk when the huge plane blotted out the sky over the tiny town as it swooped in for a landing. He thought Barrow was being invaded, but he didn't know by whom.

The airport had to divert all other traffic while the C5-A straddled the end of the runway. It was too big and too heavy to use the tarmac. In a frenzy of activity involving Colonel Carroll's National Guard unit, the United States Air Force, and MarkAir Cargo Director Ed Rogers, the unwieldy Archimedian Screw Tractor was extracted from the Galaxy's gaping jaw.

Towed to the old Navy hangar just south of NARL, the Screw Tractor awaited its chance to show the world that VECO could help the whales after all. On Sunday afternoon, Bill Allen demonstrated it to a skeptical Ron Morris. Just across the road from the hangar, the tractor, spinning its huge screws, made its way awkwardly through the sand and onto the ice. For a few embarrassing moments it slid across the slippery surface without breaking through it. When the Screw Tractor finally found a weak spot, it left a trail of thick ice in its wake. Like the ill-fated bullet a day earlier, the tractor left too much debris.

But Bill Allen wasn't finished. He hadn't spent more than a quarter million dollars not to get in on the drama's last act. The Russians were making it look too easy. They had thrown down the gauntlet to Bill Allen and his American honor. He wanted that tractor on the ice and he wanted it to work. Over the phone to Marvin King, his man at Prudhoe Bay, Allen designed a sled which the Sky Crane could tow behind the tractor to clear the broken ice. Allen drew a sketch of it and faxed it to Prudhoe.

"Put it together as fast as you can," Allen ordered his pliant manager. "Carroll says he'll give us a whirl."

King and his men worked through the night Sunday and all day Monday welding together the makeshift sled. They had to leave it partially disassembled in order to load it aboard the Hercules C-130 cargo which was standing by to airlift it to Barrow. When it arrived, Billy Bob donned a welder's mask and prepared to use the skill he learned so many years before. When he and Pete Leathard found an acetylene torch, they knew they were in business. Ordering in from Pepe's, the two men went to work and didn't emerge until the sled was complete 48 hours later. Allen called Colonel Carroll and told him he planned the test run "down to a gnat's ass."

But earlier that day, the jinxed Sky Crane, linked to the rescue's most conspicuous failures, was grounded with a fractured blade, damage that would require 100,000 taxpayers' dollars to fix. The hundreds of man hours spent furiously constructing the rush-order sled went for naught. Bill Allen's last dream seemed dashed.

By Wednesday afternoon, October 26, less than 24 hours after the Soviets first appeared off the Barrow coast, the pressure ridge had been reduced to mounds of ice separating dozens of paths which convincingly disproved its invulnerability to escape paths a quarter mile wide. All that remained between the whales and their freedom was a three-mile stretch of virgin ice.

But ironically, just as the rescuers were bridging the final hurdle, the groundswell of public support that had propelled them this far suddenly began to falter. The remarkable web of shared concern that had bound together the American people for two extraordinary weeks started to unravel. The characteristic American demands for immediate results were coming to the fore. When the whales weren't freed right away we got cranky, angry, even resentful. Just when the Russian ships gave the rescue its first realistic hope of success, Americans began to question it all.

Was the extraordinary expense justified? Was it really worth doing more? How much was too much? When balanced against these questions, the rescue started to seem ludicrous. Sympathy turned to cynicism. Talk radio, the miner's canary of American public opinion, succcumbed to the first noxious fumes.

Newspapers started printing political cartoons which mocked the lavish attention heaped on the whales. Dan Wasserman, a *Boston Globe* political cartoonist, drew one of Operation Breakout's most memorable satires: Two homeless people sitting on a subway grate donning whale costumes in an inventive attempt to solicit help.

Ben Sargent of the *Austin American Statesman* sketched perhaps the most poignant cartoon: Living skeletons of Sudanese refugees languishing near a bombed out a relief truck. Its radio broadcast the captioned message, "The world stood transfixed today by the heart rending plight of the California gray whales."

The public's empathy had peaked. The whales didn't have much time. Reacting to its audience's changing mood, the press retrenched and subtly began to adopt a more conventional role. By the beginning of Operation Breakout's second week, reporters on the scene started asking the same questions. While not mentioned in any of our reports, the three small children killed in the tragic Barrow house fire served as vivid testimony to our excessive preoccupation with the whales; a watershed of sorts. Just when things looked to be going Ron Morris' way, the first uncomfortable questions were flung at him. There weren't many to be sure, but at least a few.

Fortunately for the whales, they were too busy to contemplate their growing "image problem." Hoping for a climactic ending to justify their continued presence, most of the media stuck with the whales. By now, there were hundreds of people on the ice: a score of camera crews, dozens of reporters, the Eskimo ice cutters, Ron Morris' cadre of experts, Colonel Carroll and the National Guard, and countless Barrowans. All were urging the whales on. Eskimos said the Arctic had probably never seen so much activity in its four billion year history. Never had the Arctic ice been subjected to so much man-made stress.

But so far the ice was holding up remarkably well. While 50 million pounds of icebreakers pounded away at the ice's outer edges, millions more pounds stressed its surface. Suddenly, this desolate patch of ice was the work place to hundreds of people and all their heavy effects.

The ice was the glassy super highway allowing high speed transit for scores of commuters. It was a Southern Californian's dream, a freeway in every sense of the word, a roadway as wide as it was long, with no limits. There were no barriers and virtually no dangers. Vehicles regularly drove at speeds reaching 80 miles an hour, on sheer ice! If we spun out of control, which was not unusual, the only danger was the driver's overreaction. The ice upon which we all depended was also the landing strip and tarmac to a fleet of helicopters and even light fixed-wing aircraft.

The ice we relied on for access to the whales was the very element that imprisoned them. But as they were boldly making clear, it wouldn't imprison them for long. Just a few hours before Arctic darkness would descend upon them on Wednesday, October 25, the two whales seemed to sense that it might be their last day of captivity. The Eskimos were opening holes at breakneck speed just to keep pace with the frenzied whales. Led by Sikhu, the larger of the two, the leviathans were trying to surface in new holes before they were finished. The whales were so persistent, they were sticking their vulnerable heads within inches of the lethal chainsaws.

Malik was forced to take steps to prevent an accidental slashing. Such a catastrophe would have been particularly tragic now that the whales were so close to freedom. He split his 12-man crew in half. The lead group cut the outline of a hole with their chainsaws and moved on to mark off the next one. Meanwhile, the second crew worked on the first hole, pushing the giant blocks of ice under the rim of the hole allowing the anxious whales to surface. Instead of colliding with a deadly chainsaw, the worst the whales would bump into was an aluminum seal pole.

It was all they could do to stay in the holes. Geoff and Craig were convinced the whales could see the path to the lead. Hundreds of people piled aboard trucks and snowmobiles. They raced beyond the end of the trail of ice holes to the edge of the Soviet-cut channel.

For everyone involved in the nearly two-week-old ordeal, the final hour seemed at hand. Since he was instructed by his assignment desk to "get the whales swimming free," British photographer Charles Lawrence humorously described the various possible scenarios. Would the whales pound their flukes with added vigor as their bodies glided across a marked plane separating entrapment from freedom? Or, as a cartoon in the *Richmond Times Dispatch* amusingly suggested, once they were free, would the whales mischievously beach themselves just to drive us all crazy?

On the two previous occasions when actual news did develop—the de-icers luring the whales into the first new holes and Bone's death—there were no cameras on hand. But this was different. The whales were about to swim free, a most difficult moment to capture for sure, but nonetheless the reason we were all there. Our job was to record in words, pictures and sound the liberation of the stranded whales.

But by early Tuesday evening, the ice which had proved so reliable was starting to show strain. Large structural cracks were found leading from the breaker channels all the way to the whales. The stress of all the weight the ice was forced to support was proving more than it could safely handle. The ice was starting to break. The risks were presented in no uncertain terms. The more people and equipment that stood atop it, the greater the likelihood the ice would collapse. Those of us who entrusted our lives to the durable ice required no further elaboration. While the ominous news did not keep us away, it tempered almost everyone's enthusiasm.

Everyone, that is, except my cameraman, Steve Mongeau. A few minutes past midnight on Wednesday morning, long after the rest of were fast asleep, Mongeau casually told our host, Rod Benson, that he was going to drive out to check on the Russians. Before Rod could register his concern about driving a vehicle on the fractured ice, Mongeau had slipped away. Thinking that the special barricades put up to limit access to the ice would be unmanned at such a late hour, Mongeau figured this might be his last chance to take his camera far out on the ice without being hassled.

Driving alone and without a weapon to protect against polar bears, several more of which were spotted earlier that day, Mongeau headed out past NARL, and around the gravel cul-de-sac. At the roundabout's far end, he plunged over the frozen dirt abutment and onto Elson Lagoon, the most heavily traveled ice road to the whales. Four rescuers tending the whales watched the rapid approach of Mongeau's vehicle with alarm. The closer Mongeau got, the faster he seemed to be going. By design, Mongeau was driving straight toward the open water channel, but if he didn't slow down soon, he would fatally plow straight into it.

Cindy looked on in helpless horror as Mongeau barreled on. She stood paralyzed. Stopping a speeding truck on a sheet of glassy ice would have required more divine intervention than human skill. She didn't dare step in front of him. If she did, he wouldn't have time to stop before running her over.

When the channel finally came into view, Mongeau knew that the worst thing he could do was slam on the breaks. If he did, the truck would skid uncontrollably. Instead, he deftly swerved the truck away from Cindy and the open water channel. When the truck spun to a stop and she was satisfied the driver was safe, Cindy's fear turned to fury. She ran over to confront whoever was reckless enough to nearly kill himself and four innocent bystanders.

"There are no vehicles allowed on the ice," she barked. "What's your name? I'm going to report you."

Mongeau knew he had driven carelessly and wasn't about to deny it. But to get kicked off the ice would spoil his one chance to get the surreal night video of the icebreakers. If he picked a fight with Cindy, he knew he would lose. He tried the best tactic he knew: his skillful look of youthful innocence. He tucked his beardless chin into his chest and pretended to reach for words that wouldn't come out.

"Look, I'm *reeeelly soooory*," he added, intentionally emphasizing his thick Canadian accent. "I'm just out here to take pictures. It's my job. I promise to be more careful."

Cindy sighed with relief. After his ten long days of dealing with insatiable egos, Mongeau's apparently genuine contrition reaffirmed her faith in the human species. Her anger quickly turned to solicitude. She wasn't a policeman, she confided, so she couldn't stop him, but she warned him not to go any further out.

"It's for your own safety," she added for emphasis. With that, Mongeau drove away. But to Cindy's astonishment, he was heading straight for the dangerous ice she had just warned him to avoid.

"This guy's out of his mind," she said to Craig. "He's trying to kill himself."

Mongeau didn't want to die. Far from it. He was just a gutsy 20-year-old kid out to prove a point. He was determined to show that he had the right stuff to make it as a network cameraman. That required the willingness to take risks that could cost him his life. This assignment was his first big chance. It was an opportunity other young cameramen could only dream of. This was the fish he wouldn't let get away. Since arriving in Barrow, Mongeau had already risked his life hanging out of helicopters and chasing polar bears. So far it had paid off handsomely. Lots of his video had already aired in Japan and on several NBC News broadcasts. But the coup he would savor most lay just moments ahead.

Before retiring for the night, Sergei Reshetov agreed to keep his icebreaker away from the whales. Moscow promised he would only have to work one day for the Americans. One had already stretched into three. Reshetov and his tired crew were desperate to get home. So far, only the *Arsenyev* had been cutting ice. The water was thought too shallow and dangerous for the larger icebreaker, which sat anchored and unused in the waters off the pressure ridge. But Master Reshetov was growing impatient.

When the *Arsenyev* first sliced through the outside of the ridge, Reshetov asked the Americans for permission to bring his ship all the way to the holes. He was confident enough in his ships' sonar depth readings to risk traversing the shallow waters. The *Arsenyev* could crush in an hour what would take the Eskimos another two days to cut through. But the Americans said no. Not so much for the shallow waters, but for the safety of the whales. Cindy and Arnold worried that the whales would be too frightened to enter the breaker channels and perhaps even retreat into older breathing holes.

Reshetov was tired of relying on the Americans. While he wanted the whales freed, he also wanted to go home. He waited until he thought everyone had cleared the ice. At just past 3:00 AM, Wednesday, October 26, 19 days after the whales were first discovered, Master Sergei Reshetov ordered the *Arsenyev's* helmsman to propel the massive ship forward in a bold, headlong dash toward the whales.

But before issuing the controversial command, Reshetov weighed the risks. He knew he was about to violate standing orders from the

Americans not to come too close to the whales. He also knew that the closer his ship could get, the less distance the Eskimos would need to cover with their chainsaws. If he got too close to the whales, he ran the risk of running them over. He also realized he was giving the Americans no warning of his daring plan.

What the Soviet captain did not know was that a Canadian cameraman was alone on the ice that cold dark night on an intuitive hunch that something newsworthy might happen. The Canuck photographer's hunch paid off. His was the only camera to capture Reshetov's intrepid adventure. Ignoring rumbling warnings from the shaking frozen floor beneath him, Mongeau got out and walked to within yards of the ship's massive hull. He captured from remarkably close range the powerful sights and grinding sounds of the icebreaker's overwhelming force as it crushed its way toward the stranded whales.

His next shots were among the most enduring of the entire rescue. Lying prone with his camera right down on the ice, Mongeau framed a shot of the two gray whales surfacing frantically in the foreground while the daunting bow of the massive icebreaker loomed dramat ically in the background. For the first time since the American public became obsessed with them almost two weeks earlier, the trapped mammals looked *tiny*. Compared to the monstrous vessel towering right over them, they were. Slipping perilously down a rocking ice floe knee deep into the frigid water, Mongeau was shaken enough not to further press his luck.

Chapter 23

Free at Last

First light Wednesday morning revealed icebreaker channels just 400 yards from the two surviving whales. If anybody had questions as to how it happened, they could ask Steve Mongeau. He had the only footage. With cunning, poise, and talent, the 20-year-old Canadian had more than proved his point. He had the stuff needed to succeed. Morris never mentioned the violation to Reshetov. The Russian captain's aggressive icebreaking brought the whales closer than ever to freedom and with no apparent damage.

The excitement sparked by the pre-dawn developments was palpable all over town. Barrow took on a festive air. The whales would soon be free, and Operation Breakout over. But before it ended, Barrowans wanted to savor their glory. Residents no longer seemed frightened or unsure of all the visitors. They became more friendly, grateful their forced hospitality was only a temporary condition. Businesses closed down. The North Slope Borough Government office, the biggest business of them all, took the afternoon off. For the first time since the rescue began, classes were dismissed early. Word spread that the whales would be free by

nightfall. Teachers willingly acquiesced when the students clambered for one last chance to see the creatures that helped put their tiny
village on the map.

By the hundreds, Barrowans went to bid the whales farewell. But
once they got there, they seemed more fascinated by the media than
by the cetacean duo. After all, whales were much more common.
They saw them all the time and ate their meat at every meal. By
mid-afternoon, the line of parked vehicles along the ice looked like
a misplaced crowd awaiting a space shuttle launch off Cape
Canaveral. Dozens of pickup trucks, vans and cars sat with engines
idling, chattering animatedly in their native Inupiat. Suddenly and
without warning, Sikhu, the larger of the two surviving whales,
vanished.

Poutu, the other whale continued to surface normally in the last
hole. Malik and Arnold were stumped. Unlike Bone, who vanished
under the ice five days earlier, Sikhu was the strongest and most
vibrant of the three whales. The instant Sikhu was discovered
missing, Malik knew something significant was about to happen.
Without explanation to others around him, his dark Eskimo face
beamed with a new revelation. He dropped his seal pole and
lumbered to the icebreaker's channel just a few hundred yards away.
Craig looked at Arnold as if pleading for an explanation. At the
same instant, they dropped their poles and raced to Malik. They
simultaneously figured out what he was doing. He was waiting for
Sikhu to pop his head through the ice-littered channel.

If Sikhu did appear in the channel, he might not be so easy to see.
The channel was six miles long and up to a quarter mile wide. But
of one thing Malik was almost certain. While he could be anywhere,
Sikhu must be somewhere in the channel. Malik yanked down on the
bill of his bright red baseball cap in a nervous habit acquired over
five decades of whaling. As he scanned the water for a sign of the
missing whale, he held up a thickly calloused hand to further shield
his eyes against the blinding glare of the daylight bouncing off the
Arctic ice.

Through the sharp ice shards floating in the man-made channel,
Sikhu's head appeared. Surfacing in the water's wide expanse, the
huge whale seemed suddenly small and frightened. Its vulnerability
underscored the many traumas it had endured. Defying human
logic, Sikhu reached the channel by swimming under nearly a

quarter mile of ice. For the first time since it was found 19 days earlier, the whale was swimming in broken ice. Despite Sikhu's battered condition, the newly gathered crowd was elated. The whale was in the channel, the home stretch.

The Eskimos let out the cheer reserved for the most joyous of all occasions: the catching of a bowhead whale. Arnold embraced Malik as if he just returned from a successful whaling mission. Eleven days earlier, at the specially-convened whalers' meeting, Malik convinced Arnold and other young whalers that the whole exercise might well be a mission for Inupiat survival. If the Eskimos could convince the world that they really did depend on an animal they revered for tens of thousands of years, then maybe the world might start to understand. As the whales were about to be freed, Malik's theory could begin the test of time.

Locals, rescuers, and reporters, frantically tried to reach the suddenly distant whale. While still within the purview of Operation Breakout, Sikhu, the lead whale, was finally alone, far from the gentle hand of a well-wisher and no longer dependent upon a tiny machine flown in from Minnesota. The lead whale experienced its first moments of liberation, trying to navigate its way through the dangers of the icy sharp waters, removed from its human protectors. Sikhu's reunification with its natural environment must have been a difficult adjustment.

Poutu, the lone whale remaining in the hand-cut opening, bobbed frantically up and down. Maybe Poutu was reacting to Sikhu's underwater moans and squeaks. Perhaps through the gray whale's highly sophisticated and poorly understood method of communication, Poutu knew where Sikhu was. Poutu took one last long breath and vanished deep beneath the water. Moments later, the smaller whale surfaced within yards of its leader. It too had swum under the quarter mile of ice and emerged in the icebreaker channel. At the rate the two whales were swimming, they would be gone by morning. If all went well, the two whales would arrive in California at the end of January 1989, just about the same time as the man who gave the rescue his official blessing: President Ronald Reagan.

Bonnie Mersinger insisted that Colonel Carroll contact her the moment it looked like the whales were free. The White House was anxious to make the announcement that the operation was finally over. The whales had become the comic obsession of the humor-starved White House press corps. Each morning at the daily briefing, the customarily stuffy and self-absorbed White House correspondents bombarded spokesman Marlin Fitzwater with tongue-in-cheek questions about the geopolitical implications of the latest earth-stopping developments emanating from the Barrow ice pack. Fitzwater reveled in the levity and promised to have the last laugh.

Late Wednesday morning, Alaska time, Carroll called Bonnie to relay the rescue's latest intelligence. The whales were almost free. Bonnie ran excitedly through the corridors of the West Wing to tell Fitzwater the good news. The whales were free. So certain did the news seem, the cherub-faced Fitzwater thought the time arrived to cash in on his promise. The amiable press secretary grinned mischievously. "The whales are free," he exulted with outstretched arms.

The press corps burst into spontaneous applause. To those reporters assigned to cover the West Wing, Operation Breakout seemed over. The misconception was short lived. Colonel Carroll called Bonnie a few minutes later to tell her the bad news. The whales were not yet free.

"I don't know if you're religious," he asked her, "but if you are, I suggest you pray to whichever god you believe in." The next day, Fitzwater commented that humble pie was always his favorite.

Ever since the Russians announced they were on the way, the rescue command discussed what to do if it appeared the whales would survive. Should they tag or follow them, and if so, how? Now that the whales were in the channel, the rescuers had both their first and last opportunity to tag them to monitor their progress. Aside from the staggering problems of electronic tagging, which made tracking all but impossible, Ron Morris and the other rescuers faced an ethical problem of even larger dimensions.

Was it right to tag the whales after all they had gone through just to satisfy the curiosity of an obsessed world? Ron Morris wanted to keep his options open. The two biologists he flew in from Seattle were experts at tagging marine mammals and always carried the tags with them in the event the decision was made to use them.

Tagging a marine mammal, particularly one that weighed 50,000 pounds, was no easy task. For the electronic device to work properly it had to be shot deep into the small of the whale's back with a crossbow by an expert archer. But that opportunity never presented itself when the whales were in the holes. When confined to the small holes, the whales had only enough room to expose their heads. But even in the channel, where the whales started to surface normally, the chances were slim that the cumbersome devices could be properly implanted. It was also likely that the procedure could further stress the whales. Unlike radio transmitters attached to land animals, tagging marine mammals was extremely expensive and woefully unreliable. It was a new, unrefined technology. The waterproof radio transmitters only worked for about a month and required aircraft with special detection equipment to track them. In the ice-choked waters of the Arctic, tags probably wouldn't have stayed on the whales for more than a few days.

But beneath all the rationalizations lay a more cynical, unspoken explanation for not tagging the whales. Ron Morris had to ask himself how the American public would respond if, after spending millions of tax dollars to free the whales, the transmitters were traced to the belly of a polar bear? More importantly, what would that mean to NOAA, the agency that stood to gain so much from one of its greatest public achievements? What would happen to that fattened budget allocation about which NOAA bureaucrats were already licking their chops?

If the whales weren't tagged, the world would never know what really happened to them. Since a long and arduous journey lay ahead, maybe it was a good thing no one would find out; just the stuff of which legends are made.

Together again, the two whales swam toward the open lead some three miles through the channel. As quickly as the whales dashed through the ice littered water, news of the great escape engulfed the press corps. It sounded like the last chance to see the whales before they pounded unencumbered flukes in the open lead en route to California.

The whales stopped dead in their tracks as the commotion on the ice mounted. It was as if they suddenly became aware that once they crossed into the open lead, they would leave the blanket which draped them with protection for nearly three weeks.

Ron Morris' concern grew with the number of well-wishers who crowded the ice for their last glimpse of the whales. His first step was the most drastic. Over his walkie-talkie, he instructed everyone to immediately evacuate the area. He ordered all air traffic to stay at least four miles away from the channel and to fly above 1,000 feet. As darkness fell, a wave of anticipation swept across Barrow, catching up residents, reporters and rescuers alike. They all might well have seen the last of the whales. Nevertheless, Morris wanted Reshetov to stay overnight just in case.

After almost two sleepless weeks, the anxiety and irritability showed in the glassy eyes of almost everyone. The pressure fell hardest on Ron Morris, the coordinator and the man ultimately responsible for the rescue. When his order to evacuate the ice was openly flaunted, Morris lost his temper. In its final hour, the hour of ultimate triumph, he could do nothing but watch as his authority was yanked from under him.

Ron Morris wasn't the only one whose neck was on the chopping block. The same was true for all of us. Reporters came to Barrow to record the rescue. As it reached its climax, so too did our coverage. The United States Secret Service could not have kept us off the ice, let alone Ron Morris. Nevertheless, he fruitlessly sought to rein us in. He was at the end of his rope, his exasperation apparent to everyone.

Morris called for reinforcements. Mayor George Ahmaogak, back in town for Operation Breakout's conclusion, agreed to a special deployment of the North Slope Borough Policemen to help National Guard units guard the common ice entry points. But it would take two divisions to properly patrol 50 miles of frozen coastline and interdict the dozens of ski machines and automobiles intent on running the blockade.

Morris' edict extended to the rescuers themselves. But even his own underlings ignored him. Cindy, Geoff, and Craig had not worked so hard for so long to leave the whales at the rescue's critical last juncture. For two weeks they had risked their lives to help the stranded creatures, and they certainly weren't about to stop now. They were not out to humiliate Morris. All they cared about was freeing the whales. The trapped animals would never have made it this far without their help. Greg and Rick with their de-icers, Arnold Brower, Jr., and a skeleton crew of Eskimos joined them to keep the last few holes ice-free in case the whales were forced back by a frozen channel.

That night, around 10:00 PM, Ron Morris was socializing at

Media Central, the lobby of the Top of the World Hotel, when he learned the extent of his own emasculation. He overheard someone mention that Cindy and "the others" were still out with the whales. The lateness of the hour combined with exhaustion and one too many highballs triggered the penultimate tantrum. He stormed out of the Top of the World and into his running truck, crimson with fury. Gunning the sensitive engine, he drove to his nearest check point.

En route, he shouted invectives over his radio to everyone assigned to listen. Top members of the command monitored Operation Breakout's frequency on a 24-hour basis, but anyone working was supposed to have their radios turned on. Geoff, Craig, Arnold and Cindy were no exception. Their radios were in perfect working order. They worked, perhaps too well.

"GET THOSE GOD DAMNED ESKIMOS OFF THE ICE," Morris shouted into his hand-mike as he raced out onto the darkened ice. Everyone heard it. Everywhere, the reaction was the same. The SAR hangar command center fell dead silent. Randy Crosby searched for a face that could tell him he didn't hear what he knew he had. Instead, his eyes met Tom Carroll's. The colonel shrugged his shoulders, and lowered his head in embarrassed disbelief. It was the Eskimos for whom these two white men felt the deepest regret.

There were only about 20 people authorized to use the frequencies assigned to Operation Breakout. But almost everyone listened. Curious locals and news hungry reporters tuned in around the clock to follow the latest developments. To both rescuers and reporters, the two-way radio was an indispensable tool. For many of the Operation's key personnel, it was a lifeline. Malik, for instance, didn't have a telephone. The radio was the only way for the command to reach him. He was sitting alone after another long day quietly drinking a cup of green tea at Sam and Lee's Chinese restaurant on Natchik Street. He nearly choked when he heard the defamation blurted out over his radio.

Malik was stunned. He had argued for cooperating with the white man. He convinced his people to approve the rescue. He preached that Eskimos stood to gain by helping free the whales. Morris' eight unforgettable words had undone everything Malik had worked for. Malik didn't know how to express his anger. Eskimos believed that the fires of passion burned only in the hearts of Outsiders. As if it would somehow erase the hurt and restore the rescue to its pre-ordained mission of grace, Malik took a deep drag from his stale cigarette and turned his radio off.

On the ice, it was Arnold Brower, Jr., the probable target of the slur, who took to calming Geoff, Craig, and Cindy. His reaction was the same as Malik's. He calmly walked over to Geoff and Craig and turned off their radios. Then he pulled his own walkie-talkie out of his parka pocket, depressed the transmit button to respond to Morris: "It's out of your hands now." Without waiting for a response, he clicked off the radio. Getting back to work, Arnold wouldn't let the others even discuss the venomous remark. They had a job to do, he reminded them. If he could hum along to the tune of the indignity, then so could they.

The three worked silently on, none discussing what they all were thinking. A faint beam of light caught their attention. The closer it got, the angrier they became. They were watching the headlights of a vehicle driven by the man who had just offended them so deeply, a man who at that moment had no idea of the extent of damage he inflicted upon himself. The beam caught the four transfixed figures standing against a backdrop of the brightly lit deck of *Vladimir Arsenyev*. Morris jumped out and slammed the door behind him. As he walked toward the defiant rescuers he could make out their expressions of feigned disinterest.

"What the fuck do you think you're doing?" he shouted. "I said *no one* is to be on this ice." He ducked his head slightly before he realized he was revealing his own sense of weakness.

"You just don't get it, do you?" Arnold asked Morris, in an earnest but failed attempt to pity him. Craig and Geoff pretended to ignore the presence of the man who was clouding them in such shame. Cindy fought to contain her tears. By betraying the others, Morris had betrayed her.

Knowing he had lost Brower, Morris turned to Craig to see if the biologist would still obey him. Nothing aggravated his insecurity more than being ignored. It wasn't revenge that dictated Craig's reaction. It was fear, fear that he couldn't control his anger, that he would lash out with his fists at his small, rakishly bearded adversary. His emotion would have propelled a blow with potentially dangerous force. He had to restrain himself, but it wasn't easy. Morris kept pushing, looking for the reaction that would vindicate his own outburst.

"It's *them*, isn't it," Morris asked, pointing an accusing finger at the stoic figure of Arnold Brower. "That's all you care about." Morris had stumbled upon a theme he was determined to pound home as best he could.

"That's the only reason you're here. It's all this 'Inupiat Power' shit, isn't it? 'Hooray for the Eskimo' You can admit it. All you care about is making sure *they* look good," he shouted, his finger still pointing at Brower. "You've been on *their* side since the beginning."

"*Shut up*," Cindy shrieked. Cindy thought of Geoff, Craig and Arnold as the indispensable triad that kept the whales alive. More than that, what she refrained from saying, she didn't refrain from thinking. They were heroes and she loved them. Cindy was appalled by Morris' attacks.

Even after all the rage Morris aroused in him, Craig put aside his anger when he saw Cindy in tears. First it was Arnold calming Craig and Geoff who were furious at the slight of their Eskimo friend. Now Craig did the same for Cindy who was devastated by Morris' confrontation.

Using an English translation of an Eskimo expression Cindy didn't understand at first, Arnold instructed the two of them to "feel light." He wanted them to release a mystical weight that held down the human spirit. Cindy's empathy released an energy of warmth connecting the four together as one. Their unity had been immeasurably enhanced by the adversity thrust upon them. In the minds of those he thought he ruled, Ron Morris no longer existed.

Impervious to the human drama unfolding around them, the whales pushed on. Suddenly, they no longer seemed subject to the limitations of their own species. The whales followed the powerful beam of light from the deck of the Soviet icebreaker. To the astonishment of the whale biologists, the animals swam through water littered with jagged chunks of ice. Remaining doubts about the whales' willingness to take risks to achieve their freedom were shattered.

On Thursday morning, the whales were paying the price for their unexpected boldness. Arnold Brower was the first to discover them gasping for breath in a small hole kept open by butting their heads through the ice debris. They were bleeding profusely. The ocean water steamed from the buckets of warm blood gushing in it. They could barely manage to push their red, battered snouts through the ice that had formed overnight. The skin around their sensitive breathing holes was tender and sore. The whales seemed so close to freedom just hours before. Now they listed on the verge of death.

Before he could radio the news back to SAR headquarters, Brower noticed that a small piece of ice was stuck in Sikhu's blowhole. The more deeply the whale breathed, the wider the blowhole opened. But that only made the problem worse. The wider the blowhole opened, the more firmly lodged the piece of ice became.

Arnold jumped off his parked ski machine and ran out toward the edge of the ice. Looking across the wide channel, he knew the whale would die if it wasn't helped. He immediately probed the ice covering the newly refrozen channel. It was already thick enough to support not only him but his snowmobile. He turned off his radio the instant he heard the voice of Ron Morris exhorting him to get off the ice. Neither Morris nor anyone else had the slightest idea what was going on out on the ice and Arnold didn't have the time to explain it.

When he reached the struggling whales, Arnold scrambled on his belly to the edge of the hole, pulled off his gloves, and extended his outstretched hand toward the whale's obstructed blowholes. He gently stroked the tender area to alert the whale that he meant no harm. Apparently reassured by the Eskimo hunter's touch, the whale remained long enough for Brower to dislodge the ice. He reached his bare hand into the tender cavity and grabbed the chunk of ice. The whale writhed in pain as he pulled it out of its raw, bleeding orifice.

In the intensity of his efforts to aid the choking whale, Brower didn't even notice that Malik was right beside him, caught up in a breathless race to enlarge the small hole. Malik fished chunks of floating ice from the frigid water with his gloveless hands and pitched them over his head. Malik skated across the refrozen channel to retrieve a shovel and seal pole from the back of his ski machine. The two Eskimo whalers expanded the hole until both animals could breathe safely again.

Less than a mile from the open lead and freedom, the whales were once again confined to a tiny, frightful hole. Nonetheless, the two whales made remarkable progress through the lead before they got stuck in the frozen water. Overnight, the whales swam through almost two miles of the channel.

Arnold and Malik knew that if new holes weren't opened soon, the crisis their bare hands just alleviated would soon recur. Arnold switched on his walkie-talkie and radioed an urgent appeal for five chain saw crews to get on the ice as soon as possible. He and Malik decided to fall back on the only tactic that worked. Now that the pressure ridge was sliced away, the native crews could easily cut holes parallel to the channel, protecting the whales from its brutal conditions. If everyone were mobilized for a total and final push, the holes could be dug in a few hours.

Brower went right over Ron Morris' head to summon his own crews. He made his own decision without bothering to consult the man who was ostensibly his boss. Morris didn't overlook the insubordination. By early that morning, everyone had heard the horrible tale of the previous night's debacle. But that event appeared to have little effect. Morris lost his temper. He was willing to admit that much. But that changed nothing. He was still coordinator, and in his mind, his word was law. He reached for his radio and repeated his unenforceable declaration that no one was allowed on the ice. Only when his orders were flagrantly countermanded by his own subordinates did the nightmare sink in. His authority had been completely emasculated in the eyes of those he commanded.

Just minutes after their arrival, the first crew sawed open a new hole. Brower wasted no time waiting for the whales to make the discovery on their own. He flipped around the ends of his seal pole and shoved the blunt end in the water. He gently poked the whales so as to annoy them enough to leave the hole. After a few less than comfortable jolts to the mid-section, the whales got the message and headed toward the only haven they saw: the new Eskimo hole. For the time being at least, the whales were safe.

Morris raced out to the whales to confront Brower and his insubordination once again. When he arrived, he found the Eskimo and his crew working frantically to open new holes for the whales. No matter how he ranted and raved, Morris couldn't seem to get Brower's attention. Brower just kept digging while trying to ignore the sounds as though they came from an errant pest.

Finally, as if to swat it away, he lifted his eyes from the holes on which they were focused. He glared piercingly into Morris' eyes before he quietly uttered the same words he used only hours before. "It's out of your hands." He withdrew his gaze and returned to his task. The message was clear. If he knew what was good for him, Morris would not challenge Brower or his men again. Morris got the message and withdrew to safer terrain, the SAR hangar.

From there he contacted Sergei Reshetov aboard the *Admiral Arsenyev*. The Russian captain didn't need to remind Morris how anxious the Soviets were to get home. Reshetov also did not have to be told about what was happening on the ice. All he had to do was peer down from his perch eight stories above it. Surprising even to him, the channels his ship plowed through just 12 hours before had frozen over solid. He knew his ship's job wasn't done. There were more passes to be made before he could get home.

By noon, the *Arsenyev* wasn't alone. Bill Allen had climbed in the cockpit of his oddly named Screw Tractor and planted a huge American flag atop the cab. Amid cheers, Allen's versatile tractor plowed through the Soviet paths, spitting out smaller chunks of ice. Wrapped in the mantle of Old Glory, Allen was determined to prove his country was still the key force in freeing the whales. Billy Bob Allen was stealing the show.

"Oh Me," he exulted as he spun his way through the channels. A camera crew captured radiant shots of Billy Bob Allen driving the tractor like an enchanted child in his first bumper car at an amusement park.

Finally, after almost two weeks, Bill Allen himself was out freeing the whales. He was so excited as he twisted and turned he forgot to check his fuel gauge. When he did, it was too late. The Screw Tractor had run out of gas. By late afternoon, standing atop his idled tractor, Allen exulted ebulliently as he watched the whales swimming freely in the channel he helped cut.

"Just get a load of that Archie Bowers," he said to Pete Leathard. "Mercy, that son of a bitch sure can work, can't he?" It was the highest compliment Allen could bestow on the Eskimo leader. Now, there was no turning back. The whales were only a few hundred yards from the lead.

Operation Breakout was complete. More than two weeks and $5.5 million later, there was nothing more to do. Eskimos, their Caucasian countrymen, and Russians had cut a ten-mile path through thick Arctic ice. All they could do was wait for the whales to do the rest. As the sun set on Thursday, the 27th of October, 20 days after the whales were first found off Point Barrow, a wave of relief swept everyone. Rescuers were delighted that the whales could now swim free. Billy Bob was delighted at the prospect of finally closing his hemorrhaging checkbook, and reporters were anxious to go home.

Thursday night, Morris gave what he promised would be his final press conference. While not absolutely sure, Geoff, Craig and the other biologists were reasonably certain that shortly after dark, the whales would slip through the last vestiges of the channel and enter the unfettered waters of the Open Lead. Their Barrow misadventure behind them, the whales were almost surely free. At first light, Friday morning, Randy Crosby flew the final mission. Flying 20 miles up and down the lead, he saw not a trace. The whales were gone.

Fittingly, Malik was the last American to see the two whales before darkness fell. Petting Sikhu goodbye, he wished the two creatures the luck he knew they would need to survive on their long voyage. Ordinary gray whales would be hard pressed to make it through the multiple dangers that lay ahead. Treacherous ice floes extended for several hundred miles along Alaska's northern and western rims. Next, there were pods of killer whales waiting for weak and wounded prey. And finally, if they made it that far, the whales would have to dance through minefields of great white sharks lurking off the coast of the Pacific Northwest in search of weakened prey.

But these whales were anything but ordinary. These whales touched hundreds of millions of hearts and captivated the fickle attention of a self-obsessed world. They brought together people, industries, and nations in a way man himself never could. If only for a fortnight, the three whales were at the center of the world. They were history's most fortunate creatures.

Lucky whales.

Chapter 24

Consequences

Success or not, the media dubbed Friday, October 28, Operation Breakout's final day. If, at first light, the whales still hadn't left the ice pack, we defiantly resolved that we would. We phoned our loved ones, told them the story was over, and booked flights home.

Everyone agreed. There was nothing more to be done. Now that the pressure ridge no longer barred the whales from entering the open channel of water, the whales remained the only obstacle to their own freedom. We desperately tried to convince our assignment editors that the rescue's human aspect had concluded. From every indication, the American people were tiring of the story. They, too, had seen enough. If ever Operation Breakout gave the media and the world a chance to cut and run, this seemed the moment.

But when Malik discovered the lead whale Siku nearly frozen in the icebreaker's paths on Thursday morning, Barrow was overwhelmed by feelings of frustration. On Wednesday night, October 26, the whales seemed free. But the next morning, they once again demonstrated their penchant for getting stuck. The same faulty

293

genes that trapped them the first time did it again. The whales could not find their way out of the icebreaker channel before it froze solid overnight. Instead of finally beginning their migration, they became stranded in yet another tiny hole. It seemed like the whole mess was starting all over again. Fortunately for the whales and the weary media, the Russians remained one final night. The whales at last slipped through the channels to open water sometime early Friday morning when the icebreakers returned to clear new pathways through the ice.

After almost two weeks at 20° below zero, there was just no more left to give. From its outset, Operation Breakout was nothing more than an artificial enterprise, created not for the whales or their species, but for the media. Like any other news story, Operation Breakout needed a beginning, a middle, and, most importantly, *an end*. If it appeared that the rescue would continue indefinitely, that most critical criterion would be violated. But of course, the very notion of the rescue operating in a vacuum was absurd. The media *was* the rescue.

The contrast to Operation Breakout's final hours could not have been more striking. Barrow was the Arctic equivalent to Saigon right before the fall. People were desperate to get out.

It wasn't the NVA we feared, but Barrow itself. Don Oliver, a veteran of that frantic Indochina exodus, worked just as busily to get out of Barrow. He was helping his video editor, Steve Shim, pack all of NBC's equipment when the phone rang. It was NBC's Los Angeles bureau. Immediately, Oliver knew he wasn't going to like what he was about to hear.

Oliver rejoiced in his industry nickname, El Diablo. Yet, remarkably, Barrow and its endless privations had yet to ignite the temper for which he was legendary.

"We want you to stay on a couple of days," came the unsteady voice from Los Angeles. "You know, just in case the whales come back."

It was so cold in Oliver's Top of the World Hotel room, you could almost see steam pour out of his ears. The thought of still another day in Barrow made Oliver long for Saigon, April 1975. Watching his colleagues head for warmer climes pushed Oliver over the edge. El Diablo was about to erupt.

"In case they come back?" he shrieked incredulously, his face crimson. "We're booked on the 12:30 flight and we're not going to miss it. The whales are GONE, GONE, GONE. They aren't coming back, and if they do, that will be their problem, NOT MINE! You got that?"

The hotel's entire first floor fell silent. This was an impressive display of rage, even for the master himself. Maybe he was out for a personal best, his producer Jerry Hansen joked. We could all sympathize. Oliver, like the rest of us, had served his time. Why was his sentence extended when all other prisoners at Barrow Correctional were being paroled?

Harry Chittick, the ABC producer, walked toward us from the far end of the hall seemingly unfazed by Don Oliver's deafening outburst. Like the rest of us, he had a plane to catch. As he passed Oliver's open door, none of us spoke. We wondered how Chitticck would handle the delicate situation. Would he slip quietly past, pretending to ignore the erupting red-caped devil, or would he peak in to catch the master of rage in action.

Getting to the door, Chittick stopped, turned to Oliver and waved goodbye. Pausing in mid-tirade, Oliver turned to Chittick, flashed him a brief but warm smile, winked, stretched out his hand in a gesture of farewell, and picked up his tantrum right where he left off. Chittick laughed, hoping Oliver's latest explosion would produce the desired results. Oliver flashed Chittick a jubilant thumbs up sign.

For Oran Caudle, it was like waking from a bad dream. Just hours before, he had worked frantically to keep the North Slope Borough television studio from collapsing under the strain of 26 demanding broadcasters barking orders in half a dozen languages. Suddenly, life hurtled back to pre-Breakout tranquility. There were no more network feeds, no more pushing, no more shoving and, thank God, no more shouting. For the first time in more than two weeks, Caudle turned off the North Slope Borough television transmitter. As the light on the console faded, Caudle knew another decade might pass before it was ever used again.

But Oran's work remained incomplete. He had only a few hours to convert his global communications center into a stage ready fit to host a hundred Eskimo students from Ipalook Elementary dressed as goblins and ghosts for "Fright Night 1989." The local Haloween pageant was a major annual event on Channel 20. For Barrow's youngest residents, the whales swam free in the nick of time.

Operation Breakout helped fulfill the electronic media's technological promise of a global village. The world had been bound together in a common, seemingly noble aim. But the minute that aim was achieved, the world went home. For all the time the media spent in Barrow, few of us stayed to reflect on our impact on that remarkable hamlet we so briefly called home.

Like life itself, Operation Breakout was born, matured and, finally, died. Its death came swiftly. The story that led newscasts from Minneapolis to Moscow and Boston to Bombay one night was not so much as mentioned the next. It was time for the world to move on.

With a few hours left to kill before our flight back to the world we so desperately missed, Masu Kawamura, the Japanese correspondent, cameraman Steve Mongeau and I all drove out to Point Barrow for one last look at the site where the world had focused its attention for the last two weeks. I wondered what the endless expanse of icy terrain really looked like. Now that everyone else had left, maybe we could find out.

The only Arctic we knew was lined with cables, cords and wires. The sheet of ice we stood on so many long hours had reverberated with the sounds of man: the buzzing of helicopters, the whine of chain saws, the hum of idle engines, the chatter of human voices.

Even the throaty "FFWWWSSSSHH" of a whale exhaling depended on man. Without him, the whales would long since have died. Except for the howl of the Arctic wind, the ice would have remained utterly still, seemingly lifeless, frozen desert.

We crossed over the sandy hump that separated North America's most extreme tip from the stark white horizon of frozen sea for perhaps the 50th time. Yet it in a remarkable way, it seemed like the first. The dense early morning fog burned off to reveal a distant Arctic sun that shone brighter and stronger than on any of our previous trips. It cast a deceptive light of warmth where none existed.

For the first time since our arrival, the three of us felt alone. Not only was man gone, so was his every trace. His hand-cut holes were solidly refrozen. The windswept snow and thick blue ice were virtually all that colored the lifeless landscape. The only evidence of one of the most colossal events the Arctic had ever seen harkened back to the rescue's earliest days: a few rectangular blocks of ice pulled out of the water by the Eskimos before they learned to shove them under the ice shelf. There the blocks would remain until the brief Arctic summer would thaw them some months later.

As I surveyed the endless expanse of frozen oblivion, I couldn't imagine this was the same place hundreds of people stood just hours before. It was a completely different world, a world whose reality was emphasized by the scathing bitterness and eerie howl of its biting wind. This was the world that existed before the Whales of October. This was the world that would endure.

Encumbered by thick, heavy gear, I gazed across the Arctic emptiness realizing this was as close as I would probably ever get to fulfilling my oldest, most obsessive childhood dream. Even if it meant making a fool of myself, something that never stopped me before, I desperately wanted to live it out. I patiently waited for Masu and Steve to finish taking their last pictures.

When they started back toward the truck, I urged them to keep going. Telling them I would be but a minute only piqued their curiosity.

At that moment, Operation Breakout revealed its great reward to me. With no one to watch or poke fun, I deliberately crunched the wide bottom of my boot against the dry snow and lumbered about on the Arctic Ocean's flat, frozen surface pretending I was Neil Armstrong walking on the moon. I moonwalked like astronauts, not Michael Jackson. "Magnificent desolation," I said in a deep voice, mimicking Buzz Aldrin's first description of the lunar surface. So intent was I on believing my own delusion, I was completely unfazed by Houston's failure to respond to any of my repeated calls.

In an odd, almost undefinable way, it seemed as though everyone involved in the rescue was bequeathed a uniquely meaningful reward. Odder still, these rewards seemed commensurate with the recipient's contribution to helping the whales.

Take me, for example. I did nothing to directly help the whales. All I did was report the efforts of others. Aside from those few moments pretending I was walking on the moon, my reward came when I returned to the Lower 48. On my way back to New Jersey, I stopped in Portland, Oregon, to visit my cousins, the Sokols.

Flying from Anchorage to Portland, filth's greatest reward was finally revealed. I had a row of seats all to myself. No one dared sit next to me. Later, I showered, shaved, and actually changed clothes for the first time in two weeks. After my pictures were developed, I took my cousins and their kids out for dinner. Their youngest (and loudest), four-year-old Larry, ran excitedly across the boisterous dining room shouting that his grown-up cousin had just come back from saving the whales. If it weren't for the line of people anxious to see my photos, cherub-faced Larry might have been sent to the car. No such luck. Instead, the chubby bow-legged prankster scattered my photos everywhere. People clustered all over the restaurant. Waiters neglected their customers to marvel at scenes they all knew so well.

By Friday morning, October 28, 1988, 150 journalists from four continents, the American and Soviet governments, ARCO, VECO and Greenpeace, together with two brothers-in-law from Minnesota, had spent more than $5,795,000 to see to it that two whales stranded at the top of the world could swim safely into the Arctic Ocean's last swath of ice-free water. Their efforts dwarfed not only most human rescues, but all sense of proportion.

There were more gray whales in October 1988 than ever before in the history of the species, around 22,000. Yet they remained endangered and for good reason. Nineteenth century commercial whaling decimated the Atlantic Ocean half of the species. The North Pacific branch was all that remained. Being shallow water, shore-hugging creatures, the gray whales' survival was at the mercy of man and his insatiable appetite for fossil fuels.

The same industry that boasted of the tireless work by two of its fraternal companies to save three grays in October 1988 would threaten the entire species with extinction just six months later. Yet all the heroics and expense served only to return two whales back to sea. If marine biologists,who guessed the whales were genetically flawed, were right, Operation Breakout did more harm than good. There must be a reason nature wanted to be rid of these whales, they argued. Allowing them to pass their defects on to future generations might weaken the species, perhaps leading to still more whale strandings and maybe even more Operation Breakouts. The Eskimos could only hope.

In 15 days, the three major American television network newscasts ran more than 40 stories about those amazing whales, devoting nearly 10 percent of their programs' air time to coverage of the world's greatest non-event. Even more incredibly, coverage of the rescue supplanted coverage of the climax of the 1988 presidential campaign.

The revolution in television technology allowed more than a billion peeople to watch Operation Breakout—nearly twice as many as watched Neil Armstrong walk on the moon. In the all-important television ratings book, the rescue of three trapped whales dwarfed the single greatest achievement in the history of man.

Even Arab terrorists were affected by the world's whale obsession. Sheik Fadlallah, the C.E.O. of Hezbollah, Inc. a Lebanese-based Syrian-Iranian joint venture in the suicide car-bombing, murder and hostake-taking business, complained that the West was losing interest in playing his game. He was right, but, unfortunately not for long. Fedlallah was mad. The whales were stealing his thunder. Publicity was his business' lifeblood. Without it, his thriving enterprise might fade away.

But things could have been much worse. At least Fadlallah knew he could get back on the front page whenever and however he wanted. All he had to do was order his bearded henchman to snatch or murder another innocent American, emboldened by the fact that he could carry out his latest outrage with virtual impunity. Fadlallah knew that his latest victim's government would respond the same way it had with every other terrorist act. Call it an outrage, promise retribution, in the end, do nothing at all.

Before the whales, television's immediacy was infinitely more likely to be associated with Lebanon's venomous snake pit than with Alaska's North Slope. A cheaply-shot video of another hapless American hostage pleading his kidnappers' demands or, in the grizzly case of Colonel Rich Higgins, dangling lifeless from the end of a rope, seemed to be the American dinner hour's constant companion. That three whales became a national obsession was pathetic proof of that very fact.

In less than a decade, a band of turban-wearing Middle Eastern thugs had rendered a once great power impotent. That America would commit such tremendous resources to save three whales while doing little to protect its own citizens could only delight Sheik Fadlallah who must have danced in the bombed out streets of his beloved Beirut.

America's once legendary resolve had been reduced to saving three whales. But we couldn't even do that without asking our number one enemy to finish the job for us, a fact the United States Coast Guard used to lobby Congress to fund the construction of a third American icebreaker.

The same phenomenon that catapulted little Jessica McClune into the national spotlight two years earlier when she tumbled into a well in Midland, Texas, propelled the whales into the national spotlight. The story was simple. Either Jessica and the whales would be saved or they wouldn't. McNeil-Lehrer didn't have to cross-examine a panel of experts to dissect the issue. At least not at first. Operation Breakout started because it was easy. A wind of simplicity blowing across a world made dizzy by its own complexity.

In the beginning, nothing seemed to interfere with the story, neither the facts nor the relevance. Television producers knew everybody loved whales. Greenpeace spent the past 15 years teaching us that whales had to be saved, wherever and however they were threatened. Combine that with its slick Madison Avenue sales job, and there were the makings of a media "mega-vent."

Desperate Americans who clung to the premise that "whales are people too" made the rescue possible, only to learn they were much, much more. Up-close pictures of them struggling for survival transmitted instantly anywhere on earth, was dream television. Nothing sold like whales. The larger and longer the rescue became, the more millions of viewers glued themselves to their sets, sending ratings into the stratosphere.

News coverage of the whales earned the networks cheap, easy money without the inconvenience of soul-searching. Nobody liked constant bombardments of bad news. Give the people what they want. "*Don't worry*," went the year's Number One hit song, "*Be happy*." It seemed too good to be true, and in the end it was.

By the time the Russians showed up, Operation Breakout had transformed itself into exactly what it was supposed *not* to be.

America sought out the whales to escape its own reality, when in fact the whales forced America to confront it. The country's mindless lovefest turned into a healthy self-examination. We got the opposite of what we bargained for and exactly what we needed.

Washington Post columnist William Raspberry summed up the mood of the positivists when he called the three dramatic weeks a time when "the world was able to rise above its divisions of culture, competition, political ideology, and even the pursuit of money to join in a common, noble cause." Raspberry was right. So was Sheik Fadlallah.

Anticipating the crush of reporters desperate to get home, MarkAir scheduled a last-minute third flight out of Barrow for Friday, October 28. Euphoric Outsiders rejoicing in their Arctic liberation packed all three planes.

The Eskimos' fortnight on the cusp of national recognition was sealed behind the pressurized door of that day's last flight. When the maroon and white airliner's wheels lifted off Wiley Post's snow-covered runway, Barrow was once again alone at the top of the world. The only difference to this hardy Eskimo village was that its few weeks in the limelight had put a couple of million dollars in its pocket.

Operation Breakout gave the Eskimos of Barrow the chance of a lifetime, the opportunity to introduce themselves and their way of life to people around the world. For two weeks in October 1988, Barrow became the center of a world that all but ignored it.

For these two weeks, the tiny Eskimo hamlet seemed transplanted to some other more accessible latitude, its eternal isolation some how suspended, its bitter elements miraculously mitigated. This illusory transformation ended with the abruptness of an Arctic wind. Barrow picked up its timeless pace just where it left off.

Winter was fast on its way. While the October rescue turned out to be the coldest experience most Outsiders would ever live through, to the Eskimos it was nothing but a late autumn nip. To them, their winter didn't officially start until November 17, the day the sun slipped below the horizon, not to rise again for two and a half months. November 17 was the first of a 67 daylong night.

The year 1988-9 brought more than the customary darkness and bitter cold. It also brought the coldest and longest winter ever recorded in North America.

I went back to Barrow in January 1989 to take a second look at the place I was about to write a book about. As I stepped off the plane that dangerously cold January noon, I felt as if I had never been there before. Pitch dark at high noon.

January in Barrow made me yearn for the halcyon days of October. An ambient temperature of minus 58° was Barrow's way of saying *Welcome Back*. Nostrils and eyelids froze on contact with the cold. So too did just about everything else. Spit froze in mid-air, clattering when it hit the ground. But Barrow was lucky. It was on the coast. Just a few miles inland, temperatures dropped to 80° below zero. Dick Mackey, two-time Iditarod Trail Sled Dog Race champion, logged the coldest temperature ever recorded in North America at his truck stop in Cold Foot, Alaska, 250 miles south of Prudhoe Bay on January 21, 1989; minus 82°. It sure didn't feel like a record, Mackey said. It was just the first winter the U.S. Weather Service gave his official station a thermometer that went below minus 80°.

Isolation and depression hung over Barrow like the permanent bank of ice fog which blanketed that forlorn outpost nine months of the year. The days of Barrow's prominence seemed as remote as an ancient whaling epic. Did Barrow always seem pathetic, hopeless and remote? I asked. "Nope," Barrowans demurred, as if astonished anyone could reach my conclusion. "This is normal."

Drunk Eskimos staggered aimlessly through the frozen and deserted streets, seemingly unnoticed by nearly everyone. Unlike during the rescue, Barrow really did seem to fit its geographic location: the top of the world.

The press's relentless coverage of the non-event touched people all over the world. No matter where in the world I traveled in the next few months, almost every person I met was well versed in the plight of the whales. The whales had become international celebrities.

Cindy Lowry's reward was obvious. The whales were free. Single-handedly, she catapulted the whales from Arctic isolation to global stardom. Because of her, the California grays turned into the luckiest whales that ever lived. History's most massive animal rescue was waged on their behalf.

Greenpeace turned whale-saving into a national obsession. Their dynamo Alaska field coordinator started not just a mammoth rescue, but the biggest source of new money and members in the organization's history. Operation Breakout was an unexpected cash cow. Memberships and contributions shot up 400 percent in the rescue's aftermath, the greatest single increase up to its time.

Biologists and naturalists far removed from the scene at first claimed there was no way the whales could be spared a fate they deemed inextricable. As progress pushed the leviathans closer to that very possibility, the distant, dispassionate scientists discarded their mistaken theories. The scientists were wrong and the whole world knew it. In an attempt to salvage their credibility, they "refined" their views.

Even if the whales could get past the pressure ridge, naturalist Roger Caras tried convincing Ted Koppel on ABC's "Nightline," they could *never* surmount the myriad obstacles that separated them from their breeding grounds off Mexico's Pacific coastline. Since the whales weren't tagged for monitoring, no one could ever prove Caras wrong.

And that was just what NOAA wanted. Shortly after the rescue, the National Oceanographic and Atmospheric Administration printed up colorful brochures and passed them out to whale boat tour operators on the Pacific Coast helping sightseers identify Siku and Poutu. No damage could come its way. If the whales were found, NOAA would be vindicated, if they weren't, there would still be no proof the animals weren't enjoying their anonymity in the wet beyond.

To those who spent time with the whales, even people like me who knew little about them, it was clear this trio possessed something special. Of the untold thousands of gray whales who have died in ice strandings throughout history, these were the ones that united the world. That alone made them unique.

But there was more. After 21 days of frozen confinement, the two surviving whales conquered more than ice-covered seas. They transcended the perceived bounds of their own species. Before Operation Breakout, scientists believed that gray whales would not swim through icy waters, even to save their lives. After two weeks of proving the scientists right, the whales pulled the first of many surprises. Changing our perceptions of them forever, the two whales battered and bloodied themselves in the ice-thick water, knowing it was life's only route.

Before the rescue, science could offer no evidence that gray whales' behavior could be modified. Unlike the Killer whale, the gray whales could not be trained. There would never be any gray *Shamus*. But from the moment the de-icers were dropped to do their Minnesota magic in the new Eskimo holes, the whales were active participants in their own rescue.

If any two whales on earth could overcome the obstacles encountered clearing Barrow's ice pressure ridge, these were the whales to do it, Roger Caras and his predictions of doom notwithstanding. Science was rewarded with evidence that gray whales were even more intelligent than previously thought.

The hundreds of millions of people who watched the whale saga got one of two rewards. They were either overjoyed at the whales' freedom because they genuinely wished them well, or they were just so sick of hearing about them that they were relieved it was finally over.

For Republican presidential candidate George Bush, the whales gave him a momentary chance to lash out at his Democratic opponent. "I just hope they don't end up in Boston Harbor," the Vice President jibed when he heard the whales had swum free, referring to the nation's most polluted waterway in the very state his opponent governed.

For Michael Dukakis, the whales freedom presented his self-destructing campaign with a Catch-22. At first, the Massachusetts Governor's staff must have welcomed all the attention focused on the whales' crisis instead of their own. But when the story never ended, there was less and less time until the election, time they desperately needed to make up for blowing the huge lead they had as recently as Labor Day. The inept Dukakis campaign had to get back in the headlines. When it finally did, it was more bad news. Dukakis bad boy John Sasso, fired then rehired for the same reason—his mastery of political dirty tricks—probably wished for the biggest trick of all: re-stranding the whales.

For Ben Odom, the senior vice-president of ARCO Alaska and one of the rescue's two biggest financiers, the rescue proved fortuitous. Soon after the whales swam free, the 35-year ARCO veteran retired, just in time to leave on one of the industry's rarest and highest notes. His oil company had helped save two whales and softened the hearts of environmentalists everywhere.

Just six months after Operation Breakout's final news story was filed, Alaska, once America's most isolated state, was back in the news again. This time, the story was only too real.

At 9:00 PM, March 24, 1989, the *Exxon Valdez*, a 987-foot supertanker, left the port whose name she bore en route to Long Beach, California. On board were more than 14 million gallons of grade A North Slope crude oil pumped down from Prudhoe Bay through the billion-dollar 825-mile-long Trans-Alaskan pipelne.

After changing to an inbound shipping lane to avoid a glacial ice floe, Captain Joe Hazelwood turned over command of his vessel to Third Mate Gregory Cousins. It was 11:50 PM. Eighteen minutes later, Captain Hazelwood and the rest of the sleeping crew were jolted awake by a terrific screech which rang through the giant vessel as it struck a shoal just a few hundred yards west of Bligh Island.

The oil industry had spent the past 21 years convincing Alaskans this disaster could never occur. It was damned near impossible. A ship could never run aground, the industry promised with the slickest corporate communications its billions could buy. But to show just how ready it was to go that extra mile, the industry promised that if the impossible ever did happen, which of course it wouldn't, it would make certain that the spill would be so small, not a single cuddly otter would ever notice. Not until after North America's worst environmental disaster would the world learn otherwise.

The viscous cargo poured from a gash in the single-ply iron hull. Exxon had promised the State of Alaska and the Federal Government that it could dispatch containment equipment to any vessel in Prince William Sound within 30 minutes of a spill. Twelve hours elapsed before the first boom looped the wounded craft, too late to do anything about the 11 million of gallons destined to sully a thousand miles of Alaska's pristine coastline. It was the worst oil spill in American history.

In a seemingly calculated attempt to escape liability, Exxon blamed it all on Captain Joe Hazelwood. For months, the company succeeded in convincing nearly everyone that Hazelwood was drunk at the time of the accident. In fact, there was no conclusive evidence to support the Exxon charge, an allagation every crew member denied. Ten hours after the accident, Hazelwood's blood alcohol level was higher than the Coast Guard legal limit but below the Alaska driving limit. Toxicologists said it was likely that Hazelwood reached his test levels by alcohol ingested *after* the accident, not before.

Just six months after glowing from their greatest public high, the oil industry was reeling from its deepest low. The goodwill they worked so hard to generate in October drowned in 11 million gallons of solidifying oil that oozed its way down Alaska's violated coast.

The extent of the environmental damage defied calculation. More than 30,000 birds, and thousands of those cuddly otters Exxon promised would never notice, died. More than wildlife was devastated. So too, was Alaska's second biggest industry: fishing. Salmon, herring, halibut and pollock runs could be threatened for a decade, if not longer.

But the specter that will hang over Alaska indefinitely is that of permanent genetic damage to all species that live in or pass through Prince William Sound.

Among the potential victims were the very whales Alaskan oil titans ARCO and VECO expended themselves to save. More ominously, Exxon also endangered more than two-thirds of the entire gray whale species that swam through the Sound to and from Mexico. With the food chain poisoned, biologists could only hope that genetic mutations caused by the toxins would not be passed on as permanent species changes. The biggest company in the industry that worked so hard to save three whales threatened to extinguish the entire species. Exxon got its due, with costs could run into the billions, but unfortunately at the whales' expense.

The oilman's nightmare became the newsman's dream. Lambasted by a late-waking American public, the press returned to Alaska in a big way. Coverage of the disaster dwarfed that of the whale rescue, as well it should. Many of the same reporters assigned to Barrow in October packed their bags in a similar rush to head to another Alaskan port of call, Valdez, a thousand miles south of Barrow. That was the reporters' reward.

Sitting in VECO's Anchorage headquarters on Sunday, October 30, all Billy Bob Allen could do was stare at his desk calculator. Tallying up what his company just spent to save the whales, the liquid crystal displayed flashed an astonishing figure: $350,000. How on earth had he let himself go through that much money?

Shortly after the Exxon catastrophe, Allen got his reward. VECO won the prime contract to clean up the mess. The contract would soon mushroom to hundreds of millions of dollars. VECO's new image of whale-saver helped Pete Leathard, Allen's chief executive, land one of the biggest contracts in state history. If whales ever get stuck again, Leathard won't waste a minute to rustle ol' Billy Bob from his Colorado ranch. The first environmental job Bill Allen took brought him fame, the second brought him fortune. Billy Bob Allen's environmental conversion paid off.

Greenpeace whale coordinator Campbell Plowden waited nine months for his reward. On August 2, 1989, the Republic of Iceland announced a two-year moratorium on all commercial whaling. The crisis that brought Prime Minister Strintrimur Hermannsson's government to its knees half a year earlier finally became too much. Iceland could no longer fight the economic clout of an increasingly united world. Iceland had no choice but to get out of its $7 million whaling business.

No country on earth seemed more remote from the rarefied realm of Barrow, Alaska, than Iceland. It seemed the most unlikely place on earth to become embroiled in the affairs of a place like Barrow. Yet the tiny seafaring nation perched half way between the Old World and the New was turned on its ear by the whales of October.

While Iceland, killers of 75 whales in 1988, fell prey to a crippling economic boycott costing more than $50 million, nearly four percent of the tiny nation's gross national product, the Soviets, who slaughtered more than twice as many gray whales that same year, sent two icebreakers on a three-day diversion. The Soviets reaped praise, Iceland scorn. While serenading Moscow with cheers of "Hail the Whale Savers," the world taunted Reykjavik with jeers of "Boycott the Whale Killers."

The Soviets masterfully buried a hundred years of plunder beneath the bow of the Finnish-made *Admiral Vladimir Arsenyev* while Iceland lost thousands of jobs. The Soviet Union was the hero, Iceland, the goat.

Japan, the foreign country most interested in the whale rescue, was the world's single largest whaling nation before Operation Breakout, and was the single largest whaling nation more than a year later, killing 1200 whales in 1988 alone, almost *ten times* as many whales as the rest of the world *combined* . The rescue that captivated so many viewers from Hokaido to Honshu did nothing to stop Japan's relentless pursuit of endangered whales.

Not only did Iceland quit whaling while the Russians continued, but the Soviets were rewarded just a few weeks later. The United States, still smarting from the Soviet whale rescue, rushed tens of millions of dollars worth of emergency supplies to Yerevan, the capital of Soviet Armenia, following its devastating earthquake. Channels opened just weeks before between the United States Coast Guard, the U.S. National Guard, and the Soviet Merchant Marine were used again to get as much assistance to the Soviets as quickly as possible.

But the rescue's greatest reward went to Colonel Tom Carroll and White House aide Bonnie Mersinger. After weeks of increasingly intense telephone conversations, Carroll finally went to Washington to meet the woman who had captured his heart. Passing through the tunnel separating the two United Airlines concourses en route to his connecting flight in Chicago's O'Hare Airport, the colonel found his once sturdy stomach quivering to the hypnotizing allure of the new-age music and neon light show swirling above the long moving walkway.

What was he doing, he asked himself. He called Bonnie, who managed to maintain remarkable composure when in fact she was just as anxious as he.

"Aren't you even a little nervous?" he asked her, desperately hoping she shared his angst.

"Nope," she said confidently. "I'll see you in two hours."

The nervousness she had confidently denied just a few hours before suddenly gripped her as she watched the plane carrying her beloved colonel taxi toward the gate. Maybe she had gone too far too fast. How would the seemingly staid colonel react to her welcome present: a stretch limousine waiting outside the terminal to whisk the new couple on their first steamy, skylit tour of the nation's capital. Her fears quickly vanished after a long, passionate embrace.

Tom Carroll and Bonnie Mersinger were married on August 12, 1989. They live in Anchorage where they can be seen driving a silver Maserati sporting a license plate emblazoned with dark blue letters that read: GR WHALE.

Acknowledgments

That I had the odd thought of writing a book about such a seemingly odd event wasn't odd in and of itself. What *was* odd was that it actually happened.

The idea first struck me on my way home from Alaska. Since I rarely read books, let alone write them, I didn't have the first clue about where to go or how to get there. I did the next best thing. I called Rich Bock, publicity director for N.Y. News Corp. at G.S. Schwartz & Company in New York.

I wanted to at least say I tried before dropping the idea and getting back to reality. "Let Bock handle it," I muttered to myself secretly hoping never to hear about it again. For an instant, I forgot with whom I was dealing. I couldn't really want the idea to die, I suddenly realized. Otherwise I wouldn't have given the assignment to Rich Bock.

Not only did he call back less than two hours later with the name of an agent, but had already scheduled a dinner meeting with her that very night. "Anything else?" he casually asked before jumping on the crosstown for that night's Knicks game.

Margaret McBride was kind enough not only to invite a prospective client of dubious potential to her family's home for dinner, she made them wait several hours before realizing I was never going to show up. Then, she still agreed to take me seriously after I had royally blown my first and only chance to make a good impression.

Bock found the perfect agent. Twelve hours later, she called back.

Margaret McBride had a hot prospect. The perfect agent had found the perfect publisher, Hillel Black. Now, all had to do was cut a deal and get to work.

Jim Keys, of my Uncle Bob's remarkably affordable Indianapolis-based law firm of Klineman, Rose and Wolf, was persistent and thorough enough to make sure I had an agreement I could live with and understand.

What continues to strike me about both Jim and my Uncle Bob is their unique ability to combine the mutually contradictory attributes of competent professionalism with feverish support for University of Michigan athletics. These guys spend every season berating the institution they so claim to cherish, only to bask in the nauseating glow of yet another Maize and Blue Big Ten or, worse yet, National Championship. But just a few days later, it's right back to the same old lament: "Hah," my Uncle Bob scowls, "Those Wolves are nothing but a bunch of overpaid, undercoached bums."

His most indebted nephew learned long ago, *Nobody Argues with Uncle Bob,* particularly when he's *right.*

Thanks to Suzy Tucker at Klineman, Rose and Wolf in Indianapolis for transcribing long hours of audio tape interviews and apologies for having to endure my and Michael Richardon's off-color humor. Richardson's not nearly as bad as he sounds. Just ask his parents.

Those very parents, Mr. and Mrs. Elliot Richardson, deserve more thanks than can ever be extended. They graciously gave their son and his desperate colleague a magical place to work: their magnificent home perched atop the timeless beauty of the Cape Cod National Seashore. Was it a surprise we stayed months longer than promised and, in the end, had to be evicted?

Graciousness is a Richardson family gene. Take Michael's cousin, Nancy Bigelow. A long-lost penniless cousin shows up with an equally destitute stranger on the step of her one-room log cabin outside Fairbanks, asking just to stay onenight. "No problem," Nancy offered. "Just as long as you know its twenty miles to the nearest indoor plumbing." Almost a week later, we were still there. Stranded, smelly victims of the coldest week in the history of North America.

it took nearly eight months to write this book. Eight months in which special thanks are due to my friend and associate Mike Kelly.

He and his Hamilton Communications staff, Dawn Harris, Ted Grybowski, George Corby, Mary Pat and Jim Kelly, John Laidlaw and, yes, Pete Zangeri, kept the doors to *NY News Corp.* open and operating. Mike Kelly's cooperation and patience will be long remembered and appreciated, his Wild Irish ways notwithstanding.

So too will the true friendship and extraordinary dedication of *NY News Corp.* Marketing Director Ed Helfer, a man long overdue for a bases loaded home run. Thanks to Technical Director Jack Malick who had the good sense to stay far away from Barrow. Now, the aging sage can slide down the hill of life with all his limbs intact. To Jack, *Happy 50th.*

Thanks to my dear friends David and Vivian Relkin (much more for the latter's lemon chicken than for the former's editing), MarkAir Cargo Director Ed Rogers, who arranged Barrow transportation, and thanks, too, to Joe Schrier for his work in adaptating this story to the visual medium.

Michael Richardson and I mixed the mortar and laid the bricks. But Hillel Black was the project foreman. He took a chance on an untested author. His vision gave the book meaning, purpose and direction. He knew precisely where he wanted it to go and how to get it there.

Margaret McBride, my expert liaison to any industry I knew nothing about, told me again and again how unheard of it was for a first-time author to receive so much attention, detail and commitment from anyone, let alone a man as respected as Hillel Black. Only now, when I face the prospect of getting along without him, do I begin to realize how much I appreciate, admire and respect my new friend, Hillel Black.

Finally, to Mom and Dad, nothing could begin to describe my deep appreciation and love for you both. All I can say is *Thanks.*

TRIBUTE

What kind of a person would put up with me day and night for eight straight months, never issue a complaint—well, *hardly* ever issue a complaint—and be even more a joy to work with at the project's end than he was at the beginning? *Michael Elliot Richardson,* that's who.

Fortunately, I never understood how much work was involved in writing a book until after I signed the contract. If I did, it would never have hàppened. I panicked. I knew I needed help. There was only one person I wanted, but how, I wondered, could I lure him in?

"Don't worry," I assured him. "It will only take a couple of months and, believe me," I added for emphasis, "it won't be full time." Thank God, he was as naïve as I was. He agreed, and 228 days and 2500 hours later, we were done. The result is every bit as much his as it is mine.

To Michael Richardson, a man of the highest honor, integrity and decency, if not ribald humor, you have my deepest thanks, love, respect and heartfelt best wishes. I can only hope that *Freeing the Whales* is but the second of what will be many future collaborations.

Index